PRAISE FOR *THE HU...* *FACTOR*

A masterclass in harnessing the human element for organizational success. *The Human Factor* is a transformative guide for leaders to unlock the potential of their people through actionable insights, strategic clarity and, most importantly, the human touch.
Gethin Nadin, multi-award-winning psychologist and bestselling HR author

This book takes you on the full-circle journey of work and life with all the best, human perspectives there are out there from the many people Simon and Michael have met on their own journeys. Also, a fun and enjoyable easy read!
Elaine Bergin, HR leader

Witty and wise. This book is an essential companion for any leader.
Damian Hughes, Co-host of the *High Performance* podcast

In *The Human Factor,* Simon and Michael have masterfully distilled thousands of ideas in podcasts and from personal experiences into relevant, meaningful and actionable words. Their creative frameworks and useful tools turn people into a talent advantage.
Dave Ulrich, Ross School of Business, University of Michigan, and Partner at The RBL Group

The Human Factor is one of the most powerful and thought-proving books I have read in years. An amazing exploration of how harnessing organizational purpose, influence and inspiration can drive mission clarity – the real competitive advantage.
Eric Tinch, Chief People Officer, Sutherland

This book brings together all aspects of the human side of organisations, with a view to optimizing both individual and collective performance. It is written with authenticity, simply structured and beautifully clear. The authors offer unexpected insights, smart summaries and practical suggestions for action. It is great to generate meaningful conversations on a very important topic, particularly given the context of unprecedented change and volatility in today's world of work.
Susan Yell, HR Director, Warburtons

THE human FACTOR

How to realize the potential of
your people and your business

SIMON HUMPHREYS
MICHAEL ESAU

KoganPage

Publisher's note

Every possible effort has been made to ensure that the information contained in this book is accurate at the time of going to press, and the publishers and authors cannot accept responsibility for any errors or omissions, however caused. No responsibility for loss or damage occasioned to any person acting, or refraining from action, as a result of the material in this publication can be accepted by the editor, the publisher or the authors.

First published in Great Britain and the United States in 2025 by Kogan Page Limited

Apart from any fair dealing for the purposes of research or private study, or criticism or review, as permitted under the Copyright, Designs and Patents Act 1988, this publication may only be reproduced, stored or transmitted, in any form or by any means, with the prior permission in writing of the publishers, or in the case of reprographic reproduction in accordance with the terms and licences issued by the CLA. Enquiries concerning reproduction outside these terms should be sent to the publishers at the undermentioned addresses:

2nd Floor, 45 Gee Street   8 W 38th Street, Suite 902
London   New York, NY 10018
EC1V 3RS   USA
United Kingdom

www.koganpage.com

Kogan Page books are printed on paper from sustainable forests.

© SAP SE 2025

All trademarks, service marks and company names are the property of their respective owners.

Illustrations by Marie Trojani

ISBNs

Hardback 978 1 3986 1818 3
Paperback 978 1 3986 1816 9
Ebook   978 1 3986 1817 6

British Library Cataloguing-in-Publication Data

A CIP record for this book is available from the British Library.

Library of Congress Control Number

2024047347

Typeset by Integra Software Services, Pondicherry
Print production managed by Jellyfish
Printed and bound by CPI Group (UK) Ltd, Croydon CR0 4YY

CONTENTS

About the authors x
Foreword by Harriet Green OBE xiii
Acknowledgements xviii

Introduction: Why should you read this book? 1

1 **Strategy and purpose** 6
Introduction 6
What is a strategy? 7
The operating model 10
Alignment between mission and strategy 14
Translating strategy into meaning and purpose 16
Strategy alignment across all stakeholders 18
Strategy and change 20
In conclusion 21
Tips and tricks 22
Notes 23

2 **The case for change** 26
Introduction 26
When does change occur? 26
What are the elements of a case for change? 28
Structuring the process of creating a case for change 37
How to overcome resistance to change 39
In conclusion 42
Tips and tricks 42
Notes 43

3 **The fluidity of culture** 48
Introduction 48
What is culture and who owns it? 49
Anchoring and communicating culture 54
Culture in the eyes of colleagues and consumers 61

Culture vs climate 63
In conclusion 65
Tips and tricks 67
Notes 67

4   The importance of having a philosophy 72
Introduction 72
What is a philosophy? 72
What are some examples of philosophies? 74
Why is having a philosophy so important? 78
What factors will influence a philosophy's success? 80
In conclusion 83
Tips and tricks 83
Notes 84

5   The predisposition of a human being 88
Introduction 88
What is a predisposition? 89
The iceberg model 90
Non-conscious motives and motivation 92
The importance of self 96
How are human motivations and desires satisfied at work? 98
In conclusion 101
Tips and tricks 102
Notes 103

6   Building commitment to change 106
Introduction 106
What is change? 107
Human reaction to change 108
Building a story and narrative 112
Navigating the organizational dynamics 113
Principles for managing an effective change 114
Resistance and fatigue 118
In conclusion 119
Tips and tricks 120
Notes 121

7   The employee value proposition (EVP) 124
Introduction 124
What is a value proposition? 125
What is an EVP? 128
What does an EVP mean to the employee? 129
Building connection, belonging, engagement and advocacy 133
Delivering and measuring the EVP 136
In conclusion 138
Tips and tricks 139
Notes 140

8   The relativity of success 144
Introduction 144
What is success? 145
Relative success 147
Measuring success 150
Sustaining success 151
Success through failure 152
When doubt creeps in 154
The impact of culture on success 156
Does age influence our perception of success? 158
In conclusion 160
Tips and tricks 161
Notes 161

9   Human experience, engagement and advocacy 166
Introduction 166
Human experience 167
What is engagement, and why is it so important? 174
Why do we seek advocacy? 177
In conclusion 179
Tips and tricks 181
Notes 181

10   The role of the leader 186
Introduction 186
The purpose of leadership 187
The four-circle model 189

Leadership and philosophy 198
In conclusion 201
Tips and tricks 203
Notes 204

11   Executing the basics brilliantly 208
Introduction 208
What do we mean by 'the basics'? 208
The foundations of human motivation 210
Making the basics a way of life at work 211
Sustainability at a team level 216
In conclusion 219
Tips and tricks 219
Notes 220

12   Listening, insights and feedback 224
Introduction 224
What is listening? 225
Listening and insights 228
Insights and intelligence 231
Feedback and growth 234
In conclusion 238
Tips and tricks 239
Notes 239

13   Nurturing and developing 244
Introduction 244
A development philosophy 245
Intelligence and insights 248
Effective succession planning 249
Managing exposure 251
The power of mentoring 254
In conclusion 257
Tips and tricks 257
Notes 258

14   The role of technology in execution 262
Introduction 262
The evolution of technology in our lives 262
Standardization vs personalization 263
The importance of data quality 265
Connecting technology 269
Basics matter 272
Agility at scale 274
Emerging technologies 274
Considerations to help prepare projects for success 279
In conclusion 281
Tips and tricks 282
Notes 283

15   The dynamics of teams 286
Introduction 286
What is a team? 287
The power of a team 288
Team composition 290
The importance of culture for a team 291
Team goals vs individual or organizational goals 293
Communication within a team structure 294
Success and sustainability for a team 296
Joining an existing team 298
Virtual or dynamic teams 299
Team leadership 301
See the person 302
In conclusion 303
Tips and tricks 304
Notes 304

16   Our reflections 306

Index 308

Simon is a Global Domain Advisor at SAP with over 30 years' experience, working with clients globally on how to maximize the return on their HR technology investments. Based in Manchester, he is a co-host of *The Human Factor* podcast.

Michael is a Global Value Advisor at SAP with over 25 years' experience in delivering organizational development solutions, cultural transformations and employee engagement strategies. Also based in Manchester, he is co-host of *The Human Factor* podcast.

Marie is a Global Value Advisor at SAP, where she transforms complex ideas into clear visual concepts. Based in France, she's a dynamic mother of two daughters and a motorbike enthusiast. Marie likes to combine creativity with strategic insight.

FOREWORD
By Harriet Green OBE

Does the world need another book on the importance of human capital in the workplace?

I think we DO need a really great book on this central subject because our world of work and what powers happiness and productivity for all stakeholders is changing more now than many of us have experienced in 50 years of running organizations. Spatial factors as to where we work, societal inputs on the increasing importance of community and coaching at work, and of course technology propulsions that require us all to learn, relearn and unlearn.

I think most of us agree the workplace has changed even more dramatically in the past four years. Covid, artificial intelligence, inflation and supply-chain and labour shortages are having an impact on employees and employers alike.

So, with this in mind, what I think is very important about this book is the exploration of our employees' ever important value proposition and also our employees' responsibilities in creating a human capital nirvana where happiness *and* the increasingly important productivity of high-performance teams soars.

Why is this book important?

As leaders, our foremost duty is to cultivate environments that blend happiness with productivity, fostering thriving teams and innovative workplaces. Prioritizing employee wellbeing lays the groundwork for success, ensuring that our organizations flourish in today's fast-paced landscape.

A clear business and human capital strategy serves as our north star in navigating the complexities of the professional realm. By setting clear objectives and pathways, we pave the way for success and ensure alignment throughout our organizations.

In contemporary society, work encompasses more than traditional employment and includes various forms of contribution and engagement. Work is not just about earning income, but also about finding purpose and fulfilment. It involves leveraging our skills and talents to make meaningful contributions to our communities and the wider world. Today, work spans a broad range of activities, including volunteerism, entrepreneurship, creative pursuits and lifelong learning.

Understanding why we work is central

The fundamental question of why we work delves into the deeper purpose and motivation behind our professional endeavours. While financial stability remains significant, many individuals seek work that provides meaning, fulfilment and personal growth.

Purpose-driven work aligns with our values and enables us to make a positive impact on the world. Moreover, pursuing purpose in our work leads to greater job satisfaction, engagement, and overall wellbeing.

Creating a culture of success: nurturing happy and productive work environments

In today's dynamic workplaces, leaders wield the power to shape not just the bottom line, but also the very fabric of their organization's culture. As business leaders and HR partners, we must understand the science and art of fostering environments where positivity thrives, productivity soars, and employees feel valued and empowered.

What are we working for? Our value, purpose and measuring our impact

It is critical we delve deep into some of our economic constructs and how they are changing; for example the theme of: if our labour is free, we devalue ourselves. Many next gen workers are defining their value, purpose and how they measure themselves very differently. There's a real shift to it not being as 'cool' to work after hours and on weekends as perhaps it once was.

Here lies a huge opportunity for us all to be working on compelling consumer-grade employee value propositions to refresh or completely reset our organizations' purpose and the key performance indicators that track our progress and productivity, but most of all our happiness.

What amazing leaders do differently – time to bring it on with human factors?

1 Go big on meaning. Most employees value jobs that let them contribute and make a difference, and many organizations now emphasize meaning and purpose in the hopes of fostering engagement. But this is also the manager's responsibility. You can't just rely on incentives like bonuses, stock options or raises.

2 Emphasize learning in your team, as we continue through this world of change; my nirvana of learning over winning!

3 Focus on feedback. A recent Society for Human Resource Management survey of managers in the US found that only two per cent provide ongoing feedback to their employees. Just two per cent! Many HR bosses limit themselves to the dreaded 'performance review' and often mingle developmental feedback with discussions about compensation and promotion, rendering the former much less effective.

I have spent a great deal of time in my career on feedback! Quite simply feedback is a gift and must be a constant stream of giving. Clear, powerful performance management tools are at the heart of business's success and employee's retention.

For me, exceptional HR bosses are more important than ever with the future of work reforming around us, where we need employees to bring

200 per cent of themselves to their work, with all their honesty, vulnerability, trust, understanding and empathy to your physiological safety bond as the leader.

But the single most important part is mastering strategy: the blueprint for successful work

Behind every successful endeavour lies a well-crafted strategy – a roadmap that guides actions and decisions toward desired outcomes. It is so important that HR leaders join us as CEOs delve into the world of strategic planning, where clarity of purpose and precision of execution intersect to drive organizational success.

To unlock the secrets of effective strategy formulation and implementation, empowering leaders to navigate complexities with confidence is the lifeblood of great HR practitioners.

Why the writers of this book matter!

I have worked with both Michael and Simon, and am thrilled they have expanded their brilliant podcast series into a book because they are quite unique as HR leaders. We can all learn from them, for these reasons:

- They have the skills as superb HR partners that the world needs.
- They keep learning, relearning and unlearning as executives.
- They combine technical and life skills in a practical real way that has transformed teams.

They believe as I do that HR leaders who deliver, as part of a company's strategic plan, the essential basics of how we attract, progress, and retain great talent are essential to sustainable success. Measuring all human factors in the business, from diversity and inclusion to equity, performance and delivering daily on improvements are the most vital indicators for the team!

It is vital to get deep into the underbelly of what 'work' means today

The timing of this book is rather more important than we think because, over the last 100 years, as crisis strikes humanity it is great vision and innovation through human factors that provides the platform for repair, restoration and growth.

After the pandemic in the 1950s, Sony launched their consumer-changing first transistor radio with huge impact. After the dotcom bubble burst of 2000, amongst the debris and wreckage emerged the mighty Apple with the iconic first iPod, which changed my relationship with music forever. And in the gory undercurrent of the mid-1970s, the magnificent Microsoft was born...

As we emerge from this vortex of climate, tech, health and deep inclusion society changes, the job of changing AI and machine learning is hugely real. And, to augment these progressive technologies, we humans need to play to our creative strengths, particularly around human capital and the factors that create high-performing teams and successful organizations – read this book and learn more!

Harriet Green is a dynamic leader dedicated to living life to the fullest, serving on esteemed boards like the Singapore EDB and FTSE 100 BAE Systems, and known for her transformative roles at IBM and Thomas Cook, as well as her early achievements in the electronics industry. She is deeply committed to mentoring and business coaching globally, with a strong focus on philanthropy, community engagement, supporting the LGBTQ+ community and the Academies for Youth with Potential which Harriet founded in 2020, starting with the Lost Girls of COVID Schools in Thailand. This initiative continues to enrich young lives by providing essential skills.

ACKNOWLEDGEMENTS

We are first-time authors. Undertaking a project such as writing a book has been a new experience for the both of us. We are used to writing, and we are never shy of offering our opinion, but putting down our thoughts into a significant piece of writing has been both daunting and refreshing in equal measure. We have relished the chance to take a step back from our daily working life, and to take stock of all the wonderful conversations and interactions we have had over the years, both professionally and in our personal lives. That time to just take a moment and think about what we have learnt.

However, writing a book is something that needs a lot of support and help, and it's important for us that we recognize and call out some of those people that have been instrumental in creating this book that you have in your hands.

We will split up these acknowledgements into two primary sections – our joint acknowledgements to people that have supported us both in the process, and then some more personal acknowledgements for friends, family and those who have had an influence on us individually. Bear with us as we thank everyone, because it's important to recognize that, as with most things in life, while we can personally succeed and deliver accomplishments (and receive recognition for doing so), it more than likely occurred with support from others either directly or indirectly. We are both humble enough to recognize that without that support, this book that you hold would simply not be possible.

Our first thanks go to the group of people that helped turn the twinkle in the eye idea into a fledgling project. We want to thank Gethin Nadin and Katie King. Both are established and well-respected authors, and we are so grateful for them sharing their thoughts on how to approach an activity such as writing a book. To speak from their experiences – what we should consider in terms of topics, how to structure our thoughts, how to create a pitch for stakeholders to evaluate our proposal, and what they felt they achieved by taking on book writing. Without the inputs of these two friends, we would never have even got off the ground initially, and we are truly grateful for their help and encouraging support.

Our next step in the book development was to convince our company to support our efforts. We are very grateful to SAP for supporting us in this. SAP is a wonderful organization to work for and we are very fortunate to have such a supportive employer. Having the time and space to explore our thoughts, and an organization that encourages innovation, creativity, and entrepreneurship has been key to securing internal buy-in. For background, we have gone through many stages internally to securing commitment, including pitching our idea to our senior stakeholders, securing funding, aligning and coordinating with Marketing, and finally securing a green light. It's been a long process for sure and has taken some resilience from us to keep going, but when you are passionate about something and believe in it, all the effort is worthwhile when that final confirmation comes through.

We would especially like to thank some individuals in SAP for helping and guiding us through the processes. Firstly, Tristan Southgate was our internal sponsor and again, without overusing a familiar phrase, without him, we wouldn't be writing this! We simply would not have a book without his support, guidance, knowledge of the corporate processes and structures inside SAP. He has never doubted our intention or ability to deliver this project and has always been there to support us, encourage us, unblock impediments and introduce us to people that can help.

While we have been writing the book, we also had our day jobs to deliver. Writing the book was only going to be approved if we could assure our management team that our focus and commitments to our customers would not be impacted. We are very grateful to our line managers for their support in this. Torsten Nagel, Marie Sylvie d'Etat, Mike Theaker and Tristan Southgate have encouraged us to pursue our dream and that has been critical for us, to know that our bosses are behind us and have our backs. We have also been very supported by the market units we work in. We have taken great encouragement from our local leaders such as Leila Romane and Robert Mooney, who have again supported us throughout the writing process.

SAP is a large company, and as such, some of our internal processes are complex. We have been expertly guided through them by Ralf Heeke and he has helped us identify and fulfil all our internal obligations and needed approvals. He has done so with patience and diligence, and his support helped us navigate and negotiate our way through the approval process.

We also needed a lawyer! As stated earlier, we have never written a book before, or seen a publisher contract. Never underestimate the value of a super-helpful and patient lawyer. Nadine Heitmann took not only a professional interest in the book, but also a personal interest. Throughout the contract reviews and negotiations, she represented us superbly and with our best interests at heart and, importantly, acted at pace when we needed it.

Additionally from our tour inside SAP, we have to acknowledge and thank a number of people from our marketing teams. Over the time taken to write the book this has included Gina Prettyger, Natalie Edwards, Beata Bennet, Chrissy King, Sophie Louise Jenkins, Elaine Murphy and Deborah Phethean. All have helped us launch and run our podcast series – *The Human Factor*, which was a source of many of our conversations with amazing guests, which we reflect upon in the book. They have helped us reach our listeners, and we have been supported further by our colleagues internally and externally to amplify our message to our listeners, enabling us to reach thousands of people with these conversations.

We have to call out one person in particular when we talk about the podcast. Russell Harper is one of the nicest and most well-connected persons you will ever meet. He has introduced us to so many amazing people that have then become guests on our podcast, and we are so grateful that not only has he been super helpful, but we feel privileged to call him our friend. Russell is that person who will do anything to help and share and we have both known him now for 15 years or more. Russell, you are truly valued by us!

To write a book needs someone prepared to publish it. We found our publisher very quickly (and thanks again to Katie King for her recommendation). We very quickly established that Kogan Page was the right publisher for us, and they have been superb throughout the process. Supremely guided initially through the approval and publishing green-light process by Lucy Carter, and then fantastic support from Joe Ferner-Reeves as our editor has really made the writing stage far easier than expected. From the very first meeting with both Lucy and Joe, we knew we had the right publisher and we have never wavered from that view. That word 'patience' comes up again. They must publish hundreds of books, but we were writing our first. No question from us was too silly for them, and their advice and guidance has been invaluable.

We have mentioned the podcast series already (we will be referring to it many times throughout the book), and we must also extend our thanks to our production team that help us produce the show. Simon Burgess and Helen Doble are amazing as our podcast studio team. As we race past 50 episodes produced, the quality of their work is of the highest standard, and their support in both setting up and then running the podcast series has helped us grow as hosts. We took great pride also when our producer felt inspired to launch his own podcast series – *Life's 2nd Act: A journey into finding direction and purpose*. Give it a try. You will recognize his guests on the first episode!

And now we have reached the acknowledgement stage of actually writing the book. Time when we put pen to paper (or fingers to keyboard at least). Our source materials for large parts of the book are our conversations both through the podcast and with our customers. We are very grateful to all those guests that shared their thoughts and wisdom with us, as well as all those customers that invited us into their organizations and allowed us to talk with them. Conversation is at the heart of everything we do and learn. We have been so lucky in our careers to meet with extraordinary people and companies, and it has allowed us to learn and grow as individuals to the point where we have felt confident enough to share our thoughts in a book.

Writing is only part of the process, though. We have some amazing colleagues who have helped us review the outcomes. Mike Theaker, Jane Harrington, Dave Woolrich and Joe Ferner-Reeves have been critical to the process. They have read our writing, providing feedback on style, grammar, content, and most importantly personality. Their feedback has given us the direction and feedback we needed to ensure our writing represented not only our thoughts, but our personalities too.

We have been so lucky to work with Marie Trojani through our time at SAP. If you follow our podcast series, and our posts on social media, you will know her for her wonderful episode visualization drawings. Each episode she watches the raw footage and draws a summary of the conversation. She is so creative and the pictures she produces are art. So beautiful and also so engaging to look at. Each one is different and unique to the speaker and the topic.

Well, it was an obvious ask for us to see if she wanted to help us also with the book, and, quite frankly, this wouldn't even be a book at all without her illustrations. Every time she sends us something, we smile. Her drawings are amazing and elevate our writing to another level altogether. They say a picture is worth a thousand words. We would be happy to write more than a thousand words about how wonderful her pictures are, but we can feel our publishers tapping on our shoulders asking us for more brevity.

Personal acknowledgements

Simon

I have to start my own personal acknowledgements in an obvious place. My wife, Sarah, has been hugely supportive in the process of writing the book. Often the writing has taken place in evenings or weekends, and she has provided unwavering support during those long hours, and she makes an outstanding cup of tea! However, we both bear the scars of omelette-gate, and it took many months to emerge from that scandal.

My two daughters have also been immensely helpful. Alex and Emma have reviewed chapters, discussed topics, provided ideas and given energy to the content. Having different perspectives has helped to provide a more rounded approach to the topics we have taken on, and I'm so proud of how they have grown into strong, independent thinkers in their own right.

While trying to avoid this starting to sound like an Oscar-winning speech, I also must thank my parents, Beryl and Bernard, and sister Juli for providing encouragement and support throughout the process, including reminding me of my English teacher from my school days, who set high expectations of my writing at the time. Two friends have also been unflinching in their support of the process – Steve Bellerby and Tracey Barnes. They have challenged, critiqued, reviewed and encouraged me throughout the two years it has taken to produce the book.

I would like to take the time to call out some people who helped me throughout my career so far. Paul Robinson, George Elkington, the sadly missed Jerry Chilvers and Thomas Graybrook all provided me with guidance, encouragement, ideas, space and constructive feedback and I am very grateful for them acting as my informal mentors. I looked up to and respected them as bosses, but even though they were all very busy individuals, they took the time to work with me and guide me without imposing restrictive boundaries. They helped me find my voice and persona. While I worked for them, it always felt like I was working with them, and I'm very thankful for their patience, wisdom and counsel.

Finally, I have to say thank you to my co-author, Michael. I have known him now for over seven years, and we have forged a close working relationship. But it goes beyond that. We have both had difficult patches in our lives in recent times and we know that we have each other's back and that we are there to support each other regardless of circumstance. You couldn't wish for a better friend. Writing a book is not easy, but it has been made so much more fun writing it with my best buddy and learning from him.

Michael

Unlike my co-author, I am quite partial to an Oscar-winning speech as they often appreciate the numerous people who have helped you to become the person you are and develop the voice that you possess today. We never stop learning; we are always curious; it is very much a life's work, and for that I am eternally grateful to the people who have supported me to become the person I am today.

A huge thank you to my wonderful wife Jayne and my amazing daughters Lily and Bronwyn. Over the last 20 years I have worked in all corners of the globe and often been away from home for long periods, and Jayne has always supported me every step of the way and afforded me the space and time to grow. I am incredibly grateful for her belief in me, her guidance and being my grammar police at times! My daughters have no idea what I do exactly, but being their father has been the greatest gift I could ask for. I learn from them every day and for that I am eternally grateful.

A massive thank you to my parents Robert and Gloria. My parents are my heroes. Unwavering in their support and belief in me. Always available for advice and guidance. They have been by my side every step of the way, especially during some challenging moments. My dad has always been a constant source of wisdom, advice and has been a great role model. My mum has always given me the *hwyl* to succeed and be the best person that I can be. *Diolch am popeth.*

My brother Andrew, his partner Sue my niece Esme and my mother-in-law Eve. A huge thank you for all your love and support. It always means the world to me and your support of me and my work has been immense, and I am eternally grateful.

A personal thank you to Glenn Bracey, Paul Walsh, Hilary Wingfield and to Harriet Green who so kindly provided the foreword for our book. They will never know how much they have helped me personally over the last 20 years. They have coached me, mentored me and always been an amazing source of strength, inspiration and wisdom. I have learnt so much from them and I believe, as a product of many mentors and coaches, I would not be the person I am without them.

A huge thank you to Steve and Lisa Johnson and the team at Dynamic Business. Not only are they huge friends, but have been a real support and inspiration over the last 20 years. They operate at the sharp end of innovation and thinking, and I value our connection immensely. We also want to thank them for allowing myself and Simon to base ourselves at their offices on one of our writing stints!

Finally, my co-author and friend Simon. We became colleagues about seven years ago. I think Simon thought I was a bit of a nuisance to begin with, always having a moan and never being satisfied, but it became clear that we shared a passion for learning, making things better and striving for growth. We have collaborated on some great projects over the last five years including the podcast and now the book, and Simon will never appreciate how much I gain from working with him. Being able to write this book with a best friend has been amazing.

The Human factors THAT influence ALL ASPECTS OF work AND life

Introduction

Why should you read this book?

'People are our biggest asset.' Easy to say, and often used by business leaders when asked about what makes their organization different. But what does it mean to live up to those five words? What does the organization do to ensure that the best people are hired, retained, motivated, rewarded, appreciated and utilized? And, conversely, what does it feel like to be an employee in that same organization? Do they feel motivated, appreciated and well utilized?

Back in 2020, we were chatting around the kitchen table over a cup of tea. We wanted to engage with thought leaders and knowledgeable individuals on the factors necessary to deliver on those five words. At the time, we envisaged face-to-face meetings to sit and discuss the relevant topics, but as we planned our approach, circumstances overtook us and the pandemic locked us all in our homes.

Therefore, we pivoted and started a podcast called *The Human Factor*. In a series of monthly episodes, we invited guests to talk with us on a variety of topics related to the world of work and/or their personal experiences and development, and what influences success in either.

The episodes released were non-sequential, and we dove in and out of topics depending on our guest's expertise. What we heard were common themes emerging in the conversations. 'Get the basics right', 'Remember the human factors', 'The role of the leader is critical' and many others.

GET THE BASICS RIGHT

REMEMBER THE HUMAN FACTORS

THE ROLE OF THE LEADER IS CRITICAL

Therefore, the purpose of this book is to look at these common factors – to explore how organizations can not only deliver on those five words, but also ensure employees experience those five words in successful execution of strategies.

This is not a book about Human Resources. This is a book about the human factors that influence all aspects of work and home. But we go further than that. We also look at what motivates people, what drives high performance and how individuals can self-improve. We will explore the factors that influence whether an employee goes home after work and is able to say 'I had a good day,' and couple this with an organization being able to say 'We are investing in the right strategies to help people bring their best selves to work.'

We are two people who have worked with hundreds of organizations over the years, exploring and experiencing those challenges. We both have a natural curiosity as to what makes successful people tick, and what makes successful organizations work. We will bring together our insights and thoughts, as well as the collected wisdom we have gathered from our podcast series and from research and learnings from our company, SAP.

We have challenged ourselves to provide practical advice and takeaways from each of our chapters. We want to ensure you as the reader have pragmatic tips, tricks and advice that you can use back in your workplace, or even for your own personal development.

We have also shared personal stories, experiences and thoughts. This is sometimes difficult to convey when you have a collaborative joint-authored book and can be confusing to know whose story it is being told. We have used 'we' and 'I' in many of the chapters and we discussed whether we should label who 'I' is each time. We believe this would get too clumsy and so we have left the stories in, but not always identified which of us is the 'I'. We hope this does not diminish your enjoyment of the book or the impact of the story being recounted.

So, settle back, and let's start by exploring why human factors are so important in the world of work and in our own personal development.

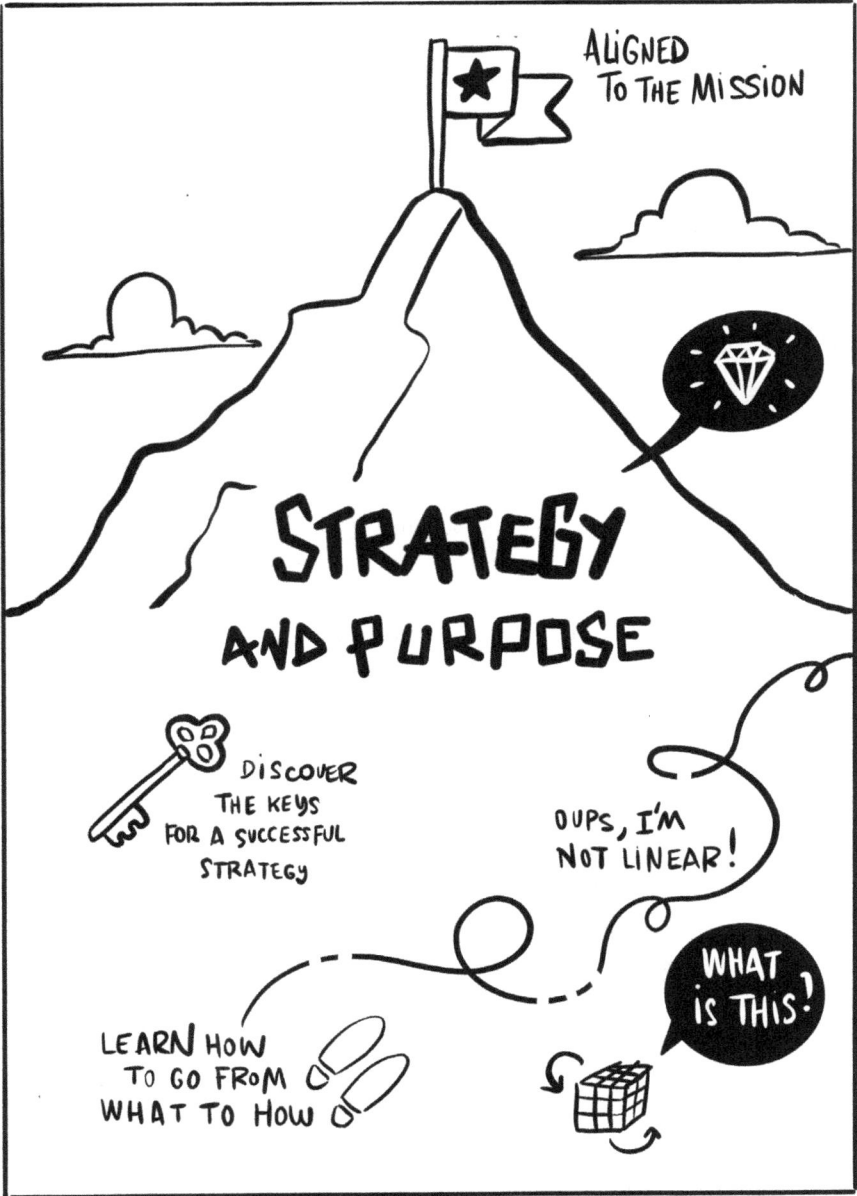

Strategy and purpose

Introduction

While determining the structure of this book, it became pretty evident that we needed to delve into strategy as early as possible. Arguably, many of the topics we will be covering are impacted in some way, shape or form by strategy and purpose.

Strategy is a word that we hear so often in our day-to-day lives, but what does it mean and what influence does it have on us as human beings? One of my favourite expressions is 'hope isn't a strategy' – it always makes me chuckle. Hoping that something may happen is a very common human trait, but often implies that there is no plan in place. We believe that, at a basic human level, we need clarity to function at our best. If I was to decide that I would like to run a marathon at some point soon, I wouldn't get very far without a clear plan or strategy that would get me fit and in a position to run 26.2 miles.

Another great example is someone who wishes to complete a Masters degree alongside their work. The Masters will require a big time investment, research and much more. Taking on that challenge without a strategy or plan could lead to demotivation very quickly.

STRATEGY
FROM MULTIPLE ANGLES

In this chapter we are going to explore the facets of a strategy from multiple angles. We will look at the literal meaning and purpose of a strategy. We will examine its role as a guiding force for teams, leaders and individuals and how the vision and strategy can determine the engagement and connection of a person. We will also explore the challenges of aligning a strategy across an entire workforce, and then turning a strategy into action and attainment of agreed outcomes.

In later chapters we will explore further differing approaches to strategy and execution, and then delve into how individuals and organizations think about strategy, purpose and execution. We will conclude every chapter with tips, tricks and advice related to that specific topic.

What is a strategy?

Over 20 years ago, I had the pleasure of sitting in the audience at a conference in Harrogate where Michael Porter was the keynote. Michael is the Bishop William Lawrence University Professor, Emeritus at Harvard University. Throughout his career at Harvard Business School, he has brought economic theory and strategy concepts to bear on many of the most challenging problems facing corporations, economies and societies, including market competition and company strategy, economic development, the environment and health care. His extensive research is widely recognized in governments, corporations, NGOs and academic circles around the globe. His research has received numerous awards, and he is the most cited scholar today in economics and business.

In the conference, the acclaimed and world-renowned professor was talking about strategy and what it really meant. I still remember it today, and the one thing that always stood out was the difference between strategy and operational effectiveness. Referencing an article from *Harvard Business Review* back in 1996, Porter stated:

> Operational effectiveness and strategy are both essential to superior performance, which, after all, is the primary goal of any enterprise. But they work in very different ways.
>
> A company can outperform rivals only if it can establish a difference that it can preserve. It must deliver greater value to customers or create comparable value at a lower cost, or both. The arithmetic of superior profitability then follows: delivering greater value allows a company to charge higher average unit prices; greater efficiency results in lower average unit costs.[1]

The key line 'A company can outperform rivals only if it can establish a difference that it can preserve' – that is WHAT the organization is setting out to achieve. That difference is key, it's the USP (unique selling proposition). It's the thing that will either sustain the organization or not. Over the course of the last 50 years, we have seen the impact of organizations not sustaining that difference – high-profile names like Kodak, Blockbuster and Motorola, amongst many others.

One of the earliest episodes of the podcast featured Harriet Green OBE.[2] Harriet is a British businesswoman who was chairman and CEO of IBM Asia Pacific and previously led three IBM business divisions: the Internet of Things, customer engagement and education businesses. She was CEO of the Thomas Cook Group from July 2012 to November 2014.

In our episode with Harriet, we discussed strategy, purpose and execution. I had the great pleasure of working under Harriet's leadership and her views on strategy were very clear. To preserve the 'difference', you had to be bold and brave and step into the spaces that others had not. Standing still was never an option. A key takeaway, however, and one that I never forget – the strategy needed to be simple. It needed to be so simple that a 10-year-old could read it and understand it.

This is all common sense, I hear you say – yet how many of us have worked in organizations where the strategy isn't clear and it isn't understood? I believe genius will always lie in its simplicity and being able to translate the strategy for everyone in the organization is a fundamental that needs to be executed brilliantly. Therefore, making sure the strategy is as simple as possible is key to this process.

Later in the book we will be looking at the complexities and challenges related to change, and many of those complexities apply to the execution of a strategy. But first we will look at strategy in the context of people and HR. Using a business design model, we will explore all the key considerations that will determine successful execution or not.

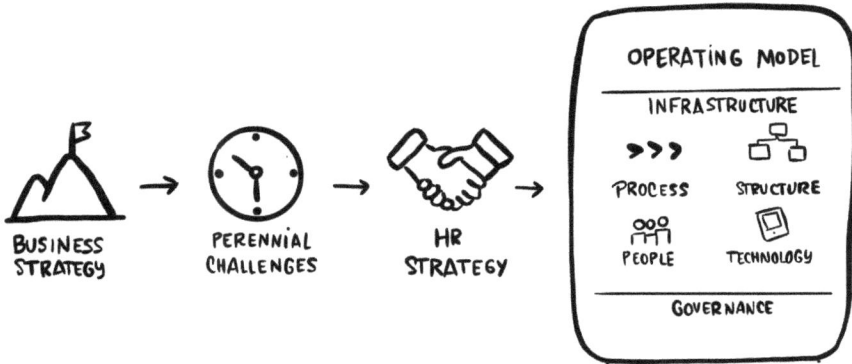

When we look at strategy through the context of people, there are many factors at play. No organization is immune from the perennial challenges. What do we mean by a perennial challenge?

For decades, organizations have had the same challenges of attracting people, building skills, developing talent, shaping a culture, being compliant and so on. These are perennial challenges, and they are not going anywhere.

In addition, the people coming into the workplace and those already there are now seeking to understand how effective the organization is in delivering on those challenges from their perspective. 'What career opportunities are there in the company?' 'How can I achieve my future career goals?' 'Is it easy to get things done here?' 'Am I being treated fairly?' 'Does the company align with my beliefs?', and so on. These questions are truly influencing their decision to join or, indeed, stay.

Therefore, there needs to be an actionable HR strategy that aligns and ensures that the key business objectives and deliverables can be met, and the perennial challenges are addressed from both the organization and the workforce perspectives. This is when you quickly move from *what* to *how*. How work is done is changing rapidly, so there needs to be a mindset of reimagination and being open to new ideas, as well as evolving legacy processes or ways of working.

$$\boxed{\text{WHAT}} \longrightarrow \boxed{\text{HOW}}$$

Let's take a look at all of the key elements and considerations that make up the operating model and influence the execution and attainment of the strategy.

The operating model

The operating model is how you orchestrate your approach and resources to execute the HR strategy: how processes need to change; how the HR function needs to be structured; the people and capabilities needed to deliver services (managers and employees as well as HR professionals); the technology to be leveraged; understanding what will be outsourced and what you'll do internally; and finally the governance mechanisms needed to manage and lead the HR function. The operating model can also enable and empower managers and employees through providing access to processes, technology and information that puts their careers and the management of themselves and their teams into their own hands – where these things belong.

We speak about the operating model a lot. What's critical is that all the elements of the operating model are connected. You can't change one element without impacting the others, positively or negatively, so the operating model needs to be considered when changing/redesigning it to better execute the strategy. We always think of the operating model as a Rubik's cube, and you twist the elements around to get the best configuration to execute your strategy.

Sourcing

Sourcing strategies have changed quite significantly in the last few years with the huge advancements in technology and automation. The technology is not the only sourcing consideration, with many organizations looking externally at various intervals to bring in people with specific skills or knowledge to support a programme or a specific project.

Infrastructure

The heart of the operating model is the infrastructure, which comprises the following four elements: processes, structure, people and technology. We will review each one in turn.

Processes

The operating model brings to life the role of HR as the custodian of people – who I believe in the future need to become super designers, amazing facilitators of change and archaeologists who can search and dig for insights and identify amazing talent.

What do I mean by super designers? I often refer to the 'employee life cycle' as the 'employee proposition' which is made up of a series of processes – these include all the transactional processes, recruitment, onboarding, performance, development, reward, learning, and the list goes on. To achieve the desired outcomes set out in the business and HR strategy, the design of those processes is a crucial piece of work. Later in the book we will discuss 'philosophy', and I believe when it comes to designing processes you are making a philosophical decision on how you want a process to behave – who can do what, who can see what, how will approvals work and many of these decisions should be linked to the mission of the organization because they are cultural decisions.

Structure

The design of the processes and how they are intended to behave will influence and inform the structure of HR to support the delivery and execution. With technological advancements and the rapid development of generative AI, we expect to see more and more reiterations of the traditional HR structure.

The opportunity to 'free up HR' to truly focus on partnering, coaching and enabling the organization to grow and develop has never been greater. With so much change and disruption, the role of the business partner is essential to coach, guide and advise the line around execution, and an influential Centre of Excellence team is also crucial to developing and delivering programmes and processes that drive required outcomes.

People

In very simple terms – what does this all mean to the people who are working for you today and those who haven't joined your organization yet? If we wind the clock back 20 to 30 years, it was commonplace for an organization to have a very clear employee value proposition (EVP).

For us, the EVP is so important. It brings to life who the organization is, the values, the behaviours, and the culture of execution. In a world where skill shortages are becoming the norm, being able to stand out in the talent market is crucial. Your EVP tells people who you are and what they can expect, and help them to make an informed decision on whether to join you or not.

TWIST

THE OPERATING MODEL

Technology

The final element of the infrastructure is the technology. Our view on the technology is clear and simple. To enable 'execution of process' without the requisite technology causes enormous problems and often huge amounts of inefficiency. However, the tail should not wag the dog, so being clear on what the technology is being designed to do is fundamental.

Employees today are also consumers, and as consumers we have been spoilt with the explosion of technology at our fingertips every second of the day. It has revolutionized our lives, so there are high expectations now of having commensurate capability in the workplace, but a point persists – if the employee doesn't know what they are executing and why, then simply having the technology doesn't matter. We are devoting a whole chapter to technology and there is much to ponder and debate, so enough on that for now.

Governance

So, the operating model is now in place, the processes have been designed, technology has been configured and the machine is in full flow. Wouldn't it be great if it was that simple? Organizations are living and breathing every day, looking to improve, evolve; legislation changes are happening on a frequent basis, a process or set of processes needs to be tweaked, and of course there is often a market unit or business unit that insists on doing something completely different.

This is where you need strong governance in play throughout to ensure all changes and decisions are made sensibly and avoid conflict. A governance model should serve to protect the strategies in play and minimize any unnecessary disruption.

The final point from the model is success metrics. Irrespective of the terminology used, whether it be key performance indicators (KPIs) or objectives and key results (OKRs), there must be agreed measures of success feeding from the business strategy through to the people strategy. One of the great frustrations with any execution or change effort is the absence of 'indicators' that tell the organization and individuals whether targets are being met or if the needle is moving in the right direction.

Later in the book we will look at the predisposition of a human being, and how measurement/progress is inherent in our DNA. There is nothing worse than applying huge amounts of effort and not seeing a reward or knowing if it has made a difference or not. For us, a process should never be in flight if there is no measure of success attached. Often the success is important for the organization as it can indicate effectiveness and opportunities for efficiency, but many of the processes that underpin the employee lifecycle need to have clear and tangible outcomes.

This is so important when communicating the purpose and benefits of the process across all employees whom you wish to gain commitment from. Otherwise, you fall into the trap of getting compliance as to its execution but not commitment to the process, which will always result in a better outcome. This is when the organization is perceiving the process to be HR for HR's sake. More on that a little later…

Translating the strategy into something that a critical mass of people can understand and are able to execute is fundamental and requires rigorous execution. It's fair to say that over the course of our careers, we have observed on more than one occasion where there hasn't been a structured process in place to align objectives, or indeed a culture where feedback and checking in on progress was commonplace. Each time I would worry greatly about the sustainability of the organization and their ability to engage, retain and attract great talent.

Throughout many of our chapters, the HOW will be examined in several ways, and each time we will look at the impact on the individual and the human factors at play.

Alignment between mission and strategy

For the moment, let's take a pause on strategy and look at the 'mission' of an organization. For many years the mission statement of an organization was often highly visible on the walls of an office, or on posters lining the hallways. There would be an expectation that everyone was aware of it, could recite it and believe in it. The reality, however – and the proof is always in the pudding – is whether individuals believed it and whether the organization itself was committed to it. That is why aligning the mission, strategy and values is incredibly important.

A mission can be described in different ways, but common descriptions state it is the reason the organization exists, the values it holds dear and how it wishes to be perceived by customers, employees, stakeholders and so on. Missions are often tightly aligned to the brand of an organization, in some cases almost synonymous, and from all our conversations on the podcast it is becoming clear why that is super important. Not to make assumptions, but you may be asking: 'Why is that so important?'

We reflect to Episode 14 of the *Human Factor* podcast with David Hieatt.[3] David is the co-founder of Hiut Denim. Our conversation with David was all about growing your brand through your people, and Hiut Denim is a great example where the mission, strategy and brand are completely aligned. Hiut Denim are a jeans manufacturer with a simple strategy. They make high quality jeans, and only jeans. Their mission is not to make the most jeans, but to make the best jeans in the world, sustainably. Their brand is a commitment to that mission, moving to a 'made to order' model to reduce waste and offering customers free lifetime repairs. The Hiut Denim mission, strategy and brand is a commitment. A commitment to the people who work there, and to the consumer who is buying their product.

There are many other examples of brands being synonymous with their mission – Nike is a great example with: 'To bring inspiration and innovation to every athlete in the world',[4] and also Starbucks: 'To inspire and nurture the human spirit one person, one cup, and one neighbourhood at a time'.[5] I personally have always loved Google's mission: 'To organize the world's information and make it universally accessible and useful'.[6] It literally does what it says on the tin. The mission brings to life who the organization is and what it stands for. As prospective employees and customers, we make big decisions based on whether we believe that mission to be true or not, and this is very much the reason why the alignment of mission and strategy is incredibly important.

Do the actions of the organization reflect the mission? Do the behaviours exhibited day to day reflect the values of the organization and what is important? Is there a congruence between what is said and what is done, and how is the culture of the organization perceived?

These are the questions being asked every day and on which long-term decisions are made. We would argue that in an era full of change and rapid technological advancements, keeping people loyal to a brand or mission is getting harder. It can be brittle, and the moment someone perceives you are not being true to it – you are in trouble.

Translating strategy into meaning and purpose

People coming into employment today are looking for meaning and purpose in their work. Haven't we always been looking for meaning and purpose, I hear you say? Well, yes, but were previous generations as vocal about it? The DNA of a human being hasn't changed over the last 100 years, but how we view work, our expectations and our preferences have shifted significantly and events like the Covid-19 pandemic acted as a huge catalyst to bring much of that to the forefront. From a very young age, the need to achieve has been ingrained in all of us, but it can be demotivating when you believe the work you are doing is meaningless or lacking in purpose.

A story that many of us will have heard is the janitor who was working at NASA back in 1962. Whether the story is true or a myth, it's a great story and a great example. President Kennedy was visiting that day and noticed a janitor carrying a broom. He interrupted his tour, walked over to the man, and said: 'Hi, I'm Jack Kennedy. What are you doing?' The janitor responded: 'I'm helping put a man on the moon, Mr President.'

The janitor understood the importance of his contribution. He truly felt he was a valuable part of something bigger than himself, and his attitude created a feeling of self-confidence in his mission. He wasn't merely a janitor; he was a member of the 1962 NASA Space Team.

It's a great story, and a great example of where someone appreciates what they are doing is contributing to the ultimate strategic goal. Now, is this the case in every organization? Probably not, but it certainly should be the aspiration. A question that I ask often is, 'What needs to happen for a person to go home at the end of the day and say, "I had a great day"?' I know the answer will be determined by many factors and not one single thing, but I know from my own experience that when I feel misaligned with the strategy and delivering work that is not strategically aligned, the level of de-motivation quickly rises and so does resentment. There is no worse feeling than delivering something that will not influence an outcome that is considered important.

Referring to Episode 5 of the *Human Factor* podcast with Harriet Green OBE on the importance of aligning strategy to purpose, she shared: 'If you are not positioned with an authentic believable commitment, a powerful set of values that really drives diversity and inclusion, that not only hires superb people but progresses and retains them, then you will lose that war for talent.

If you lose the war for talent and you don't have great people, then you certainly won't have great clients, and that is the end of a business.'

One of the reasons for writing this book and ultimately starting the podcast is the sheer number of factors that determine what success is (relativity is everything), but one thing that is apparent is the enormous impact of brand, mission and values on how the workforce feels about their connection and engagement to the organization. A red thread through so many conversations has been the importance of the 'basics' – doing the basics well. It all starts and stems from the mission and strategy. These are the human factors, and there are so many at play.

Strategy alignment across all stakeholders

Building the strategy is one thing. Thinking about how it will be executed is another. The biggest challenge, however, is alignment across all stakeholder groups. It's no accident that many organizations will repeat each year the importance of SMART objectives. In our opinion, translating the strategy into SMART objectives that can be effectively aligned or cascaded across the organization is arguably one of the most important processes and fundamentals. It requires rigour and a real commitment, and the consequences of not doing it well can be disastrous for the organization and the individual.

Over the course of the last 20 years, I have held dear that providing every individual with meaningful, aligned and tangible objectives is crucial. An absolute non-negotiable. Many years ago, I was asked to join an organization that was going through a recovery period, and I was asked to develop and implement a performance and development culture and framework. My starting point was to understand the current state, and I did this by spending time with team leaders and individual contributors. I always asked two questions:

1 Can you share your goals with me?

2 Can you help me to understand how you receive feedback and support to achieve your goals?

It quickly became apparent that there was no goal setting at all, and absolutely no feedback. Individuals were coming into work, doing their best and going home. I then discovered that voluntary turnover was over 40 per cent, sickness was through the roof and recruitment agencies were living on site to help keep the flow of talent coming into the organization to meet service levels. An absolute mess and a soul-destroying experience that demonstrated no understanding or appreciation of the needs of a human being – something we will cover in a specific chapter a little later.

From an organization perspective, the process of aligning goals is critical to prevent people from undertaking work that in simple terms isn't supportive of the organizational strategy. Again, this sounds obvious, but we have observed individuals and teams working on projects or pieces of work that are not aligned and don't have any strategic relevance at all. Technology has existed for some time to assist and enable this crucial process, and can identify when goals are being set that don't align and this enables leaders to course-correct. It also provides the organization with the visibility and transparency to see progress and updates.

Doing this work manually is quite frankly a thankless task, and achieving the level of alignment required is almost impossible. Providing any kind of aggregated update on progress would require a manual collation effort on a gargantuan scale.

From an individual perspective, it's all about achievement. Having a purpose, a stretch, a challenge, clarity on why I am here, what I am being asked to do. Tapping into the psyche and DNA of a human being. I believe the principle of providing every individual with clarity on their goals/objectives should apply irrespective of role. The 'human need' is the same and I believe the classification of groups – white collar, blue collar – has been a major hindrance in the effectiveness of such an important process.

Later in the book, we will cover the role of the leader. The onus and expectation on leaders today is only increasing, and you can argue that success and failure very much sits on their shoulders – but ensuring that every person who works in the team is crystal clear on what they are being asked to do and getting regular feedback on how well they are doing has to be one of the most important things a leader has to do.

The alignment of the strategy isn't something that just happens at the beginning of the year. Of course, most of the heavy lifting is done then, but the follow-ups, regular touchpoints and feedback loops must happen on a regular basis. It's all about finger on the pulse, acting with integrity and making sure the human in the team feels engaged, connected, appreciated and has an important role to play.

Strategy and change

Developing a strategy and aligning across an entire organization is not a linear process. While translating the strategy into goals that can be cascaded throughout is a crucial element of the whole process, it doesn't mean that everyone will support or indeed agree with the direction taken and what it means to a team or an individual.

We spoke to Eric Tinch in Episode 37 of the *Human Factor* podcast, where the focus was on 'Influencing the C-suite'.[7] A vastly experienced leader, Eric is the HR Director for Sutherland Global. He has 25 years' experience of driving change and transformation and is currently leading a significant programme across the 70,000 workforce in Sutherland. During the episode, Eric was very clear: 'Change is the hardest thing you will do in your life.'

It wasn't only what Eric said, it was how he said it. He meant it. He would often tell his board the story of a man who lived in a small apartment and had won the lottery. He was about to move his family to an eight-bed mansion. Eric would ask the board: 'How long do you think it will take before they realize what they have lost, and all of a sudden the change they have made doesn't feel as appealing?' See Chapter 6 for the full story.

It is easy to assume in that scenario that the change would be positive, but this is the complexity of change. What works for one person may not for another. As human beings we go through a whole range of emotions related to change. Some adapt straight away, some will push back, some will get angry, and some will not change at all. This is reality, and in later chapters we will dive into the complexities of getting organizational and individual commitment to change.

In conclusion

Organizations are 'living and breathing' every day. They are dynamic, fluid, disruptive and disrupted. They can't stand still; it's innovate or die. However, you must take your people with you every step of the way. More than ever, there must be a clear convergence between organizational and individual success, but as we have discovered on our podcast, it is not an easy thing to do – hence why the connection and engagement of an individual to an organization today can be brittle at times.

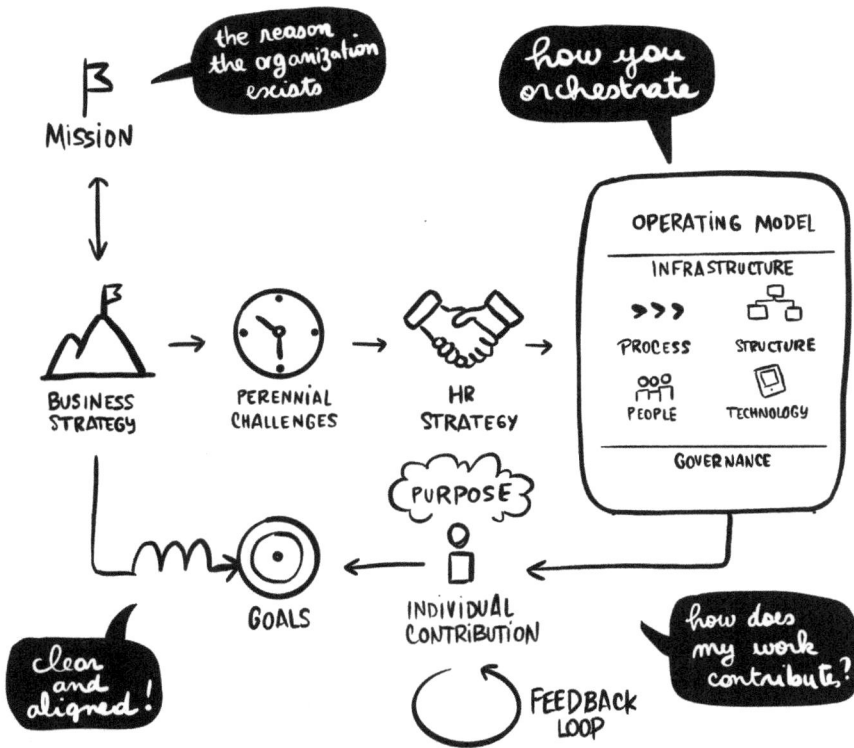

Tips and tricks

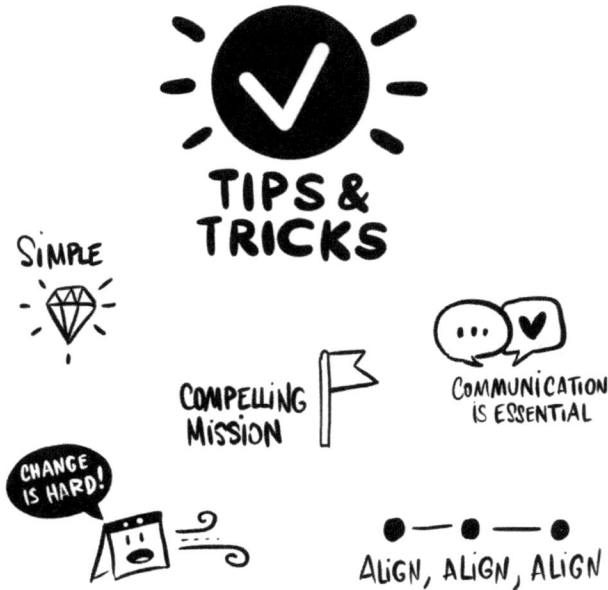

1 Strategies that are simple in design and clearly highlight competitive difference are more likely to be understood, accepted and executed.

2 The mission of the company needs to be compelling, irrefutable and reflected in the strategy and day-to-day culture of the organization.

3 People coming into the workplace today have different expectations and preferences (where and when they work) to other generations. Being able to communicate the strategy, mission and purpose and EVP to this audience is essential to competing in the talent market.

4 Aligning a strategy across an organization is one of the most important processes. Remember that everyone is relying on clarity and feedback to perform at their best. Nobody wants to be working on projects that don't matter!

5 A mission and a strategy is living and breathing. Therefore, always make sure that it is understood, that leaders understand it and that the culture of the organization reflects the values and behaviours that bring the mission and strategy to life. Change is hard. It never ends. Communicating something once often isn't successful.

Notes

1 M Porter (1996) What Is Strategy? *Harvard Business Review*, https://hbr.org/1996/11/what-is-strategy (archived at https://perma.cc/N8B6-P2DA)

2 *The Human Factor* podcast Ep 5: Delivering On Your Purpose – Executing The Basic Fundamentals | *The Human Factor Podcast* by SAP, https://podcast.opensap. info/the-human-factor/2021/08/17/the-human-factor-ep-5-delivering-on-your-purpose-executing-the-basic-fundamentals/ (archived at https://perma.cc/ 2AXL-5CW8)

3 *The Human Factor* podcast Ep 14: Growing Your Brand Through People | *The Human Factor Podcast* by SAP, https://podcast.opensap.info/the-human-factor/2022/04/01/the-human-factor-ep-14-growing-your-brand-through-peopleguest-david-hieatt-co-founder-of-hiut-denim-and-co-found/ (archived at https://perma.cc/X8HB-7JRJ)

4 Nike (2024) What is Nike's Mission? Nike.com, www.nike.com/help/a/nikeinc-mission (archived at https://perma.cc/3XSR-LJ3S)

5 H Peiper (2023) A new mission for Starbucks, Starbucks Stories & News, https://stories.starbucks.com/stories/2023/a-new-mission-for-starbucks/ (archived at https://perma.cc/Z3BF-AKQN)

6 Google (n.d.). Our approach – How Google Search works, www.google.com/intl/en_uk/search/howsearchworks/our-approach/ (archived at https://perma.cc/M5Z7-EF7A)

7 *The Human Factor* podcast Ep 37: Influencing the C-Suite | *The Human Factor Podcast* by SAP, https://podcast.opensap.info/the-human-factor/2023/11/17/the-human-factor-podcast-ep-37-influencing-the-c-suite/ (archived at https://perma.cc/V7MT-2WBD)

CHANGE
is the only
CONSTANT

in life

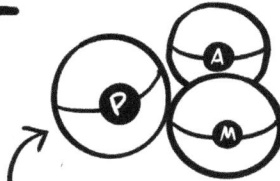

The case for change

2

Introduction

If there is one thing that can be relied upon in life, it is that change is constant. Whether that is at work or in our personal lives, we all experience change regularly. But change can also trigger reactions – such as anxiety, stress, fear, excitement, anticipation, ambivalence, apathy and many others.

In this chapter, we will explore when and why change occurs. We will examine the human factors involved in enabling a change, and what drives success versus failure. We will examine the constituent elements of a case for change as well as exploring the differences between personal and organization change. Having identified the elements of a case for change, we will then build upon how this can then be delivered successfully – how we can apply structure to the process, what commitments are needed, who is likely to be involved and how we can evaluate and differentiate success from failure.

We will explore how some organizations have successfully established their case for change, as well as pitfalls that can occur in the process. Finally, we will conclude with tips, tricks and advice when considering a case for change, which can be applied to work or personal change.

When does change occur?

Change comes about when there is a discontent with the current state of things; we change when there is a need to avoid pain, or in the pursuit of a gain. Change can be something small and personal, for example changing your golf swing, to an organization-wide change such as implementing a new corporate strategy. However, it is likely that we all go through a similar thought process when thinking about a change. Sometimes the thinking process is brief and may even be subconscious. Other times, the thought process could take days, weeks, months even.

In the introduction, we mentioned reactions to change or even the thought of change. Neuroscience has determined that when we experience uncertainty or ambiguity, we activate the part of our brain called the mediodorsal thalamus.[1] This area of the brain helps us problem-solve and triggers decision making. The more the uncertainty, the more this area of our brain must work. This is what defines how we react to change. For some, the reaction is more biased towards fear and anxiety. To others, the reaction could be more towards excitement and anticipation.

As we process our thinking about the change we are considering, we examine potentially a lot of input data – what does the change involve, what are the consequences if the change is unsuccessful, what are the benefits of a good change, how will I be able to assess the risks, what don't I know yet and so on. Clearly when we are changing our golf swing, this is a different level of processing when compared to enacting a change to corporate strategy, but we are still assessing the same elements – should I change my golf swing, does my swing need changing? What will I gain by trying to change my swing? How long will it take to change, and should I change during competitions or only in practice for now? How easy will it be to change? Am I tweaking my existing swing, or am I doing a radical overhaul on how I use the golf club? Is it just driving that needs to change, or is it every swing that I need to change?

Our overall feeling towards that change will be driven by these thoughts. What makes us human is that we don't all react to those thoughts in the same way. For some, that new swing change is something to be feared, causing anxiety and stress. For others, it's an opportunity to gain a competitive advantage, leading to a boost in self-esteem.

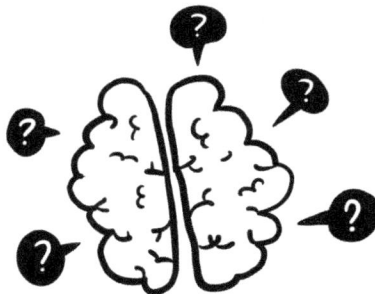

And this is the challenge when we switch our attention to making organizational change. Organizational change triggers similar thinking and emotions as changes in our personal lives, but increases in complexity because the outcome can impact on potentially hundreds or thousands of individuals. We can influence how that change is perceived through our change management approach, but we ultimately have less control over it when compared to changes in our personal life.

Deciding that we want to change, though, does not guarantee success. We have gone through the thought process that we need to change, but we also need to build commitment to it and then we must also execute the change. We will explore commitment and execution later in the book, but first, let's explore the basic elements of change, so that we can ensure we don't miss anything when building our case for change, and thus give ourselves the best chance possible of making a successful and sustainable change.

What are the elements of a case for change?

Drivers for change

As we discussed earlier, understanding why we want to change is often the first step. What is causing us the discontent? Has something become unsustainable that will need addressing, or is it a change towards that something new that I anticipate will be beneficial. Why do I need a change in my golf swing? – is it the avoidance of pain (for example, my drives are going off to the left all the time), or is it the pursuit of a gain (for example, I want to hit the ball further and a change in swing is needed to achieve that)?

Clearly identifying the driver for change will help us in identifying the case for change, but will also help us articulate to others why the change was needed. For organizational change, understanding the current as-is state gives us a well-informed view on the start point. Are we pursing gain, avoiding pain, or maybe a bit of both? This 'discovery' element ensures that our knowledge is as complete and current as possible and allows us to also establish a baseline of the current state. What is causing the pain? How painful is it? Who is it painful for? How long has this current state been like this? How are we doing things today, and what have we tried in the past? What are the benefits of alleviating the pain? Who will experience these benefits?

In Episode 3 of *The Human Factor*, we spoke with Elaine Bergin.[2] Elaine is the Director of Colleague Experience at British Telecom (BT). We discussed the change that was underway at BT with regards to their transformation of the HR function, including, but not limited to, a system replacement. Elaine was clear that the discovery phase was very important:

> What is the problem statement with where we are right now? You know, really start lifting the lid on things, digging underneath, understanding what the root cause of the issues [is], even if sometimes the root cause of the issues is of your own making.

She noted that this was not always easy, and sometimes made for a degree of awkwardness inside the organization:

> Recognizing the moment at which things are not working for you any more, and you've got to change them, sometimes means facing into the demons of what it was that you created in the first place.

This discovery grounds our case for change and allows us then to explore the opportunities to be different. We can build our argument for the change. We can start exploring what changes we want to consider, and what the different options are, as there may not be one obvious direction. Which leads us to defining the change and helping us to create the argument for change.

What is the change?

It is essential that we can clearly identify what the change is, while being able to define what success looks like. We have established at this point that we need to change, but what exactly will that look like when we seek to deliver it? Until we know and can define it, it will be almost impossible to create our case for change adequately.

If we go back to how change can cause fear, it is in part because of uncertainty. By clearly defining the change, we are eliminating some of that uncertainty. Vagueness here is not our friend and can result in misalignment of expectations and ultimately dissatisfaction.

Reflecting again on our conversation with Elaine, she also pointed out that it's not uncommon for a case for change to be named, to bring life and shape to it, but, more than that, to also build a connection:

> Even just the name of what it is that you're trying to achieve generates a story and a connection for people and if you can do that in a way that everybody understands, even better. It speaks to people.

We have observed many change initiatives when working with our customers, and while naming the project is sometimes treated as a bonding exercise or as a way of injecting some energy into the team, it can also be a way of bringing it to life in a meaningful way. A well-chosen name articulates what the change is seeking to achieve, and can inspire. It also gives the change substance. It becomes more real. Maybe having a name makes it more relatable, less remote and less scary? Of course, the choice of name will still take careful thought – 'Operation Mincemeat' may not invoke the reactions you are seeking.

As we continue to develop and give more detail about what the change is, we also must ensure that the outcome will not only deliver an organizational change, but one that also can be adopted by people that it influences.

Another of our podcast episodes, Episode 10, was with Jane Harrington and Nicola Johnson from Bentley Motors.[3] Jane was the HR Digital Transformation Manager, and Nicola the Head of People Development and Transformation. Bentley Motors, as with any automotive organization, is undergoing a significant transformation in the marketplace with its transition from the internal combustion engine to electrification of vehicles.

To help this transition, they also went through several internal transformations to ensure the workforce was and is equipped for this change. One of their biggest learnings from the work they were doing was to ensure that, when they designed new ways of working or new processes, they considered the impact of the change on the workforce. According to Jane:

We need to constantly remind ourselves, working in HR, that there's a human being on the end of every process.

Be authentic, be purposeful, and make sure that we're doing things for the right reason.

Change consequence

We must also assess the consequence of the change: not only the benefits and risks with making the change, but the risks of *not* making it. Often the strongest competitor to a case for change is doing nothing at all. We need to be able to articulate what the risks are with continuation of the existing state, and ensure that there are sufficiently compelling reasons to do something differently. If we don't make this organizational change, will the current situation continue (which might be unpleasant), or could it get even worse (even more unpleasant)?

For example, we are considering replacing our recruitment process. Today's process is failing to attract candidates of sufficient quality. The risk of doing nothing is not only that we continue to fail to attract desirable candidates, but potentially we will risk increasing attrition and reducing employee engagement. By not filling roles, more burden is placed on our workers, leading to an increase in dissatisfaction with the organization, and therefore people deciding to leave.

Clearly then, the risks of doing nothing can be both significant and compelling, but if we assume these are known and don't articulate them, we risk our case for change not securing the commitment and/or funding it requires.

Resources

Our case for change also needs to clearly identify what it needs to effect the change. It needs to be clear with the assumptions, the resource needs, the costs and the timeline. All of these ensure absolute clarity on how the change will be delivered, and, should any of these areas be diluted, then we can set the expectations for how the change will be compromised as a result.

An argument and a justification

Our argument has established the context for the change, the evidence we have collated and what we believe is necessary, such that we can persuade ourselves or others to accept it. With it, we have sought emotional commitment.

However, the argument on its own is insufficient. We also need to justify the change by providing further detail on what is needed to make the change occur, typically in time or money. Likewise, we need to detail what the benefits of the change will be, again often in time and money saved. This justification gives us also a means to prioritize our change against other changes and create a timeline in terms of urgency. From this we can also secure our financial commitment.

If we make an argument for our case for change without a justification, we may attract interest, empathy, excitement for it, but not the commitment to make it happen. Let's take an example from our personal lives. Consider that we have lived in our house for some time and we then decide that the house is draughty and cold. The windows are not as insulated as they used to be. Our argument is clear – we are cold. The windows are contributing to this. If we change the windows, we will lose less heat to the outside. We want to change the windows. But new windows will cost us thousands of pounds. Can we justify spending that money on windows, and, if yes, can we justify spending that money now if we also need to fix the kitchen and the roof and other areas?

If we make the justification without an argument, this can lead to scepticism, a lack of belief and a potential to misalign expectation in what is being delivered. In our analogy above, a salesperson has arrived at our front door, offering us the chance to change our windows and save ourselves a large amount of money on our heating bills. Here, the case for change seems justified – if I pay to replace the windows, I will save money on bills. The problem is, Do I believe it? How much will I really save? How much more important is it to save money on the windows if I can save money on fixing the roof instead? What if I like the windows as they are?

Therefore, we can see that any case for change needs an argument and a justification to secure full commitment. If either or both are missing, we are likely to struggle to secure adoption and/or a return on investment in the future, if we can even proceed that far.

Stakeholders

As with any change, we need to identify the stakeholders of the change. A golf swing might be a very easy example, in that our only change stakeholder is ourselves. In our house example, though, we may need further stakeholders to be involved, for example other people living in the house who might have other priorities. The window supplier to provide quotes, examples of materials, project timelines, etc. We may need to borrow money and therefore need a loan.

When we go to our organizational change example of a new recruiting process, our stakeholder list will likely include the Recruitment team, HR leadership, Finance leadership, maybe Procurement teams or external third parties need to be involved and so on. Identifying the necessary stakeholders is key to securing a successful outcome and avoids delays later in the process if we must include additional people that were originally forgotten.

These stakeholders will have differing expectations and requirements from the case for change. As such, early identification of the stakeholders and what they need to commit to the change is imperative. We recommend that discussions with stakeholders start with the outcome and work backwards: 'If I were to undertake this change, what would you need from me to commit to supporting and approving it?' For the Finance team for example, this could be more than an identification of the cost profile and expected benefits. The Finance team may also require payback periods to be defined and cashflow projections, so by working backwards from the outcome, a clear set of requirements can be identified so that the case is complete at the first time of asking, rather than going through an iterative process of submission, improvement, re-submission etc.

This part of the change is not easy. Many change initiatives have failed due to either failing to identify and involve the right stakeholders, or failing to sustain the momentum with those stakeholders.

In Episode 17 of the podcast series, we talked with Ann Hawkins and Helen Adams from Walgreens Boots Alliance.[4] Walgreens Boots Alliance is a collective group of retail pharmacy chains. Walgreens is based in the United States, and Boots is based in the United Kingdom. They also have a number of pharmaceutical manufacturing and distribution companies. Ann was the Transformation Lead and Helen was the Senior Director in Global HR. They were responsible for deploying a global change to their workforce, which is approximately 330,000 employees in eight countries.

In our conversation, we explored their approach to stakeholder management in some detail. They reflected: 'We needed to do an incredible amount of work pulling together and managing the expectations of the HR and IT teams in each of the markets.'

More importantly, these expectations were not a static concept. They evolved, developed and grew/changed as time progressed. What they found was that the technology aspect of their change was reasonably well accepted: 'Every leader that we spoke to could understand how hard it was to get data and get quality information, and that meant we got that hook.'

However, having got the hook for the change imperative, they had to consider other aspects: 'The case for change was less from an IT perspective because [the system] was chosen, and it was more around gathering HR around that idea of a central global platform.'

Towards the end of the episode, we asked Ann and Helen for their tips and tricks from the journey they had been on. Three of their observations were focused on the stakeholders in particular:

1 Who are the right people who will challenge you in the right way? Who will help you celebrate successes in the right way but will also be that critical friend at the right times to help drive you on.

2 Make sure you're clear on your influencers and your decision makers. Really nail those and then get the partners in place to man-mark them.

3 Alignment, alignment, alignment.

Structuring the process of creating a case for change

Now that we have identified the ingredients for the case for change, how do we apply a structure to the process in the context of effecting organizational change? In 2019, we (the authors) and a colleague, Mike Theaker, initiated a piece of work that investigated how structure could be applied to the creation of a case for change.

We wanted to ensure that this structure would ensure that our case for change encapsulated three key aspects – Purpose, Approach, Mindset:

1 Is the purpose of the change well understood?

2 Is the approach to the change clearly identified?

3 Will the case for change enable the right mindset to be adopted to ensure successful and sustainable change?

Your Case For Change | Purpose Approach Mindset Framework

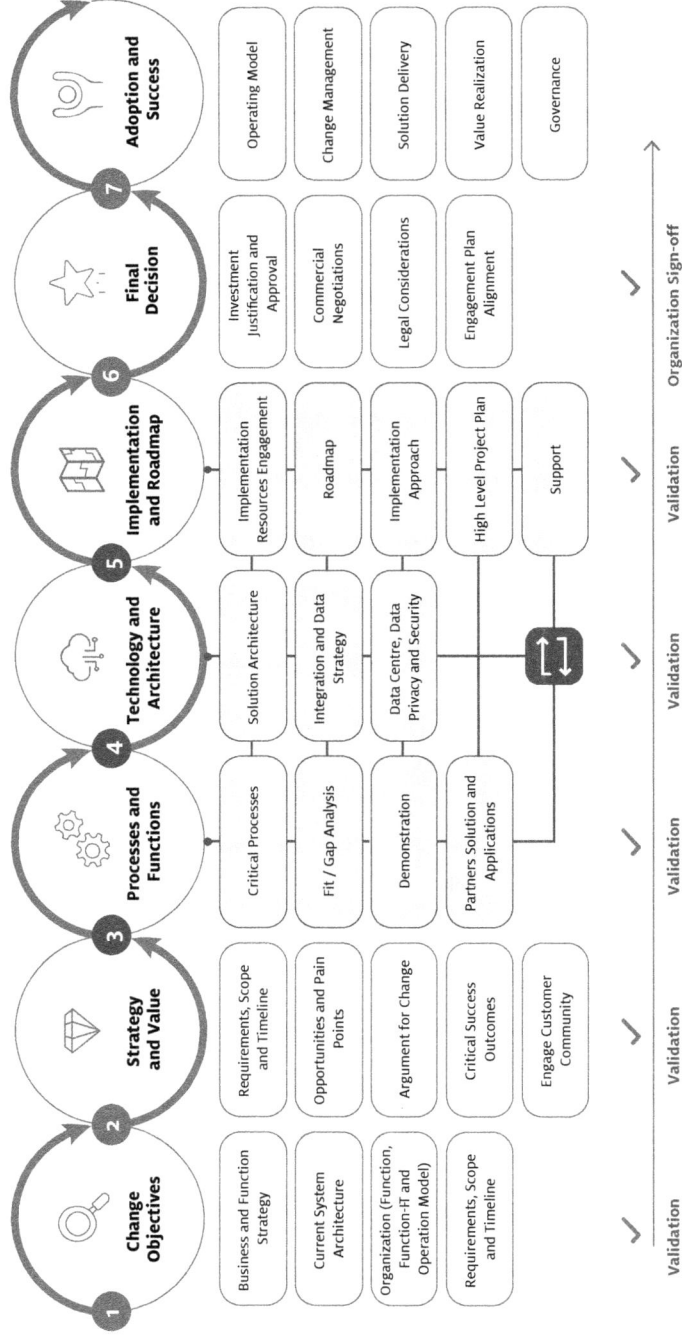

	1 Change Objectives	**2** Strategy and Value	**3** Processes and Functions	**4** Technology and Architecture	**5** Implementation and Roadmap	**6** Final Decision	**7** Adoption and Success
	Business and Function Strategy	Requirements, Scope and Timeline	Critical Processes	Solution Architecture	Implementation Resources Engagement	Investment Justification and Approval	Operating Model
	Current System Architecture	Opportunities and Pain Points	Fit / Gap Analysis	Integration and Data Strategy	Roadmap	Commercial Negotiations	Change Management
	Organization (Function, Function-H and Operation Model)	Argument for Change	Demonstration	Data Centre, Data Privacy and Security	Implementation Approach	Legal Considerations	Solution Delivery
	Requirements, Scope and Timeline	Critical Success Outcomes	Partners Solution and Applications		High Level Project Plan	Engagement Plan Alignment	Value Realization
		Engage Customer Community			Support		Governance

Validation — Validation — Validation — Validation — Validation — Validation — Organization Sign-off

Continuous Stakeholder Management and Value Case Socialization

We identified a number of phases and activities that should be considered. While it is critical that the Discovery Phase and the Strategy & Value Phase are undertaken first, the subsequent phases of Process & Functions, Technology & Architecture and Implementation & Roadmap are more likely to be on an as-needed basis. Some changes will not require technology, for example, or will not be supported by third parties, but most organization changes will go through the same process, if not necessarily all of the outlined activities.

We also found that phases 3, 4 and 5 tended to become more iterative as the change became more clearly identified. As such, these phases may be non-linear in how they are undertaken. What is important is that activities were not forgotten about, leading to an incomplete case by the time we are seeking organizational sign-off.

What we then observed was that it was human nature to jump straight into phases 3, 4 and 5 and start solutioning what the change could look like and deliver. However, without phases 1 and 2, this often led to difficulties in securing that organizational sign-off because the case for change didn't have a sufficiently strong argument. The justification was often well documented, but the argument was weak and, as we observed earlier, this then led to a lack of commitment when needed.

What we also found as we created this framework was that it applied to all cases for change, whether it be for organizational change, purchasing equipment or even making lifestyle choices in our personal lives. The fundamental principles still applied and the process of creating the case for change were common, even if some of the activities weren't required. And, unless we ensure the case for change is humanly desirable and organizationally, technically and economically feasible, then it is unlikely to secure the commitment needed.

Dr Vikas Shah MBE DL is a highly respected entrepreneur and philanthropist. He wrote in his book *Thought Economics: Conversations with the remarkable people shaping our century* on this last point, and it remains as true today as when he wrote it.[5]

These are the fundamentals to a successful case for change.

How to overcome resistance to change

We started this chapter acknowledging that change can be daunting. As humans, we are constantly having to evaluate changes in work and our home, and sometimes it also becomes overwhelming. Not all change will lead to a better state, and we hopefully recognize those instances. We have explored those personal changes, where we are in control of the decision. But organizational change, especially at scale, is much more complex. We will need to consider many opinions, backgrounds, agendas and, regrettably sometimes, sabotage for political reasons. How do we work through these considerations for our case for change?

If we have built our case for change on solid foundations, with good discovery and alignment of our argument and justification to value, then we are certainly well placed. We need to ensure we communicate regularly with our stakeholders and seek their ongoing commitment to support the case.

We discussed how to work with the C-suite in particular when discussing change in Episode 37 of the podcast series.[6] Our guest for that episode was Eric Tinch, who is Chief People Officer for Sutherland. Sutherland is a global provider of business process and technology management services. They underwent a global transformation in 2023, going live with a new people solution accessible by all their employees.

Eric shared his thoughts with us in a fascinating conversation. One of his first observations was to keep things simple and remove the complexity:

> The first thing I try to just take the complication out of the conversation. Every opportunity I have that means to find a consistent approach. To straight talk, that straight talk must be embodied in the why. Why it matters and if we can get on to why it matters, then we can understand well – Here are the advantages. Here are the disadvantages. Here's what happens if we do nothing.

Having that clear, simple messaging helps explain the change to all levels in the organization, but also consistently. Everyone understands what the change means. Eric then identifies that we also need to set the context for the change – how long will it take and what it will take: 'Articulate what the change is. Articulate how long it'll take. Articulate what it will involve relative to a shift in our human's life or their day-to-day activity.'

For him, this was particularly important to consider:

Articulating the timeline early and often and then tying that back to why it mattered. It's critically important.

Eric then talked about advocates and adversaries. And for him, they served very specific purposes in securing a case for change: 'I use adversaries to help me understand the potential barriers as they see them. I use the advocates to help me understand that perception of the road ahead. Utilizing both to help create a balanced approach.'

He acknowledges that not all his stakeholders will agree with the change, but that the goal of getting 100 per cent acceptance and buy in is not always possible, nor needed. 'I think there's a misconception when it comes to driving change or when it comes to affecting a process. I think there's a misconception that you must convince everyone to come to the middle. It simply will not happen. You're trying to shift the balance more toward advocacy. If you can shift the balance more toward advocacy, it's like flowing water, right? Eventually, more is going to flow toward advocacy.'

Our question back to Eric was how to deal with not securing 100 per cent acceptance for the change proposal. His perspective on this was: 'There is no utopian perspective where you end up saying, of the ... people I have, 100 per cent of them are inside. Well, if I can get 71 per cent, if I can get 68 per cent, maybe I can take the guys who are still adversaries and utilize that group to keep me grounded, utilize that group to help me understand that we're not yet done.'

Eric talks passionately about being the change evangelist. He observed: 'A word I use softly with my own leadership team is you must *evangelize* these processes. And there are times that it gets a little bit exhausting. You've got to go to every meeting. You've got to continuously have conversations about how well or, you know, in some cases when things aren't going well, being straightforward and honest with the masses and with the other stakeholders around the organization about the effort, whatever that effort is.'

We asked Eric how he kept his own personal energy at the right level, especially when the change was occurring over a significant period of time.

> I keep going back to the mission at hand, and whenever I am just completely exhausted myself, or if I look at the team and I can tell that they're getting a little bit worn, especially if it's a multi-year transformation that you're driving, I'll take everyone back to the mission. **This is why we are here. This is why it matters.** It sounds so simple.

In conclusion

We started this chapter with the premise that change is constant. We have explored the different aspects of creating a case for change, and it's important to recognize that this is not always easy. However, a structured approach will always help, and as such we have outlined the Purpose,

Tips and tricks

TIPS & TRICKS

ROBUST DISCOVERY

WORK BACKWARDS

START BASELINE

KEEP AN EYE ON ENERGY LEVELS

SOCIALIZE THE CASE FOR CHANGE

1 Ground any case for change upon robust discovery.

2 Baseline the existing situation so that future improvements can be measured. If actual baseline figures can't be obtained, use assumptions.

3 Start from the point of case acceptance and work backwards. This helps understand expectations of what is needed to secure buy-in.

4 Socialize the case for change often as it is being formed, and ensure stakeholders are routinely aligned.

5 Keep an eye on personal energy levels. Remind yourself of what you are trying to change and why it matters.

Approach, Mindset framework, as well as advice and guidance from some of our podcast guests that have been through significant changes in their organizations.

Each change journey will also be different, with differing start points, stakeholders, challenges and benefits. What we have covered here though are the common elements, whether that is for personal or organizational change.

Notes

1 Massachusetts Institute of Technology (2021) How the brain deals with uncertainty, https://news.mit.edu/2021/how-the-brain-deals-with-uncertainty-1014#:~:text=Functional%20brain%20imaging%20had%20shown (archived at https://perma.cc/F37N-BHFQ)

2 *The Human Factor* podcast Ep 3: Is Technology the Catalyst for a Transformation? | *The Human Factor Podcast* by SAP, https://podcast.opensap. info/the-human-factor/2021/06/17/the-human-factor-ep-3-is-technology-the-catalyst-for-a-transformation (archived at https://perma.cc/B64P-ZG9W)

3 *The Human Factor* podcast Ep 10: The Attraction of Talent in a Digitally Changing Environment | *The Human Factor Podcast* by SAP, https://podcast. opensap.info/the-human-factor/2021/12/17/the-human-factor-ep-10-the-attraction-of-talent-in-a-digitally-changing-environment/ (archived at https:// perma.cc/K728-PLJR)

4 *The Human Factor* podcast Ep 17: The Dynamics of Organizational Change | *The Human Factor Podcast* by SAP, https://podcast.opensap.info/the-human-factor/2022/05/27/the-human-factor-ep-17-the-dynamics-of-organizational-changeguests-helen-adams-senior-director-of-global-hrnbs/

5 V Shah (2022) *Thought Economics: Conversations with the remarkable people shaping our century*, Michael O'Mara

6 *The Human Factor* podcast Ep 37: Influencing the C-Suite | *The Human Factor Podcast* by SAP, https://podcast.opensap.info/the-human-factor/2023/11/17/the-human-factor-podcast-ep-37-influencing-the-c-suite/ (archived at https://perma.cc/C32J-KCX2)

the culture will be tested every day

The fluidity of culture 3

Introduction

I recall our earliest brainstorm for the book and deciding our structure, topics, etc. We lost count of the number of times we mentioned the word 'culture', so we had to include a chapter on it, but then you stop and think about the complexities and risk of ending up down a rabbit hole. However, throughout the book, we have committed to grounding our topics and not ending up in the proverbial rabbit hole, but instead focusing on some of the elements that we consider to be important related to culture.

It's a word that is spoken about on a regular basis. We think it's a word that most people would understand if asked, but what do we do with something which isn't physical, can't be touched, is intangible but arguably has more influence on what we think about our workplace more than anything else? It is also challenged and influenced by the changing context in which we live and work. It doesn't stand still; therefore, it needs to remain fluid and flexible.

If we consider, for example, the impact of the pandemic in 2020, overnight organizations had to shift to remote working. It gave rise to new ways of working; it provided employees with a greater work/life balance and the ability to fulfil tasks that were perhaps not achievable previously owing to having to be in an office location. The impact on culture was immense. Leaders were connecting with their teams in different ways, utilizing platforms like Teams and Zoom became the norm. It created a new culture.

Now, in 2024, however, we are seeing adaptations of that. Organizations have been wrestling with what to do with remote working, but we are seeing a desire to return to more 'traditional ways of working', and having their teams return to the office. In some cases, it is perhaps for three days a week, but in more extreme cases it is full-time. What impact will this have on culture? We suspect a fair amount of tension, resistance, and it is highly likely people will move on to pastures new. This is the other side of culture when it isn't conducive to the individual.

We will reference in this episode the conversation that we had on the *Human Factor* podcast with Sue Yell; a conversation that focused entirely on culture.[1] With over 25 years' experience in the HR sector, Sue Yell has been HR Director for Warburtons since 2011, where she has worked with the executive team to define and deliver the business's growth plans. Sue is responsible for the development and delivery of the people management strategy and the people agenda, which is now seen as essential to the organization's success.

Warburtons is a great example of an organization with multiple generations working side by side every day. It is still family owned and has always stayed true to its roots in Bolton when the business started in 1876, almost 150 years ago. Culture is everything to Warburtons. We asked Sue what culture meant to her, and this was her response:

> The culture of a business absolutely defines the environment, the personality, the atmosphere, the relationships, and of course importantly, the performance outputs. It really does represent a set of shared beliefs, norms, values that very much influence how people think, feel, and behave.

Through the chapter we will explore several areas. This will include what is culture, who is accountable for it, how is it communicated and anchored within an organization, and what happens when it becomes a 'bad' culture and the impact this has on the workforce.

What is culture and who owns it?

The word 'culture' has many different meanings. For some it refers to an appreciation of good literature, music, art or food. For a biologist, it is likely to be a colony of bacteria or other micro-organisms growing in a nutrient medium in a laboratory Petri dish.

However, for anthropologists and other behavioural scientists, culture is the full range of learned human behaviour patterns.[2] The term was first used in this way by the pioneer English anthropologist Edward B. Tylor in his book *Primitive Culture*, published in 1871. Tylor said that culture is: 'that complex whole which includes knowledge, belief, art, law, morals, custom, and any other capabilities and habits acquired by man as a member of society.' Of course, it is not limited to men. Women possess and create it also.

We want to focus in on the idea that culture is the 'full range of learned human behaviour patterns'. At the beginning of our book, in Chapter 1, we explored strategy and all that it entails. Irrespective of organization and its size, when you move from strategy to execution, you have a decision to make on how you wish to execute. This is very tightly connected to philosophy, which we cover in Chapter 4, but if there is no stated vision on how you wish people to work – the behaviours that you wish to see and even the behaviours you don't – then how can you expect to cultivate a culture that is aligned to the organization you aspire to be?

Let's take the analogy of a school for a moment. Speaking as a parent, it was something that I was keen to understand when selecting a school for my daughters. I wanted to understand and get a feel for the culture. Schools are often very clear on their vision, their values and behaviour. We will touch on 'reinforcement' a little later in the chapter, but just by speaking to the headteacher and spending some time in the environment, I was able to get a feel of what the 'culture' was like. Did it feel supportive? Did it feel progressive? Did it feel a little strict and perhaps a bit more tightly controlled?

In the school environment, you sense and feel that the culture is very much set by the headmaster or headmistress. On a welcome evening, they stood in the main hall and presented the vision of the school, bringing to life the culture and the emphasis on behaviours and outcomes. I believe that was the same when I was in school, and it certainly was for my parents. In an organization, however, is this always the case?

Therefore, who owns the culture within the context of an organization? As you would expect, there are multiple thoughts and opinions on this. One view, which we support, comes from the *Harvard Business Review* in their article 'Company culture is everyone's responsibility'.[3] In their view, the importance of culture has only risen since the pandemic due to the advent of remote working, a greater recognition and intensified push for diversity, equity, inclusion, and belonging (DEI&B) and the challenges with attracting talent. Culture has become a strategic priority with impact on the bottom line. It can't just be delegated and compartmentalized any more. Therefore, culture-building has now become more of an approach where everyone is responsible. In many organizations there is a gap between the existing culture and the 'desired' culture – the culture needed to support and advance the company's goals and strategies. In a new culture-building model, everyone is responsible for cultivating the desired culture.

This approach assigns different roles in defining and developing the culture. This happens through formal roles as well as informal spheres of influence and reflects how organizations operate these days. It also establishes clear accountabilities for results. While the actual implementation of this approach may vary based on the type, size, age and structure of the organization, the general distribution of responsibility can look something like this:

- **Board of Directors**: Guide the definition and development of the desired culture, ensuring that it aligns with business goals and meets the needs of all stakeholders.

- **CEO and senior management team**: Define the desired culture and cultivate it through leadership actions, including setting objectives, strategies and key results that prioritize culture-building, and designing the organization and its operational processes to support and advance the company's purpose and core values.

- **Human Resources**: Design employee experiences that interpret and reinforce the desired culture. Also implement strategies and programmes that enable the rest of the organization to fulfil their culture responsibilities, such as offering training programmes that develop leader capacity for culture-building and employee engagement; and developing culture guidebooks, processes such as performance management and systems such as rewards and recognition programmes that nurture the desired culture.

- **Compliance, Risk, and Ethics department**: Provide input to the CEO and senior management team on the definition of the desired culture from the perspective of ethics and risk. Also ensuring that execution on the desired culture across the organization aligns with the company's risk management strategies through tools such as ethics decision trees, processes such as a whistleblower programme and systems such as compliance monitoring that align with the desired culture.

- **Middle and front-line managers**: Deliver employee experiences that interpret and reinforce the desired culture. Also implement culture-building strategies, cultivating employee engagement with the desired culture and fulfilling the culture-building responsibilities of employees.

- **Employees**: Provide input to the CEO and senior management team on the definition of the desired culture and culture-building programmes and tactics by providing insights on how the desired culture aligns with or differs from the actual culture, customer perspectives, and employee needs and expectations. Employees should provide feedback on existing culture-building efforts and ideas for new ones. Also create, adhere to and enforce routines and norms that interpret the desired culture, and align their attitudes and behaviours with the desired culture.

We believe employees expect someone to 'set the tone' and champion and model what the culture should be. In Chapter 10 we discuss the role of the leader, and setting an example is an important aspect of leadership. There are no leaders without followers, so the emphasis on leaders to be modelling the culture of the organization every day is super important. The moment they don't or there are inconsistencies in application or care, you will quickly see confidence and belief impacted lower down the organization.

As humans we can experience multiple cultures in one day. If we take the *HBR* culture building model, we will see the creation of culture follow a similar vein. There is the overall organizational culture in your place of work, but on a day-to-day basis I am part of many small teams led by different people. Culturally each of those teams can be very different, and much of that is dictated by the person who is leading the team.

When I leave work and join my six-a-side football team, the culture will be different again, and after football I will return home to my family, and within our home we have our own culture. We determine how we do things, how we behave, the behaviours we don't tolerate, our 'rules' if you like. Very much reinforcing the point of the *HBR* model, without any guardrails there would quite possibly be anarchy, but it is still the responsibility of everyone in the home to sustain the culture.

So, when we stop and think about culture and what it is, for us it is the behaviours that truly underpin how the organization wants to work and what it believes are the behaviours that will create an environment that people want to work in, is fair, inclusive, supportive, and progressive.

In Chapter 4, *The importance of having a philosophy*, we touch on the philosophy of David Hieatt and the team at Hiut,[4] but what also shines through was the culture. They have developed a clear and defined culture, extremely inclusive, where everyone has a voice. The production team manage their schedule to meet production. They have 15-minute clarity meetings every week to discuss what they have learned or to find out something they don't know. There is no tea or biscuits; it's 15 mins sharp. They celebrate birthdays, and on a regular basis they will all go out. As David says: 'It's important to go out, connect with your people, have a dance and a chat.' We love that.

Very early in my career, during an open forum, a question was asked to a senior leader around how he viewed culture, and he gave quite a funny answer. In simple terms, he said: 'It's how things are done here. Our customs, our practices, and the behaviours that we wish to see on a day-to-day basis to drive the business forward.' He then went on to say: 'I am also realistic [enough] to know there is a shadow culture, which is the one when the senior leaders have gone home or are out of the office,' and he winked at me. We knew what he meant. As children, we didn't always behave the same when the grown-ups were not around or had gone to bed!

We now have a baseline picture that describes what we mean by culture, leveraging the insights from the *HBR* article to suggest what a new culture-building model could look like, so there is clear accountability for the setting of the culture, but ultimately everyone then has a part to play in cultivating it and making it a reality. In the *HBR* article, it noted that many organizations have a gap between desired and reality. That is the constant challenge, and what we will look at next. How do we anchor the culture, how do we communicate what it is and means, and how do we then reinforce it?

Anchoring and communicating culture

Like anything in life, if you don't communicate effectively what you hope and desire to happen, then don't be surprised if it doesn't. Even worse, it manifests to become the opposite of what you hoped for. This absolutely applies to culture. There is an element of 'you reap what you sow'. Far too many assumptions are made in life, and one of the worst is assuming that a message has been received and understood.

We have dedicated a whole chapter to the employee value proposition, which is Chapter 7, and we strongly believe this is the natural starting point for new employees and existing employees to truly understand the culture of the organization. It provides clarity on the strategy, the vision, purpose and the fundamental behaviours. It brings to life and articulates the culture and the commitment required from all employees to help cultivate, nurture and realize it. It is part of the psychological contract between the organization and the employee.

How does it get communicated and anchored, however? By 'anchored', we mean made into part of the fabric, understood, visible to many and felt. We could write a whole book on the various ways of communicating cultural expectations, but one thing that must be stated is the absolute need for a clear plan. Again, that sounds so obvious, but we observe on so many occasions the absence of a plan. There is too often an assumption that something exists, people have been told about it and therefore know what else is to be done. This is a big mistake.

Anchoring cultural expectations requires a clear plan. Below are some ideas and suggestions for communicating and anchoring. We will share some of our personal experiences, and also what we have learnt from others including Sue and her team at Warburtons.

1. The delivery mechanisms

Genius will always lie in its simplicity, and being able to communicate a clear message to a large group of people requires simplicity, but also a commitment and conviction. It can't be ambiguous. Whether it is a video from the CEO or a structured cascade delivered through individual teams, the message needs to be consistent and clear.

I have observed and been part of teams that have delivered cultural change messages in very creative ways. One of them was 'The Big Picture', a creative way to bring to life in visual terms what the organization was seeking to create and cultivate. Teams were gathered in workshop style to experience 'The Big Picture' and understand what it meant, and through facilitation were asked for their input, concerns and observations. It remains one of the most powerful ways that I have seen an organization engage around a common vision and culture.

Both Simon and I have had the great pleasure of working with Warburtons for several years. I remember my first meeting with Sue Yell and her team. It was a memorable meeting for several reasons, one of them being that I got Sue's name wrong. Thankfully she forgave me! I remember walking into the head office reception and being met with signage celebrating their place on *The Times* Great Place to Work List. As I walked through the office, I could see a huge amount of information related to values and behaviours on walls in bright colours that just drew you in.

I then sat down with Sue, and she proceeded to share with me who Warburtons were, their strategy, the culture, the behaviours. The DNA and conviction came to life in the space of a 30-minute conversation. A commitment to quality, care, ambition, responsibility and sustainable success.

In terms of a delivery mechanism, Sue shared that as Warburtons grew across the UK, they created a cause called 'Painting Britain Red'. It was nothing more complex than a map in all locations which turned more and more red as new bakeries and warehouses were opened across the UK. It aligned the whole business and provided a clear line of sight that everyone understood, including their own role in it. An extremely powerful example of aligning a workforce towards a common goal with a highly visual delivery mechanism.

2. The organizational anchors

Anchoring a culture is the next challenge. We are going to focus on the behaviours that are considered essential to building the right culture for the organization. Developing behaviours does not happen overnight. This is one of the biggest assumptions made.

Giving and receiving feedback will always be one of the best examples. There is an assumption that everyone can do this. That is simply not the case, and the reasons for this are varied. Many people have had bad experiences receiving feedback; others are fearful telling someone something they may not wish to hear; some may feel the culture does not support it. It is a behaviour that requires nurturing. In some cases the skill needs to be built, but in the main it needs to be identified and communicated as a behaviour that is central to the effectiveness and development of the culture.

Within the *HBR* article, one of the key stages falls on HR, which is the design of experiences, programmes and processes that will anchor the culture into the everyday fabric of the organization. So where do they need to show up? How can you create a red thread through processes and all experiences? Working from the employee value proposition, let's look at the different processes in which the behaviours of the organization can be anchored, measured and reinforced. We also classify these processes as the 'perennial challenges' which lie very much at the heart of culture.

If we look below, we have very much looked at the processes from an organization perspective:

- **Recruitment and onboarding** – finding individuals who fit the culture of the organization.

- **Performance and goal-setting** – assessing individual behaviours versus competencies.

- **Learning and development** – supporting individuals with focused development interventions versus competencies.
- **Succession and development** – accurately identifying individuals with desired behaviours and competencies.
- **Reward and recognition** – targeted approaches to identifying and recognizing exhibited behaviours.
- **Legal compliance** – ensuring individuals have the skills and capabilities to meet requirements of the role.
- **Feedback** – facilitating peer-to-peer feedback.

However, in 2024, the individuals who are yet to join an organization will also be considering many of these processes. Their questions and thoughts will include the following:

- What career opportunities are in this company?
- How can I move into new roles?
- How can I achieve future career goals?
- How can I get fulfilment from my current work?
- Will I be treated fairly?
- Is it easy to get things done?
- Does the company align with my beliefs?

This is where a culture is well and truly tested, and the point is very well made in the *HBR* article. We have observed with many organizations that they are experiencing a high percentage of turnover within the first six to 12 months of someone joining. We believe this will be in part due to cultural perception and the commitment of the organization to behaving and growing in a certain way that aligns with the expectation of the employee.

If an organization is committed to developing a culture, then anchoring the desired behaviours into the day-to-day fabric of the organization and the processes that will enable and underpin the culture is crucial. The processes need to be designed to reflect the behaviour of the organization, and there must be a clear focus on execution and outcomes. It simply cannot be that there is a process in flight which is not being engaged with and is not measurable. There must be a discipline and rigour, otherwise it is merely process for process's sake, and this is when people disengage and question the purpose and value.

Developing behaviours, however, does not happen overnight. It is not enough to simply say: 'The programme is live; it has been rolled out', and that is the extent of the enablement and communication. It needs reinforcement, and it needs success. Mini celebrations that celebrate cultural changes or impacts. We will touch on reinforcement shortly.

3. The rule of 6,7,8 or 9

I have had the privilege of working with some great communicators in my career. It has led me to observe and try to understand some of the great practices when it comes to landing and reinforcing a message or building behavioural habits over a sustained period.

The rule of

7

REPEATED EXPOSURE IS VITAL

1
2
3
4
5
6
7

If you want to nurture and grow a progressive culture that truly aligns a whole organization, you need to be communicating A LOT. Not for the sake of it, but to make sure that programmes, messages, policies are landing and understood. In Chapter 6 we focus on building commitment to change, and communication is central to building that commitment and understanding.

Being very candid here, and perhaps talking from personal experience, culture work can be a challenge owing to the previous experiences or perceptions of the workforce. There may be a heavy amount of cynicism: 'We have heard it all before and nothing ever happens or changes.' You perhaps will need to overcome or not be perturbed by that resistance and stay true to the course you are on. This is one of the main reasons why communicating successes is super important.

I will share a personal story from my time at Premier Farnell. We deployed our SAP SuccessFactors technology as a key element of our business transformation, of which people and culture were a central pillar. We went from entirely manual/paper-based to automated overnight. We asked people to fill in their people profile online, so we could start to build some talent intelligence.

I remember, one week into using the technology, I was asked if I knew of any fluent Polish speakers. I did a talent search, and found 33 people who classed themselves as fluent. That little quick win was passed to the Group Head of Communication, and it was included in a blog post from our CEO that night. We saw a huge spike in the completion of profiles, and it provided a visible sign of the cultural shift. This is how you start to get connection and buy-in.

In the specialism of marketing, they have the Rule of Seven. The Rule of Seven asserts that a potential customer should encounter a brand's marketing messages at least seven times before making a purchase decision.[5] When it comes to engagement for your marketing campaign, this principle emphasizes the importance of repeated exposure in enhancing recognition and improving retention. Repeated exposure is vital because it builds familiarity and credibility, fostering trust and influencing your audience's behaviour.

I have long joked with colleagues (and not to just copy the original rule) that you may need fewer than seven ways to land a message, and you may need more. A part of establishing a culture may involve the sharing of knowledge or information. It may also require skill building across a large volume of people. Some parts of the work will require a longer investment of time to realize the required outcome, and this is particularly true when it concerns changing behaviour or forming new habits which very much lie at the heart of culture. They don't happen overnight, and may require revisiting on a regular basis.

Colin Camerer, a behavioural economist at the California Institute of Technology, conducted some research on habit formation.[6] One popular idea suggests that it takes 21 days to solidify a habit. Colin found that on New Year's Day when a resolution was made and the 21 days were up, only 9 per cent of people stuck to their goals. A hallmark 2009 study on habit creation found that habits developed in a range of 18 to 254 days; participants reported taking an average of about 66 days to reliably incorporate one of three new daily activities – eating a piece of fruit with lunch, drinking a bottle of water with lunch, or running for 15 minutes before dinner. Consistent daily repetition was the biggest factor influencing whether a behaviour would become part of an automatic daily routine.

Therein lies the fragility of creating and sustaining a culture. If new behaviours and habits don't form, the culture will be tested. Sustaining a culture requires a concerted focus and effort. Strip away assumptions, have a programme and plan in place that reinforces key messages at regular intervals, and run refresher sessions on critical processes to ensure understanding and ability to execute. This absolutely applies to leaders who are responsible for teams.

Part of your plan must focus on reinforcement, but also recognition. This is how behaviours are celebrated and recognized. It's how you establish a culture of modelling and best practices.

4. *Reinforcement*

We mentioned earlier in the chapter that schools are often highly effective at setting out the culture of the school, what is expected in terms of behaviour and what isn't. We observed that when our daughters attended secondary/high school, they would come home with badges on their blazers, and we would ask what they were for. Children were recognized for demonstrating behaviours and upholding the values of the school. It was a highly visible sign of attainment and reinforcement of what is important in the school.

Cultures are fluid and need to flex, and reinforcement is a big aspect of that. Celebrating together, recognizing on a peer-to-peer level appreciating the efforts or contribution of an individual when they helped you or someone else in the organization, or better still the end consumer or customer. Recognition is a hugely powerful way of cementing the right behaviours, so they are repeated time and again and serve as an example to others.

Ultimately the true measure of the culture will always reside with the individual, whether that is a colleague or consumer. Culture very much resides in the eyes of the beholder and their perception of the experience and behaviours demonstrated. That is the reality and that is what organizations must influence every day.

Culture in the eyes of colleagues and consumers

Sue Yell shared with us during our conversation her ultimate test of culture:

> Warburtons has always focused on having a very strong and positive culture where employees can believe in the company values and are proud to be part of something. So for me, the real test is at 4.30 am in the morning on a wet November [do they think] 'I'm going to phone in sick'? Or do they think, 'Do you know what I'm proud of? What I'm part of? I work with a great bunch of people.' Because that discretionary effort is so important for a business like ours, we are totally built on an ethos of quality and service. Everyone understands our purpose and all our noses are pointing north.

It really is a very powerful statement and one that absolutely reflects what is sometimes the binary nature of culture. The difference between compliance and commitment. Is this something that I am proud to be a part of and am I appreciated for it? The individual is ultimately the one who determines that. Am I proud to work here? Is this an organization that develops and takes care of its people? Is my voice welcomed and heard? That is culture in action.

We believe the consumer is the other barometer of culture. We are all consumers and we have more than an eye for sensing the culture from the very beginning. We can almost sniff out when we believe the culture is, dare I say it, rotten. From a consumer perspective it is all about behaviour. Whether we are in a shop or a restaurant, I believe we carry with us an expectation that the person serving us is polite, attentive, helpful and you believe committed to helping you have a great experience. Some may argue that none of those matters, but referring to Chapter 1 and Michael Porter's definition of strategy, it is about perceived differentiated value.

Of course, value means different things to different people, but it was a point reinforced in our conversation with Dave Ulrich on the *Human Factor* podcast.[7] Dave is the Rensis Likert Professor at the Ross School of Business, University of Michigan, and a partner at the RBL Group, a consulting firm focused on helping organizations and leaders deliver value. He has published over 200 articles and book chapters, and more than 30 books. He edited *Human Resource Management* from 1990 to 1999, served on the editorial board of four other journals and on the Board of Directors for Herman Miller for 16 years; he has spoken to large audiences in 90 countries, performed workshops for over half of the Fortune 200, coached successful business leaders and is a Distinguished Fellow in the National Academy of Human Resources.

Our conversation with Dave covered a huge amount of ground, including the evolution of HR as the custodian for people. Dave placed a huge amount of emphasis on value and in particular the end consumer. He shared: 'The biggest challenge in your job today is to help your company succeed in the marketplace. If your company doesn't have a successful customer or an investor, there is no workplace. The challenge of HR today is to create organizations that succeed in the marketplace, because without a marketplace, there is no workplace.'

In a fiercely competitive market where customer loyalty is perhaps difficult to retain, the culture of the organization needs to shine and shine bright. Are you an organization that I respect and value, an organization that I wish to be associated with? Do I believe there is a genuine care in your behaviour and a commitment to me as a consumer? So much of society has become quite binary, things are very black and white. Standing out in the marketplace requires a culture that drives behaviours that are finely tuned to customer success and delight. Without it – I'm sure many of us have been on the receiving end of appalling service, we know the consequences. We will absolutely take our custom elsewhere, and I believe in this instance you get the very tangible impact of a poor culture on the commercial success of the organization.

Later in the book we will touch on advocacy, and I believe this is very closely linked to culture. Am I willing to proactively shout about an organization and recommend them because I respect who they are culturally? That is the acid test – do I respect their behaviours, but also what it feels like, the visceral connection. This applies to colleagues and consumers.

Culture vs climate

A visceral connection speaks to emotion and a feeling. Culture very much describes and articulates how things are done. The purpose, the vision, the key behaviours. Is it possible however, to be part of an organization where you respect the culture and are perfectly OK to operate in it, but you are not overly happy? On a personal level, it doesn't feel great. Is that possible? Is that in fact the reality for many people? We discuss that very point in Chapter 9 on human experience, engagement and advocacy.

In Chapter 10, *The role of the leader*, we discuss climate. This is the perception and feeling that someone has of working or being in an organization. While the organization is working very hard to build a progressive and

supportive culture with all the building blocks and guardrails, it can all fall apart if the individual experience doesn't marry with that.

What happens if your leader/manager is not committed to the execution of processes? What happens if you don't see or experience the behaviours that the organization is trying to nurture and develop? What happens if you feel too many people are not being sincere and respectful of the culture and are almost dismissive of it? It doesn't take long for attitudes to shift, and the mindset becomes: 'Well, if they are not going to do it, why should I?' The climate can start to feel a little toxic, poor performance is tolerated and there is a clear difference in effort and attitude between team members.

What happens in that instance? Do you lose faith in the organization or your line manager? Or both? Is this the point when individuals start to look externally for new opportunities, is this the moment when 'quiet quitting' starts to happen and discretional effort fades away? Feedback on Glassdoor starts to question the culture of the organization. Customer net promoter scores start to drop; engagement scores plateau or start to decline.

This is the reality, unfortunately, and this is when the foundations of a culture begin to get eroded, and people lose hope and belief. At an individual level, you may still be committed and maintain your own standards, but when the collective is not on the same page or rowing in the same direction, there will be an impact. This is the challenge with culture.

Both Simon and I are huge football fans. We will often relate culture to the world of sport and football. If you take the example of a struggling team, you can see with your own eyes when players are not putting in maximum effort, they are not helping each other or covering for each other, and it is clear that something is not right. In football terminology, you will hear the phrase: 'The manager has lost the dressing room', and often that is the case. It could be that some players have become disillusioned with the manager and his tactics/strategy, or some players have not been given a chance in the team and are getting frustrated, or the same player is being picked every game despite not playing at all well. Perhaps the manager has criticized the team in front of the media. All of this will test the 'culture' of the team. Are they aligned and connected as a group, or are they in effect rebelling at the culture and 'downing tools'?

This is where the resolve of the organization must kick in, and there needs to be a proactive plan to underpin it. The organization needs to be listening across multiple processes and events for this, and it needs to act. Preserving a culture is not linear or easy. There must be an acceptance of bumpy moments and denial is not a strategy. There may be times when the culture turns sour and there may very well be good reasons for it. In those moments, leaders must step up. Employees who have perhaps become disillusioned will want to see that their voice has been heard and understood. If we refer to the *HBR* article guidelines and the expectation of the employee, it is twofold – to cultivate the culture, but also to feed back what is working and what isn't. Culture is fluid, it doesn't stand still, and it can flex from one week to the next.

Throughout this book, and indeed the podcast, we are striving to highlight that organizational success is dependent on countless factors all coming together in harmony. This includes the organization always having their finger on the pulse, understanding what is working, what isn't and acting. We believe that most employees will retain faith and hope when they trust that leaders are always listening, acting with integrity and prepared to act. It is the absence of action that often frustrates and diminishes hope.

In conclusion

Culture is something which will always fascinate us. It isn't physical, you can't touch or see it, but you can feel it and sense it. It sends a message to the external world and consumers.

Sue Yell very kindly joined us on the podcast, and the episode focused entirely on how to nurture and sustain a progressive culture. It was an extremely rich conversation with many takeaways, but I wanted to share three that really stuck with me. We believe they truly sum up what a culture-led organization looks and feels like:

- There is a famous saying within Warburtons that the family have been restless since 1876. *Complacency is not an option.* The people working in the organization today are the custodians of the values and DNA, and need to leave it in a better place for the next generation.

- While the values and behaviours are non-negotiable, the culture must flex. It needs to appeal to the next generation so there is relevancy in the organization. This dynamic can be very complex, but this is a great example of having your finger on the pulse.

- In Sue's view, there are several elements that influence culture, and she highlighted resilience and environment. The culture of all organizations is tested every day and much of this is external. Building resilience into the fabric of the organization is fundamental to cope with and react to this pressure and change. The second point is an environment where everyone feels able to contribute and take risks. Does the organization provide timely feedback and overcome any failures quickly?

Complacency is not an option. That sums it up. Be curious, restless, always alert. Understand what is changing, what is happening, what needs to flex, what needs to change. The culture will be tested every day – that is life – so the foundations need to be rock solid to surface what isn't working and acting.

Tips and tricks

1 Be clear on the behaviours that are important to your organization and which you believe will be the bedrock of the culture you wish to create.

2 Have a clear strategy for anchoring your culture through your processes and ways of working.

3 Encourage individual ownership. Have your voice heard, take risks and responsibility for actions.

4 Celebrate success, communicate widely and recognize contributions that are truly aligned to the culture of the organization.

5 Build an effective listening strategy that is built into the right places at the right times, to ensure an accurate picture of what is happening within the organization.

Notes

1 *The Human Factor* podcast Ep 25: Building, Shaping and Retaining A Great Culture | *The Human Factor Podcast* by SAP, https://podcast.opensap.info/the-human-factor/2022/12/16/the-human-factor-podcast-ep-25-building-shaping-and-retaining-a-great-culture/ (archived at https://perma.cc/PBV7-M6J8)

2 Palomar College (n.d.) Human Culture: What is Culture? www.palomar.edu/anthro/culture/culture_1.htm#:~:text=The%20term%20was%20first%20used (archived at https://perma.cc/UVJ6-NC23)

3 D L Yohn (2021) Company culture is everyone's responsibility, *Harvard Business Review*, https://hbr.org/2021/02/company-culture-is-everyones-responsibility (archived at https://perma.cc/7KPF-ADWL)

4 *The Human Factor* podcast Ep 14: Growing Your Brand Through People | *The Human Factor Podcast* by SAP, https://podcast.opensap.info/the-human-factor/2022/04/01/the-human-factor-ep-14-growing-your-brand-through-peopleguest-david-hieatt-co-founder-of-hiut-denim-and-co-found/ (archived at https://perma.cc/K79P-Q8XM)

5 University of Maryland (n.d.) Marketing Rule of Seven, www.umaryland.edu/cpa/rule-of-seven/#:~:text=The%20Rule%20of%207%20asserts (archived at https://perma.cc/R8U6-C59F)

6 J Solis-Moreira (2024) How Long Does It Really Take to Form a Habit? Scientific American, www.scientificamerican.com/article/how-long-does-it-really-take-to-form-a-habit/#:~:text=A%20hallmark%202009%20study%20on (archived at https://perma.cc/2HR7-EL79)

7 *The Human Factor* podcast Ep 44: Dave Ulrich – The Development and Evolution of HR | *The Human Factor Podcast* by SAP, https://podcast.opensap.info/the-human-factor/2024/05/15/the-human-factor-podcast-ep-44-dave-ulrich-the-development-and-evolution-of-hr/ (archived at https://perma.cc/LZ7B-PQYM)

As humans
We want to be

INSPIRED

The importance of having a philosophy 4

Introduction

We are going to explore philosophy in this chapter. Don't worry, we aren't going to go into an academic discourse on Friedrich Nietzsche or René Descartes. We will explore what it means to have a philosophy, whether that be individually or organizationally. What does having a philosophy enable you to do, and how does the absence of a philosophy manifest itself in the day-to-day activities of life or the office?

We will explore the supporting human factors such as beliefs and behaviours, and we will then see how this influences values and principles. This chapter is not intended to be scientific or academic, but we do need to understand how all these factors gel together to truly understand the importance of having a philosophy.

We will support our exploration with some science, but also with the conversations we have had in the podcast series from several different perspectives, industries and also personal developments. We will also see how personal philosophies have formed organizational change and examples of where it has worked or not.

Finally, we will conclude with our tips and tricks on the importance of having a philosophy.

What is a philosophy?

There are several varying definitions of what a philosophy is, but most are built around the concept that it is a guiding principle for behaviour. A framework, if you will. It's important for us to be clear though on what the difference is between a philosophy and a belief.

A belief is an acceptance of something to be true; it is typically subjective. I may believe in a religion, for example, or that my football team will win this weekend. These beliefs don't necessarily need proof to sustain that acceptance, and if you watched my football team, you would clearly see a lack of proof to sustain that belief (but that's another story).

A philosophy, though, is a collection of beliefs and values that influence my behaviour. It is often referred to as a principle or set of principles, but it is also objective and based upon observational evidence. An example of this may be: 'I don't expect anything, so I can't be disappointed.'

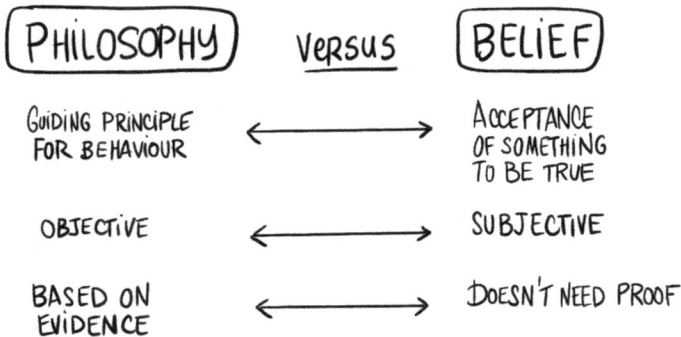

PHILOSOPHY   VERSUS   BELIEF

GUIDING PRINCIPLE FOR BEHAVIOUR   ←——→   ACCEPTANCE OF SOMETHING TO BE TRUE

OBJECTIVE   ←——→   SUBJECTIVE

BASED ON EVIDENCE   ←——→   DOESN'T NEED PROOF

Our philosophy can be formed by other factors too, not just beliefs. Perceptions, thoughts and feelings also help form our philosophies. But all these factors can exist not only at a conscious level, but also at a subconscious level. And this is what makes exploring our philosophies so difficult. We may not even be aware of what is informing them without considerable self-reflection.

People don't care how much you know until they know how much YOU CARE

In 2022, we were joined on the podcast series by Russell Martin, the then manager of Swansea City Football Club.[1] Russell is an ex-player, with a career spanning over 500 games. His playing career was spent predominantly at Norwich City FC from 2009 to 2018. He also represented Scotland at an international level, achieving 29 caps. Since retirement as a player, he is now a manager, initially at Milton Keynes Dons, before joining Swansea City in 2021. In 2023, he left Swansea to join Southampton.

Our episode with Russell was on the topic of 'The power of the philosophy'. We will draw on that conversation throughout this chapter. Early on in the conversation, Russell summarized well what a philosophy meant for him: 'When I took over as a manager, I wanted to do it in a way that reflected me as a person, so I wanted the team to reflect me on the pitch and my personality. I want the way we behave day in, day out, to be something that I enjoy being part of and I'm really comfortable with.'

We covered how he had developed his philosophy, which he then described as building over time: 'The values and belief system that I've built over a number of years, from my childhood through my football career, through my relationships with other people and that's all helped shape what I want to be as a football manager.'

However, we are starting to get deep and existential, and that is not our aim. Let's explore some examples of famous philosophies in action.

What are some examples of philosophies?

Sport is an industry often associated with philosophies. One of the most famous examples is from the world of football (or soccer for our transatlantic readers). Pep Guardiola was an acclaimed Spanish footballer, playing for Barcelona Football Club. The club played a style of football that valued possession and pressing the opposing team when out of possession of the ball. Towards the end of his career, the club began using a different style of play, prioritizing a more physical approach, and this was a contributing factor to Guardiola leaving the club.

The natural evolution for him at the end of his playing career was to explore coaching and management, and he returned to Barcelona to coach the B team. It was here he brought his philosophy to light, based on the beliefs he learnt while a player from Johan Cruyff and others.

Guardiola embraced the chance to explore his philosophy, and the team enjoyed success. So much so that when the first team coach, Frank Rijkaard, left the club at the end of the 2007/8 season, Barcelona promoted him to manage the first team. What followed is one of the most successful managerial careers of all time. Winning trophies managing Barcelona, Bayern Munich and currently Manchester City has validated his philosophies on how the game should be played, albeit supported by the financial backing of some of the most powerful clubs in the world.

What is notable is how Guardiola requires acceptance of his philosophies from his players. He has to communicate what they are, help the players understand their roles in them, overcome resistance and ensure total commitment to how they should be executed. Those players that don't work within these constraints are usually moved on from the club. And so Pep's philosophies have become the clubs' philosophies also. The club may of course have supplementary philosophies that run in parallel, but to be truly successful, they can't have competing philosophies. They must not only co-exist, but also be harmonious and aligned.

CO-EXISTENCE   ALIGNMENT   ACCEPTANCE

In the opening chapter of this book, *Strategy and purpose*, we discussed alignment, and the same principles apply here too. Our organizational philosophies must align with our leaders' philosophies to ensure our overall strategies are executed effectively.

Looking at another example, in a different industry, takes us to Apple Inc. Apple originated as a technology company, creating personal computers, tablets, mobile phones and more recently wearable technologies such as smart watches. A tipping point came though when their marketing strategy adopted a new philosophy – that Apple products improved our lives. Now they were no longer selling technology but selling enablement of dreams.

In an article for True Digital Park, four key philosophies are credited for the success of Apple:[2]

- **Be the best, not the first** – it is well-known that the first to market is not always the most successful. By focusing on quality rather than the need to be quick to market, they ensured that their products were designed better, more reliable and therefore higher quality.

- **Find an enemy** – taking on well-established providers for Android and Blackberry phones, Apple took an aggressive approach to be better than, rather than as good as. And they marketed this, tapping into the human behaviours of choosing a side and building brand loyalty.

- **Focus on user experience** – Apple don't sell phones or tablets. They sell solutions to problems, and are very clever about how they tap into our values as consumers. I am no longer buying a phone, but a device that will help me manage my finances or communicate with friends. I now have a device that will call the emergency services for me if I have a serious fall, and as such, it's a lifesaver.

- **Empathy** – Apple communications are designed to be empathetic with the challenges faced by their consumers. They seek that deep connection with their customer base and so appear sincere and caring.

It is these philosophies, initiated and nurtured by Steve Jobs and his management team, that lead to Apple gaining considerable market share and brand loyalty.

In 1998, two Stanford University PhD students founded Google. Larry Page and Sergey Brin created a search engine that would go on to become a world-wide phenomenon valued at approximately $1.86 trillion, as of February 2024. In their early years, they wrote their philosophies down as '10 things we know to be true'.[3] These have evolved over time, but remain in place to guide the company and its employees in their mission to organize the world's information and make it universally accessible and useful. The 10 things are as follows:

1   Focus on the user and all else will follow.

2   It's best to do one thing really, really well.

3 Fast is better than slow.

4 Democracy on the web works.

5 You don't need to be at your desk to need an answer.

6 You can make money without doing evil.

7 There's always more information out there.

8 The need for information crosses all borders.

9 You can be serious without a suit.

10 Great just isn't good enough.

Each of these 10 things underpins how they operate their business and set the tone for the company. These philosophies outline how they want the business to run and their expectations of how they want their employees to approach work.

Your company doesn't have to be a global superpower to be driven by a philosophy. Earlier in the book we introduced Hiut Denim Co. We spoke with the co-founder of the company, David Hieatt, in episode 14 of *The Human Factor*.[4] The episode was titled 'Growing your brand through people'.

With only a handful of employees, Hiut Denim Co make high quality, tailored jeans and list royalty among their customers. Their motto or philosophy, is: 'Do one thing well', and they use this to drive focus and attention within their business:[5]

We make jeans. That's it. Nothing else. No distractions. Nothing to steal our focus. No kidding ourselves that we can be good at everything. No trying to conquer the whole world. We will just do our best to conquer a bit of it. So, each day we will come in and make the best jeans we know how.

David spoke with us about how he brings that philosophy to life on a day-to-day basis. His perspective is: 'If I grow people, I will grow my business', and 'I'm going to hire you. I'm going to show you some stuff to help you fly. Then I'm going to get out your way. I'm going to create a space for you to do the best work you've ever done.'

From these examples, we can start to see how having personal and organization philosophies not only drives commercial success, but also secures engagement and buy-in from both the workforce internally and consumers externally. We will also explore later in the chapter the concept that philosophies need to be more than just words. They need to be ingrained in how the organization runs. The execution of the philosophy is just as important as the philosophy itself.

Why is having a philosophy so important?

In the previous section, we explored examples of philosophies from different organizations and individuals. We now need to explore why having a philosophy is a good thing and conversely, the impact of not having a philosophy.

As can be seen from the examples, the philosophies of an organization are not its mission statement, nor are they its business strategy. The philosophies are the framework for how we want to realize those strategies and mission. They are the guiding light to us and our workforce and will help to determine and drive the organization's culture. In the previous chapter we discussed culture at length, and how it can be a very fluid concept. Philosophies can and sometimes need to change, but often help provide continuity and consistency.

The examples of the philosophies we gave allow the organization to understand what is expected of them in terms of behaviour and approach. They aren't specifically related to job descriptions, but are more generally about how they are expected to act as representatives of the organization.

However, the philosophies may also articulate how the organization works with and treats customers, and so is not limited to just internal boundaries.

Articulating a philosophy can improve the perception of an organization in the marketplace. If we take the Hiut Denim Co example, the philosophy of 'Do one thing well' is multipurpose. It's guiding the employees to prioritize quality and attention to detail. It's guiding the company strategy to focus solely on the manufacturing of jeans, rather than diversifying into other products. It is also making a statement to the marketplace, not just that they only make jeans, but also that they value quality at a fundamental level.

In Chapter 1 on strategy, we discussed our conversation with Harriet Green, OBE. We talked with Harriet about delivering on your purpose, and this is tightly linked therefore to philosophy. The quote we gave was:

> If you are not positioned with an authentic, believable commitment, a powerful set of values that really drive diversity and inclusion that not only hires superb people, but progresses and retains them, then you will lose that war for talent.

If we flip that around, and show that we are positioned with an authentic, believable commitment, then we can connect at a deeper level with both employees and potential employees. We can drive higher engagement and loyalty from our workforce and enhance our employee value proposition to candidates considering joining our company. Using Google as an example, as a candidate I will know not only what the job role is and the salary expectations, I will also now have an insight into how the company operates and treats its customers and employees. I can make a more informed judgement as to whether my own work philosophies align with Google's, and therefore increase the likelihood that I will enjoy working for them and thrive in their workforce.

As we saw in the quotes from Russell Martin, the philosophies of an individual or an organization also share the personalities of the individual/ organization. Players considering joining Manchester City and working under Pep Guardiola will know that he expects hard work and flexibility, but he will also help develop their growth at a personal level.

What we observe therefore is that having a philosophy helps articulate beliefs, principles and values. It helps define the culture of an organization. It helps employees and candidates assess what the company stands for and its expectations of how it will operate. It helps build a connection, be it with the employees, with candidates or even with customers. That connection then develops a bond which drives loyalty.

Does having a philosophy guarantee those outcomes? No. That is down to whether the philosophy is one that resonates with those you are seeking a connection with. Can we achieve success without a philosophy? Yes, but have we got those deep connections in place to ensure a sustainable future for that success?

What factors will influence a philosophy's success?

Success is a relative term. So much so that we dedicate a chapter to it later in the book. Success is not always profit or winning. It could be surviving under difficult conditions. The other initial observation is that the way philosophies are perceived can be subjective. One person may love a certain philosophy, whereas another may hate it. However, let's look at the qualities that will help a philosophy create the conditions for success.

Ingredients of success

AUTHENTICITY   TIME   EFFORT   RESILIENCE

A crucial factor with any philosophy is that it must be authentic. For that authenticity, the philosophy must be meaningful and resonate at a personal level, but it also needs to be a living part of the organization. Words on a wall will not drive success. Successful philosophies need to be demonstrably in action every day, at every level of an organization. For example, a company's philosophy of more relaxed working would be undermined if a manager tells their team that they must wear a suit for a meeting with the CEO. Either the CEO isn't living that philosophy by expecting people to wear suits, or the manager isn't living the philosophy if their perception of a meeting with the CEO requires a suit.

Time is an important factor. Philosophies take time to embed into the culture of the organization. They take time to become the way people operate by default. Some philosophies may also need time to evolve to a point of acceptance, with feedback leading to refinements.

But it's worth also sharing that some industries are more dominated by results than by philosophies. The sports industry has seen many examples where a person has joined a club, tried to impose their philosophy on to how the club operates and how the team plays, only for results to be disappointing, and the manager departing. When the philosophy is challenged, either the philosophy must adapt or commitment to it must be restored. If left unresolved, belief and trust in it is eroded.

But this is not as easy as it sounds – just change the philosophy. And that is because it's based upon beliefs, values, principles and feelings. Philosophies can evolve and change, but it's rare to see an organization radically change a philosophy without significant effort and time. In reality, in the sports industry, we often see a change in personnel rather than the existing person changing their philosophy.

This is not always the case, though. In 2023, we discussed 'The ingredients of success' with Maggie Alphonsi, OBE.[6] Maggie is a former Rugby League World Cup winner with England Rugby.

In our conversations with her, we talked about the 2010 World Cup, when England were runners up to New Zealand. She described how they were forced to reflect on the defeat and look at their philosophies. At that time, Maggie felt: 'We spent a lot of time focusing on team first rather than person first.' And that: 'We had one leader, one voice. But the rest of us, I always feel like, when things became difficult, we didn't know how to step up.'

Therefore, those underlying philosophies were potentially holding the team back from realizing its full potential. In 2014 they reached the final of the competition against Canada. This time, their philosophy was different. To give themselves maximum agility to respond to on the field circumstances, they had to 'make sure that they're all leaders and that they are able to coach and self-manage themselves'.

Their philosophy then evolved to become:

Try and create 15 leaders on the field so they can all be accountable for their decisions and direct themselves ... I think that's absolutely brilliant and that's how I see the best teams.

A key factor for philosophies is resilience, especially in the early days. Back to the world of sport, and Russell Martin. When results do dip, discontent can surface in the customer base – in this case, the supporters. Russell commented on this aspect and observed: 'You have a press conference after a game where you're emotional depending on the result, but also trying to remind the supporters of why we're doing what we're doing, where we're trying to go. Remind them of the vision.'

We have used similar observations elsewhere in the book, when discussing the case for change, the strategy, the culture and now the philosophy. It's important to articulate what they are, why they are needed, where the organization is in respect of them and what they will support in terms of vision, strategy and mission.

But this is a book about human factors; these too play a part in philosophies, not just in what that philosophy is and how it has been formed, but also in how it is executed and sustained. As we saw with the conversation with Russell, his philosophies have been built over time based upon his experiences, observations, beliefs and principles.

In another of our podcast series, we had a conversation with Marie-Noëlle Gagnon.[7] Marie-Noëlle is the Chief Talent Office at Cirque du Soleil. She described herself as follows:

I'm probably the fruit of many mentors.

This comes up on a consistent basis. People often form their own philosophies based upon observing people they admire or learn from. Many people remember that teacher that influenced them, or the boss they worked for, or sometimes that family figure who instilled values in them.

When we are consuming a philosophy, as humans we want to be inspired. We want to align with people and companies that share our values, and thus we tend to gravitate towards people and organizations that have similar philosophies to our own. That connection, that bond, that sense of belonging can be enhanced by a shared philosophy.

At SAP, we run an annual survey across all our employees. One of the key questions asked is: 'How proud are you to work for SAP?' Pride in working for a company can be influenced by many factors, but a company's philosophies will be a key consideration:

- Does the company I work for share the same values, principles and beliefs as I do?
- Do we share the same philosophies?

In 2024, in an internal survey, 90 per cent of its employees stated that they were proud to work for SAP, which is testament to SAP's philosophies, values and leadership style.

In conclusion

In a chapter about philosophy, we must acknowledge that philosophies are inherently personal. We have explored how we originate and develop our own philosophies, but the articulation of them is just as important. Bringing them to life in such a way that inspires, motivates and leads others. When done well, a philosophy can be a guiding light for individual and organizational success.

Tips and tricks

TIPS & TRICKS

COMMUNICATE

REFINED (BUT...)

AUTHENTIC

BUY IN TAKES TIME

ALIGNED

1 Organizations need to communicate their philosophies, both internally and externally.

2 Gaining buy-in to philosophies takes time and effort.

3 Philosophies must be authentic and adopted by the whole organization. They must not become just words on a wall.

4 Philosophies can be refined and evolve, but be cautious with radically overhauling them.

5 Ensure philosophies are aligned with the business strategy and the organization's mission.

Notes

1 *The Human Factor* podcast Ep 15: The Power of Philosophy | *The Human Factor Podcast* by SAP, https://podcast.opensap.info/the-human-factor/2022/04/13/the-human-factor-ep-15-the-power-of-philosophyguest-russell-martin-head-coach-swansea-city-football-club/ (archived at https://perma.cc/G8RC-F766)

2 True Digital Park (n.d.) 4 Apple Philosophies That Brought Its Remarkable Success, www.truedigitalpark.com/en/insights/articles/20/4-apple-philosophies-for-success_1 (archived at https://perma.cc/53J5-WRNF)

3 Google (2024) About Us – Google UK, https://about.google/intl/en-GB/philosophy/ (archived at https://perma.cc/LY2W-RBXF)

4 *The Human Factor* podcast Ep 14: Growing Your Brand Through People | *The Human Factor Podcast* by SAP, https://podcast.opensap.info/the-human-factor/2022/04/01/the-human-factor-ep-14-growing-your-brand-through-peopleguest-david-hieatt-co-founder-of-hiut-denim-and-co-found/ (archived at https://perma.cc/2T8R-PDJD)

5 Hiut Denim Co. (2023) Our Story, https://hiutdenim.co.uk/pages/our-story (archived at https://perma.cc/2HPE-LAZD)

6 *The Human Factor* podcast Ep 34: The Ingredients of Success | *The Human Factor Podcast* by SAP, https://podcast.opensap.info/the-human-factor/2023/08/18/the-human-factor-podcast-ep-34-the-ingredients-of-success/ (archived at https://perma.cc/N6JK-HPXD)

7 *The Human Factor* podcast Ep 31: Creating The Greatest Show on Earth | *The Human Factor Podcast* by SAP, https://podcast.opensap.info/the-human-factor/2023/05/22/the-human-factor-podcast-ep-31-creating-the-greatest-show-on-earth/ (archived at https://perma.cc/B6SK-5FTH)

WHAT MAKES a Human TICK?

The predisposition of a human being

5

Introduction

If you are going to write a book about the human factor, it would be remiss of you to not explore what makes a human being tick. Why do we do what we do? When we started writing this book, we didn't want to assume any prior knowledge from you, our reader. Through our experiences on the podcast and my own experience over the last 20 years, getting to the depths of what makes a human being tick is often not considered, and is often generalized.

This chapter is going to break that down and how the manifestation of who we are can have a significant impact on our motivation, engagement, wellbeing and mental health. It's important to acknowledge that there are many studies related to the study of humans, human motivation and psychology, but we will be leveraging what we believe best explains and details what is often a very complex topic.

When we started the podcast, we were inherently curious – and still are. A real desire of mine was to understand how a human shows up irrespective of industry, and the manifestation within that industry – whether it is sport, entertainment, television, big business or small business. What is important to the human and what impact does the environment have on outcomes? That is our quest, and will continue to be.

We will start this chapter looking at the predisposition of a human being. That statement itself often brings huge debate. Are we predisposed in one direction or another; is that true? Are we not just disposed in certain ways – e.g. a person who is always smiling, funny and laughing might be considered to have a sunny disposition? Well, this is the argument that we are looking to work through in this chapter, and what we believe underpins everything that we do.

What is a predisposition?

To be predisposed means to have a 'tendency or inclination beforehand'. The key word for us is *tendency*. Tendency means 'inclination towards a particular characteristic or type of behaviour'. Therefore, are we predisposed towards a certain direction? Would we know this consciously or even sub-consciously, and how can we influence it?

How much of who we are is influenced by 'nurture' when growing up, and how much by 'nature' and what we bring with us? Nobody has a definite answer to that question, it's impossible; but there is evidence to suggest that genetics can influence how we are predisposed.

How does a predisposition therefore manifest itself on a day-to-day basis? As human beings, when we wake up in the morning, get dressed and go to work – what are we bringing with us? What is guiding and orientating us throughout the day? What dictates how we think, how we behave, how we act? What influences how we feel in a certain moment or situation?

I have completed many surveys across my career which indicates my perceived strengths, weaknesses, blind spots, preferred team roles and much more. All those surveys were completed honestly and consciously, but largely speak to a conscious preference (respondent methods), and are we always aware of what is influencing us consciously? What about the unconscious? The stuff we don't know – what about that? That is the predisposition and influences our tendency towards a type of behaviour or characteristic.

The research that we will reference throughout this chapter is that of David McClelland.[1] According to Wikipedia:

> Born in Mt. Vernon, New York, he was awarded a Bachelor of Arts from Wesleyan University in 1938, an MA from the University of Missouri in 1939, and a PhD in experimental psychology from Yale University in 1941. He taught at Connecticut College and Wesleyan University before joining the faculty at Harvard University in 1956, where he worked for 30 years, serving as chairman of the Department of Psychology and Social Relations. In 1987, he moved to Boston University, where he was awarded the American Psychological Association Award for Distinguished Scientific Contributions.

His research built on Henry Murray's study of motivation[2] and largely dictated the focus of his work for the next 30 years. McClelland argued that operant methods (i.e., tests where a person must generate thoughts or actions) were more valid predictors of behavioural outcomes, job performance, life satisfaction and other similar outcomes than other methods. Specifically, he claimed that operant methods had greater validity and sensitivity than respondent measures (i.e., tests calling for a true/false, rating or ranking response).

McClelland had a clear point of view that operant methods were a more valid way of predicting behaviour than respondent measures, and it's something which McClelland argued for often, against normal convention. He made it his life's quest to prove that 'operant methods' with clear coding was a much more reliable predictor.

I was very fortunate to study McClelland's work, and to get certified to practise his work. It was a real privilege and provided a completely different lens through how I viewed people and worked with people. Life wasn't the same again, and to this day massively informs my thinking and how I live my life. It all started with the iceberg model for me. I had seen an iceberg being used as an analogy to describe the layers of a person which are not visible and the parts that are, but this was adding an extra layer.

The iceberg model

Why is an iceberg a useful analogy?[3] Most of an iceberg is below the water line, and only the tip is usually visible. This is very much the same with human beings. On a day-to-day basis, our behaviour and skills are visible to other people, but other parts are often not seen unless consciously disclosed. Below the surface you will see things like social role, your own self-image, your traits and your values. From my experience of working with senior leaders across all corners of the globe, many operate from their values. A value can be described as 'something that is important to us' and is conscious and self-reinforced. Their behaviour and actions very much driven by 'what is important', and you may argue: what is wrong with that?

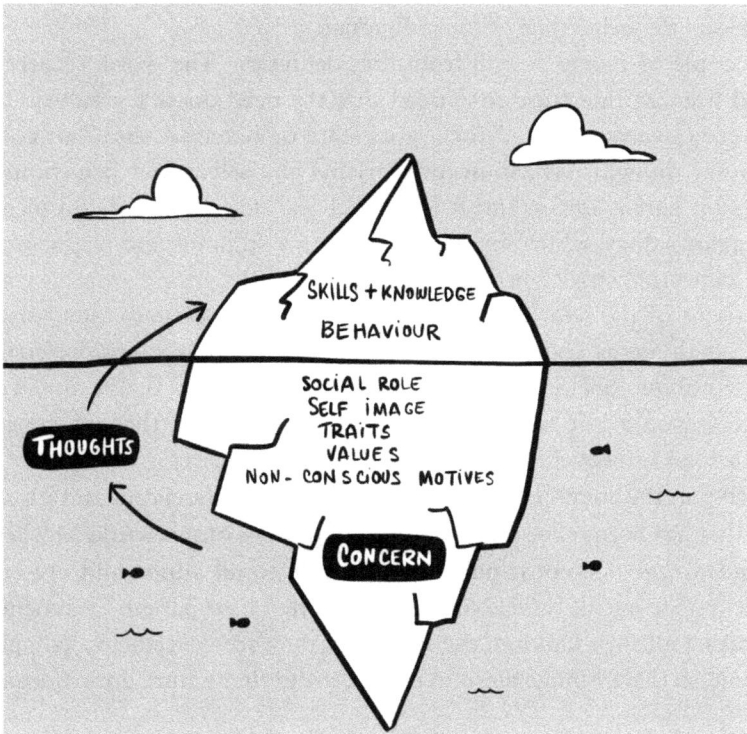

In short, nothing; but there is an important consideration – while something is important, do I enjoy doing it? In life we know there are things we must do, and many things are important – but what happens to us and our motivation if that thing must be repeated over and over, and I really don't get a buzz or sense of joy from doing it? That was largely the crux of McClelland's work: how to maximize our motivation by better orientating ourselves and our behaviour.

Right at the bottom of the iceberg are the non-conscious motives which, without undertaking some of the work that McClelland designed, are non-conscious to many of us. It became clear to me while working with our global leaders that many were largely in denial about their motivational profile because they didn't recognize that side of themselves. They had lived a life through the lens of 'values' which are reinforced by parents, education and society and that is what provided them with their compass in terms of behaviour.

McClelland's definition of motivation is as follows: a recurrent concern for a goal state or condition as measured in fantasy, which drives, directs and selects the behaviour of the individual.

A couple of things to pull from that definition. The word 'recurrent' is crucial because the study concluded that the need doesn't go away. It is a recurrent (always-on) need for a goal state or outcome, and that concern drives our thoughts which, in turn, orients and selects our behaviour. The always-on part is important. It is natural and doesn't require an incentive like Pavlov's dogs, which involved providing a stimulus and response.[4] The word 'concern' can also be replaced with 'need'.

In terms of the word 'fantasy', our need for a goal state then emanates from our thoughts and imagination which are non-conscious. Referring to the point about 'operant methods', McClelland deduced that a simple questionnaire would not be able to measure and capture the non-conscious thoughts, and so developed a unique coding system.

Earlier in the chapter 'nature and nurture' was referenced, and it's something that has been reflected upon through the lens of this work. McClelland concluded that non-conscious motives apply to all adults and are largely formed by the age of three. Now, you will often hear parents comment that they raised all their children the same, but they are nevertheless completely different, so there is huge merit in the argument that nature does indeed play a role.

So, let's look at what the motives are and how they can help us to maximize our motivation and energy.

Non-conscious motives and motivation

Henry Murray's study of human motivation came up with a ton of descriptive labels, and McClelland was keen to build on that work but also to simplify it. I believe he inherently wanted to make it more accessible, more practical and to assist people on a day-to-day basis. What sets McClelland's work apart (in our humble opinion) is the accuracy of the study and how relatable it is to the individual. His definition disclosed that motives 'energize and orient behaviour' based on thoughts. Our motives are self-energized and 'always-on', which then begs a very important question – if they are always-on, surely they need managing?

Absolutely. Like anything in life, too much of something can be bad for our health. Our motives are no different. It is important to note and highlight at this juncture that there is no relationship between the motives and intellect.

As human beings we learn through growing up about social norms and understanding what is socially acceptable. How to behave in front of other people, respect for elders and not shouting at the top of our voices in a crowded church. We would describe this as displaying self-control. If we think of our motives like energy taps inside us, self-control would be the safety valve to turn them off. I will cover this again at the end of this section.

So, what are McClelland's social motives?

- **Achievement** – the need to achieve a self-imposed standard of excellence.
- **Affiliation** – the need to maintain and restore close friendly relationships.
- **Power** – the need to influence or arouse emotions in others.

Achievement

Excellence is all relative. Excellence to one person is climbing the highest mountain in the world, whereas to someone else it is running a half marathon. It is self-imposed and concerns 'self'. When I was a young lad, I would do 'keep-me-ups', where you keep the football in the air without touching the ground, in the garden. I would set targets and wouldn't go in for my tea until I achieved it. If the target was 50 and the ball dropped on 49, I started all over again.

Another example of achievement is someone who has very clear career goals and their focus is on achieving them. Going back to the point about self-control, what happens if achieving that goal means I am there for hours, and it gets dark? Is there a point where you just stop? Well, it's easier said than done, and we will provide an explanation as to why.

Affiliation

Relationships are important to people. In the case of the affiliation motivation, the need is for the sake of the relationship alone. We often hear about lifelong friendships, friendships since the beginning of school, or work colleagues who became close friends.

To some, relationships are the only important thing, sacrosanct, and must be maintained and always preserved. This need will vary from person to person. We will all have this need, but for some it's everything and they invest a lot of time, energy and commitment into maintaining them. In the event that they are disrupted, great lengths will be taken to restore them.

Power

In hindsight, McClelland wished he had labelled this motive 'influence' because of the connotations of the word 'power'.

The study found that there were two sides to the coin when it came to power: 'socialized' and 'personalized'. In simple terms, when someone exhibits 'socialized power' in an exchange with another person, the other person will leave feeling better for the exchange. This depicts behaviour that is supportive, coaching in nature, advising, empathetic, etc. On the other hand, when 'personalized power' is displayed in an exchange, the other person will leave feeling worse. This will depict behaviour that is aggressive and controlling, as well as providing unsolicited feedback which is not empathetic at all.

We see clear evidence of the power motive from a very young age. Let's consider the baby in the cot who will not stop screaming unless they are picked up, or the baby in the high chair who drops the plastic keys waiting for someone to give them back. What do they then do? Drop them again and again. We learn from a very young age how to arouse emotions in others and to influence. Out of the three motives, this is the one where the self-control valve is arguably the most important.

The study concluded that alcohol can artificially stimulate the power motive, which can lead to an array of emotions and consequences and can inhibit our ability to apply self-control in certain situations.

Understanding ourselves can be complex. We are a cocktail of so many different parts. Some of it we know, and some of it we discover as we go along. For myself personally, being able to understand and practise McClelland's work was very much life changing. It provided a completely different lens for understanding myself, but also others. Being able to better understand the driver of behaviour and the manifestation of my experiences, when my mood was low, or if I felt that my motivation was low. It's helped me to make decisions about the work I enjoy, the situations where I operate at my best, and has explained things that happened early in my life.

Before, we move onto the next section on 'understanding self', I want to close out on the point about self-control. This has been touched on many times, but it really is a crucial point. Our motives provide an energy, they give us a buzz. They orient us towards a goal state (irrespective of what that is), but what happens when our behaviour oversteps the mark or is inappropriate? What happens when it 'takes control' of us? How does that impact us personally, but also others?

I believe one of our greatest challenges as people is marrying the intent of our actions with our desired impact, and it is something we probably do hundreds of times a day. At work, at home, with our children, friends, teammates, and other relationships. How are we best managing our motivation to drive the optimal outcome for you and others?

Understanding the motives for me is fundamental, but there is much more to us as people. How do we better understand our 'self' in all facets? How do we build the awareness of 'self' to better understand why we do what we do, have increased awareness around our self-control valve and mastery of our minds and thoughts? How do we piece this puzzle together so that we can maximize who we are from a performance and motivation perspective, continue to grow, and above all else be healthy and happy?

The importance of self

We were very lucky to be joined on the *Human Factor* podcast in two separate episodes by Danny Donachie[5] and Glenn Bracey[6] to explore and gain a deeper insight not only into self, but also our minds. Danny is a performance coach working with high-profile business leaders and world-class athletes. His background is in professional football, initially as a player, transitioning to the role of medical director at several Premier League teams.

He has a master's degree in leadership from the Tavistock and his work is informed by over 30 years of meditation practice. His interest in growth and performance was stimulated during childhood in his own quest to emulate his football-playing father.

For 30 years Glenn has been deep diving into two intimately connected areas: understanding **performance**, and our **authentic self**. In that time, he has worked across the world, sharing learning with around 15,000 people, and noticed that in their learning (including mindset, emotional based training), there is little or no learning on awareness. He has worked with wilderness survival teams (Bear Grylls), FBI-trained hostage negotiators (UK Police), in 30+ industries (public and private) and coached professional athletes across football, rugby and track.

They were fabulous episodes, and in both we were super keen to explore the power of the mind and awareness. Throughout the podcast series we have tried to challenge all assumptions (including our own) and really get to the heart of a specific topic. I have known Glenn for almost 20 years and his coaching has been a huge part of my growth and development. Very early on in our relationship, he helped me to better understand my mind and self; focusing heavily on my 'psychological self' and 'aware self'.

The aware self is full of acceptance for who we are. Calm, quiet, methodical and peaceful. The psychological self is almost the opposite. Full of noise, contradiction, doubt, fear and much more. I think this quote from Glenn sums it up:

Our psychological self is searching for all the things that our aware self has already got, and all I need to do is learn how to stay with my aware self a little bit more, and then imposter syndrome fades.

Our psychological self will play real tricks on us. It will take us away from who we really are, where our energy and buzz come from, and can really make a huge impact on our performance and mental health.

We have touched on imposter syndrome elsewhere in the book, but there is no better example of the psychological self playing tricks on us, convincing us we are perhaps not good enough or feeling confident enough to impart some knowledge or wisdom to someone else, believing that your point of view is worthless: 'What could I possibly say that would be of benefit to somebody else?'

Our conversation with Danny followed a similar vein, by looking at the conscious and subconscious mind. As Danny progressed through his football career following in the footsteps of his father, he found aspects of his game, and in particular his ability to kick a ball with his left foot, were not to his desired standard. He would practise and practise, but one evening on the way to a match, he did some mindfulness work and in the first 45 mins of that match, his left foot was like a wand. It was at a level Danny had not experienced before. He found that it didn't last, and the level dropped to what it was previously, but it opened his eyes to the power of the mind and the unconscious and he has invested a huge amount of his life learning and applying how to better understand and manage this aspect of self. This quote from Danny very much captures what he believes:

The mind and the unconscious are the most important and the biggest thing that's going to impact our performance over the long term.

What has fascinated me for most of my career and both of us during the podcast is the complexity. Nothing is linear and straightforward. It is almost as if there are competing forces at play on so many levels. At a motivational level, we have a deep need to achieve an outcome or goal state; however, our focus on values may conflict with the things which motivate us and give us pleasure. On top of this, you then have the challenge of the mind and the different versions of self. Is it therefore a surprise that terms such as imposter syndrome have become so commonplace? Being able to understand self at a deep level is not easy. I have often called it my life's work.

So, let's now put this into the context of the organization. Let's imagine an organization that employs 10,000 people. As we have discussed earlier in the book, the organization has a strategy to deliver, but to do so it needs to harness and maximize the contribution of those 10,000 people. Based on what we have covered in this chapter so far, how easy is it for the organization to achieve this?

How are human motivations and desires satisfied at work?

We have covered a fair amount of ground in this chapter, perhaps overly simplified in parts, but to summarize, when a human being gets out of bed in the morning and comes to work, they are bringing many things with them. They are bringing their predisposition, their values, their thoughts and all the things that are happening in their life. When you go into work you don't hang your life up at the door, it's all part of your whole self. You can't split out employee from person.

We believe there is an onus on every organization to create structures, frameworks and guardrails to facilitate the whole self. How can the organization learn about all their employees, and how can the employee feel empowered to take ownership and control of their journey at work? This is the convergence that needs to be created, culturally enabled and supported. We have touched on first line managers and leaders many times, but they have a pivotal role to play in supporting this work.

For too long, we have either not considered or ignored that a human being needs certain things to happen during their working day for them to feel fulfilled, motivated and engaged. When you look at any Gallup study on engagement, is it a surprise that global engagement scores are still low?[7] The future of work requires a rethink and a re-design, but it doesn't need to be revolutionary.

There are three episodes of our podcast that immediately come to mind when considering the desires and motivation of a human being at work. David Hieatt and his team at Hiut Denim is a great example of teams being encouraged to take ownership for their growth, performance and excellence.[8]

As David said himself: 'I'm going to hire you. I'm going to show you some stuff to help you fly. Then I'm going to get out your way. I'm going to create a space for you to do the best work you've ever done.'

Every week the team at Hiut Denim will have a clarity session for 15 minutes. An opportunity to ask questions, learn about something they are interested in or simply don't know and need to know. This speaks to the motivation of a human being. We thrive on clarity and feedback. It speaks to our need for achievement. The production team at Hiut Denim are also accountable for the working schedule. They are fully empowered to build a schedule that delivers on production targets, but also provides some work/life balance.

In episode 41 of the *Human Factor* podcast we spoke with William Lankston.[9] Will has worked at the Timpson Group for 13 years. The Timpson Group is a family-owned retail business based in Manchester. Today, Will is Managing Director of Timpson Direct. Timpson have become synonymous with their philosophy of creating happiness enabled by their upside-down management model. Will believes that the key to the growth of the group has been the continual development of the culture of upside-down management. He feels a culture based on trust and kindness works when Timpson recruit colleagues with an amazing personality. At Timpson everyone is equal, and it is William's job to make sure his colleagues are happy in their jobs.

There are only two rules at Timpson – look the part every day, and put the money in the till. Outside that, teams are empowered to make decisions. If one of their store locations wants to paint their walls pink, they are encouraged to do that. If they want to look after a parrot for a customer who is going on holiday, they will do that too. Every member of staff is asked to rate their happiness out of 10 every week. It is by far one of the most important metrics in the business. Teams are empowered and trusted to make decisions. It is therefore not a surprise that Timpson has long-tenured staff who are integral to their amazing journey.

The final soundbite comes from our conversation with Osian and Catrin, a husband and wife who started their business Crwst from their kitchen.[10] Based in West Wales in the lovely town of Cardigan, Osian and Catrin quit their jobs with a dream of owning and building their own business. They are a great story for a multitude of reasons, but the main one is excellence.

From a team of two, in seven years they have become a team of 71 delivering a variety of products through their physical locations and online. They are developing talent who are moving within the business; they are growing the skills of their employees every day, but the thing that binds them is excellence. Their standards and consistency of experience is so high. When they were a team of two, they crafted their goals, some of which were audacious, and one of them was to have their products on the shelf for sale at the famous department store – Harrods. Today, their products are for sale in Harrods. It's an amazing story that absolutely speaks to the motivations of a human being.

I became a fan and advocate of Crwst two years before I sampled any of their products. They did an amazing job of bringing to life who they were, why they existed and the care and love they put into excellence. They make some of the most amazing brunches, cakes, doughnuts and jarred products, including Osian's famous salted caramel.

The conversations with David, Osian, Catrin and Will were super important. They really got to the heart of self and being able to be the best version of yourself every day. Striving, growing, feeling empowered, valued, trusted and connected.

In conclusion

This chapter was important to us, and very much sums up why we wrote this book. Simply being able to truly understand self is a big task. Understanding who we are and being able to truly maximize who we are every day is not easy. In simple terms, we get in our own way. I call it a life's work and when you have your motives, values and mind converging on each other, it's easy to see why doubt and a lack of confidence can creep into focus. When we then layer on top our work environment, the picture becomes even more complex. Is the organization creating the climate and conditions where you can perform at your best? Do you feel as if the organization knows you and encourages you to grow, have a voice, feel empowered and able to make decisions?

As we progress into the next decade and beyond, the design of work will be vital to truly leverage the skills and brilliance of every employee. Being able to attract people that will thrive in your culture and take your business forward. Creating a climate where people feel safe, feel able to bring their whole self and have the support when it is needed.

This is the collective challenge that we all face.

Tips and tricks

TIPS & TRICKS

BE HONEST WITH YOURSELF

SPEND SOME TIME

TALK TO SOMEONE YOU TRUST

RECOGNIZE YOUR BEHAVIOUR

PRACTISE BEING WITH YOUR AWARE SELF

1 Spend some time looking at the motives and try to identify with the descriptions to see if it matches with your perception of self.

2 Recognize whether your behaviour is being driven by values or motivation. If you are using language such as 'I really ought to', that is a statement being driven by importance (values). You are doing it for that reason, and not necessarily because you will get a buzz from it.

3 Talk to someone who you really trust. Someone who will support you, but also challenge you. How do they see you and how would they describe you? Share the motives with them and ask which they think could be your dominant motive.

4 Take some time out for reflection. Learn some breathing exercises to give you some room for clarity and space. Being with your aware self requires practice and the ability to recognize when you are slipping into your psychological self.

5 Be honest with yourself. Experience has shown me that we don't always prioritize self, and it can come at a cost. Don't live your life through the lens of somebody else. Re-assess your values on a regular basis, tap into the things that speak to your motivation. It's OK to course-correct, stop doing some things and start some new things. Live the life that gives you growth, contentment and happiness.

Notes

1   Harvard University (2019) David McClelland. Harvard.edu, https://
    psychology.fas.harvard.edu/people/david-mcclelland (archived at https://
    perma.cc/L875-XE2F)

2   Wikipedia (n.d.) Murray's system of needs, https://en.wikipedia.org/wiki/
    Murray%27s_system_of_needs (archived at https://perma.cc/W9PF-TVZC)

3   www.linkedin.com (2023) The Iceberg Model of Behavior: A Vital
    Framework for Leaders, www.linkedin.com/pulse/iceberg-model-behavior-
    vital-framework-leaders-shankar-subramanian/ (archived at https://perma.cc/
    V2KJ-J3RB)

4   S Mcleod (2024) Pavlov's dogs study and Pavlovian conditioning explained,
    Simply Psychology, www.simplypsychology.org/pavlov.html (archived at
    https://perma.cc/S7ND-C4TW)

5   *The Human Factor* podcast Ep 29: Performance and Growth – Tapping into
    the Unconscious Mind | *The Human Factor Podcast* by SAP, https://podcast.
    opensap.info/the-human-factor/2023/03/17/the-human-factor-podcast-ep-
    29-performance-and-growth-tapping-into-the-unconscious-mind/ (archived at
    https://perma.cc/KKM4-NUE7)

6   *The Human Factor* podcast Ep 28: Understanding Self | *The Human Factor
    Podcast* by SAP, https://podcast.opensap.info/the-human-factor/2023/02/28/
    the-human-factor-podcast-ep-28-understanding-self/ (archived at https://
    perma.cc/LAV3-TN89)

7   Gallup (2024) State of the Global Workplace Report, www.gallup.com/
    workplace/349484/state-of-the-global-workplace.aspx (archived at https://
    perma.cc/6PHT-CLWJ)

8   *The Human Factor* podcast Ep 14: Growing Your Brand Through People |
    The Human Factor Podcast by SAP, https://podcast.opensap.info/the-human-
    factor/2022/04/01/the-human-factor-ep-14-growing-your-brand-through-
    peopleguest-david-hieatt-co-founder-of-hiut-denim-and-co-found/ (archived
    at https://perma.cc/9BQR-K3HD)

9   *The Human Factor* podcast Ep 41: The Happy Organization | *The Human
    Factor Podcast* by SAP, https://podcast.opensap.info/the-human-factor/
    2024/03/13/the-human-factor-podcast-ep-41-the-happy-organisation/
    (archived at https://perma.cc/MT3V-344W)

10 *The Human Factor* podcast Ep 46: The Power of Brand Advocacy with Catrin
    and Osian Jones | *The Human Factor Podcast* by SAP, https://podcast.opensap.
    info/the-human-factor/2024/07/18/the-human-factor-podcast-ep-46-the-
    power-of-brand-advocacy-with-catrin-and-osian-jones/ (archived at https://
    perma.cc/QS8N-QEUR)

genius lies IN SIMPLICITY

Building commitment to change

6

Introduction

If ever there was a chapter where we need to strip away assumptions, it is this one. It is fair to say that the creation of a strategy, a clear philosophy, a progressive culture and a clear case for change will have a big bearing on whether commitment across a wide spectrum of people is achieved or not. When you then add on top the predisposition of us as people, and don't forget we are all different and can react differently to change, we can start to appreciate the complexities of change.

In this chapter, we will do our best to highlight the differences between building a case for change and building a commitment to the change.

The reality is, we change every day. Something in our life will be different every day. That is almost a guarantee. Some of it we will instigate, some will be instigated externally to you. Some changes we will really like, some we will tolerate and there will be some that cause us to become quite angry and perhaps a little irrational. As the saying goes, 'The only constant in life is change', and it is so true.

Look back over the last 20 years and look at the technological explosion in our lives. Just think how much has changed and the difference it has made to the way in which we live our lives. My parents are both in their 70s and very often they will comment that they can't keep up with the pace of change; and that is one of the inevitable outcomes of change, that some people can be left behind. Sometimes that is through choice, but there will inevitably be a consequence to that, which we will cover a bit later in the chapter.

In this chapter we will explore change from multiple angles, firstly breaking down what it means, our reactions as humans to it, and also how we can become more effective in gaining a commitment. We will also discuss the other reality of change, which is how tiring and draining it can be. Before all of that, and as we have done with many of the chapters in the book, let's start at the very beginning, strip those assumptions away and look at what change is from our perspective.

What is change?

A couple of extremely wise souls (thank you Glenn and Hilary) coached me early in my career to think more deeply about what change really meant. As we mentioned in the Introduction, it is so easy to fall into the trap of thinking that everyone knows what change is, so we just need to tell people what the change is, and it will happen. We are being a little glib with that comment, but researching for this chapter, we were looking at statistics related to successful change programmes and an article in *Harvard Business Review* confirmed that 70 per cent of change management programmes fail to achieve their desired objectives.[1] Something is clearly not working.

This chapter will primarily approach this subject from the organizational perspective. We will touch on personal change, but the complexity with change largely resides within an organization, with the complexity of scale and differing priorities often a significant barrier/challenge and this is where those two wise souls really helped me with the following pieces of advice:

- Change will only occur when there is discontentment with the current state. It's easy from a personal perspective. If you wake one morning and you don't like your hair style, you can choose to cut or restyle your hair. That change is within your gift if you are discontented with it. However, when you are looking to change within an organizational context, who else is discontented? We will cover this in the section on navigating the organizational dynamics later in this chapter.

- Change only occurs for two reasons – a need to avoid pain, and a need for a gain. There are no other reasons for change. Some people naturally gravitate to the prevention of pain: we see this with people who buy cars with long warranty coverage who don't want the pain of any expensive repairs; and then there will those who prefer the soft top car for a little bit of cruising around which is a gain. In the organizational context, not falling foul of compliance or legislation has become a very legitimate reason for accelerating change and the prevention of any resulting pain, for example.

We recognize there will be many other definitions and approaches to change, but those pieces of wisdom have influenced our collective thinking for some time and have proven to be extremely wise and helpful advice.

Too often when we observe change programmes, the desired impact of the change is missing. The reason or need for the change is usually clear, but what will happen when the change is implemented across the organization? What are the desired outcomes, how will the organization know if the change has been successful or not? This is the crux of the issue when it comes to building a commitment to change, and let's not beat about the bush, it is hard work and no small undertaking. In other chapters of the book we will discuss communication, managing a message, etc, but the key usually is getting someone to change behaviour. Habit formation doesn't happen overnight, and we struggle with this personally, so imagine doing it for an organization of 100,000 or more.

We often cite the personal example of someone in December making a commitment to lose weight. That is the need, and often the answer is: 'I need some equipment or a gym membership' (the solution). So, we now have a treadmill in the spare bedroom and for three weeks we are in there using it. We then have a few days off and we don't go back. Behaviour has not been changed, the change has fallen flat, but we have a very expensive solution taking up valuable space in the spare room. It's a story that will be recognized by many people.

We all react differently to change. Some of us are very high on acceptance – 'it is what it is' – while some will moan and resist as long as possible. It can be a very broad spectrum. Let's therefore explore in a bit more detail how we as human beings interact with change, and what our various reactions are.

Human reaction to change

Many people will be familiar with the Kübler-Ross Change Model.[2] Developed in 1969, Dr Elisabeth Kübler-Ross wrote about the Five Stages of Death, also known as the Five Stages of Grief, Five Stages of Loss, or just the Five Stages. She identified these stages as defence mechanisms or coping mechanisms for change, loss and/or shock.

Since its formation, the Kübler-Ross model (or Kübler-Ross Change Curve) has been extensively used by individuals and organizations to help people 'understand their reactions to significant change or loss'. Today the model holds true for anyone going through an extremely traumatic experience, or other change situations like work and business. The Kübler-Ross Change Curve model has been accepted worldwide to explain the change process. As the basic human emotions experienced during personal loss, change, death or a dramatic experience remain the same, this model can be applied effectively in such situations.

It is important to reiterate that our reaction to change differs from person to person. It is all relative to the individual, and the time spent at any of the stages below will vary from person to person and usually depend on the situation. What we recognize, and this is one of the reasons that the Kübler-Ross Change Curve has been used extensively across the world, is that change will invoke a reaction and needs to be managed.

Let's imagine a fictional scenario. An organization is undergoing a transformation. It will involve significant restructuring, new operating models, role definitions; there will be some new branding (associated with the organization), significant changes in ways of working, new reporting lines and the introduction of new technology.

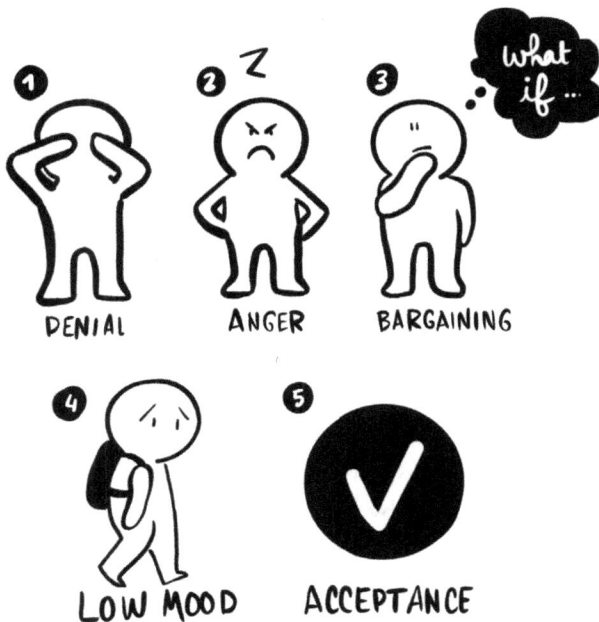

The stages associated with the model include:

- **Shock and denial:** This is the most common reaction to significant change. Depending on the personal level of impact, some people will be in shock, but also denial – unwilling to accept all or certain aspects of the change.

- **Anger:** Shock and denial can quickly move to anger. Unhappiness about a change in reporting line, a change in job definition… it doesn't matter what it is, but when people don't accept a change or understand it, anger can quickly manifest.

- **Bargaining:** Anger moves to bargaining. How do I live with this change? What are my options? How do I deal with it, how can I avoid it, what can I influence? We are natural problem-solvers at heart, but this is still not accepting of the changes happening.

- **Low mood:** At a certain point, the mood of the individual will be impacted and for some this can be quite severe. Engagement drops considerably and there is almost a feeling of lost hope and disconnection. The energy becomes really low, and individuals can sometimes 'check out' mentally.

- **Acceptance:** This is the stage that an organization is aspiring to achieve from the moment any change is shared, when the change is accepted and understood. For some individuals it can take considerable time to reach this point. As I mentioned earlier, some will accept immediately, but many people may struggle.

We have a rhetorical question to ask at this stage, which explains why we have included the Kübler-Ross model in the chapter. Are human reactions to change considered enough when organizations communicate change? Or do we assume that people will understand it or just need to get on with it; almost a 'like it and lump it' mentality? That sounds very harsh, and it is not our intent to criticize, but we believe this to be a very serious point. We are naturally creatures of habit and like doing things in a certain way or as we have always done them. Giving that up is hard. Self-preservation can kick in, and it can have a material impact on the person, not just the employee.

There is also an assumption that some change is good, and it is assumed that it will be met positively by all. This is a lesson that Eric Tinch shares with his executive team.[3] Eric's episode on the podcast was discussing how to influence the C-suite, so a big emphasis on change. Eric told this great story which he shares regularly with the board:

> Imagine a family living in a small two-bed apartment, very cramped, but have lived in the community for most of their life. They win the lottery, a

large sum and decide to buy a big mansion with loads of bedrooms and loads of space. You would assume that is a marvellous change for that family. However, they have moved from their community, their friends, and their daily life. How long do you think it will take that family to feel some regret, some sadness and perhaps resent the change they have made?

Nothing can be assumed, and this is the immense challenge when communicating and building a commitment to change. In many respects it is almost like a fork in a road and determining the route you decide to take. For example, when a change message is communicated, the first steps are to raise awareness and build understanding and to seek a positive engagement from individuals and teams. Based on how well this is done largely dictates that fork in the road. The individual will either form a positive perception or a negative perception.

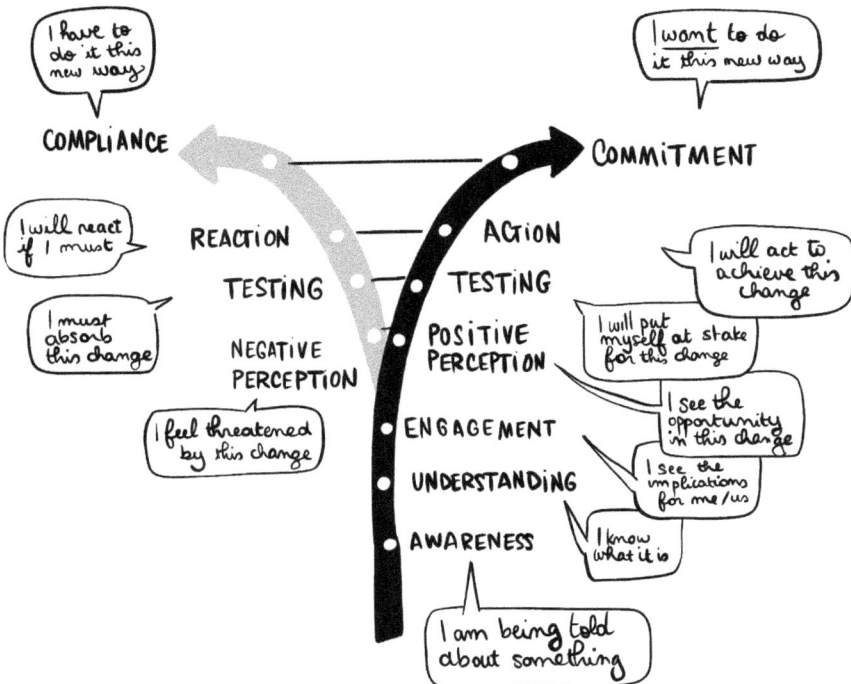

If someone forms a negative perception, they may go through many of the stages from the Kübler-Ross model. They may reach a point of acceptance eventually, but their execution of the change will be met with compliance rather than commitment. It goes without saying that the aspiration when communicating any change is engendering high acceptance to the change resulting in high levels of commitment. That is the ultimate task and test.

So, with that crucial context in place, let's shift our attention to the work required to build that commitment. In an organizational context, no change is a given. We covered this point earlier: if other people don't agree with the need to change, then why would they support it? It therefore requires a clear narrative and argument – a story, if you like.

Building a story and narrative

In Chapter 2, *The case for change*, we covered some of the following points, but we will point out some of the subtle differences that may appear the same on the surface but require a different appreciation and focus.

For example, building a case for change is an integral and essential element of any organizational change, irrespective of whether investment is being requested or required. However, the building of a case for change can be a discrete and siloed piece of work with the goal of securing support and approval from a senior board of directors. It can often be completed without any engagement from the broader organization, and this is an important point that we really wish to highlight.

A truly effective case for change should not only seek approval for a change, but also articulate what needs to happen to gain commitment from the wider organization to the change that is being proposed. For example – an organization is seeking to introduce new technology to enhance the execution of processes. It will involve changes in the ways of working, simplification of approvals, workflows, enhancements to the behaviour of certain processes such as goal setting, performance reviews and succession planning. The case for change needs to not only secure investment in the technology, but to articulate the commitment required from the senior leaders to make the change a reality.

Therefore, the story being told is not only a narrative that details the 'need' to change, but which articulates what will be different, the impact on the business, the incentive for the workforce, the effort needed, the timescales and the need for rigour and reinforcement.

Navigating the organizational dynamics

We believe one of the great skills of influencing change is to understand what else is happening within the organization. Most organizations are a hive of activity, with change happening left, right and centre. We see too regularly that stakeholder management and alignment often only happen towards the end of a change process – that time when the business case has been produced and it needs to be socialized to garner support. That is often too late.

Stakeholder alignment needs to be constant. It is part and parcel of organizational dynamics. It is unrealistic to assume that a set of senior stakeholders will be aware of all changes happening in the organization at a detailed level. They may not be aware of 'needs' to change or 'opportunities' to change. Likewise, the person who is seeking to make a change, may not be aware of plans that are already in flight and being socialized. It was a great pleasure to spend time with Elaine Bergin from

BT on *The Human Factor* podcast and I will always remember her comment that a huge part of driving change is 'commercial sensitivity' and knowing when the right time is to really push and seek support.[4]

Getting early buy-in and support from stakeholders is essential, even at the embryonic stage. We were joined on the *Human Factor* podcast by Celyn Jones.[5] Celyn is an actor, writer and filmmaker and the co-founder of the film and TV production company Mad as Birds. Celyn joined us to discuss 'Performance through art', and how you get the right talent at the right time to be able to make or complete a production. What became apparent, however, from very early in the conversation is the relationship between production and change management.

Way before anyone even thinks of saying 'action' and sometimes before a word has been written on a script, Celyn and his partners at Mad as Birds will be meeting with a whole variety of stakeholders to build support for a potential idea or story. This can be extremely hard yards and incredibly complex. Your ability to tell a compelling story that you believe will be appreciated by the public lies at the heart of the process and is essential to getting support from film bodies and production studios. When we finished the conversation, we immediately compared it to the process within an organization, and a key takeaway was having those conversations early and often.

We will often advise colleagues when looking to influence change that they shouldn't be perturbed if, at first, they don't appear to be getting any traction or support. This part of the process requires patience, perseverance, and a belief in what you are communicating. The change that you hope to manifest and realize across the organization starts at this point. Finding that one stakeholder who believes in what you are telling them is a key first step. Building a level of commitment needs sponsors, advocates, cheerleaders and people who are willing to tell your story on your behalf.

The skill of building a commitment should never ever be underestimated and requires thought and a very clever articulation of what you are saying. The skill is in being able to articulate it at a macro and micro level, and for that there are a few principles that we would recommend considering.

Principles for managing an effective change

For this section, we are going to stick to some simple principles that have stood us in good stead over the last 20 years. We believe that 'genius lies in simplicity' and is a crucial principle. Throughout the book and in our acknowledgements we detail that we have received a huge amount of support, coaching and mentoring to help us on our way.

I always refer to a coaching session with Harriet Green during our time at Premier Farnell. We were executing a huge amount of change across the organization, and I took away from that session several key principles which helped to create a phenomenal foundation. It's not every day that your CEO is taking the time and effort to coach you on some of these principles, and that was principle number one.

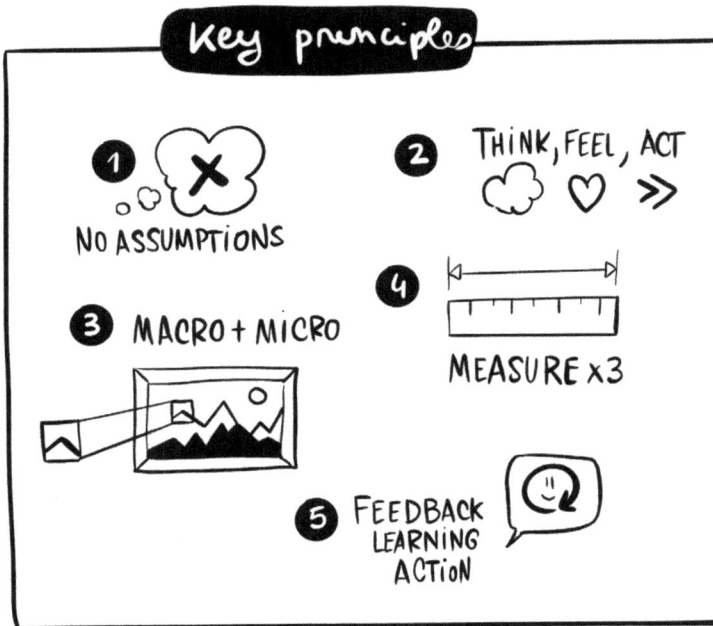

Principle 1 – No assumptions, complacency or going through the motions

We have reiterated the point about assumptions many times throughout the book and this was the day it really hammered home for me. To gain the level of commitment desired, there can be no complacency or making assumptions. Expect resistance and challenge and at no point can there be any going through the motions. Commitment must be earned, it's as simple as that.

Principle 2 – Think, feel, act

Whether we were presenting to Harriet's direct reports or to a team working on the front line, the principle remained the same. When constructing any message, we were encouraged to follow:

- Think – what do you want people to think about what they are being told?
- Feel – crucially, how do you want them to feel? How can you make that visceral connection, so they understand the purpose of what is being shared?
- Act – be explicit on how you want them to act. What will they be doing differently?

Principle 3 – Macro and micro

Taking a group of senior leaders through the context and background of a change will require a macro view and a micro view. It's a skill to avoid getting into the weeds and too much detail without establishing the broader organizational context, but this is essential work. Never assume that all leaders will be supportive, receptive or knowledgeable about what is being shared. This is reality, and don't allow words like 'should be supportive' or 'should be receptive' to creep into your mind. Just don't assume and earn that commitment.

In terms of the micro, we hope that Harriet doesn't mind us sharing this principle. As a CEO Harriet was our sponsor and would provide feedback on every change programme – and we learned very quickly that unless we answered the following question, we were being sent back to the drawing board.

For any change that would impact people, we were asked, 'How will this influence the life of Lizzy sitting in the contact centre?' In many ways a simple question, but we were not always clear, and this is when you really start to focus and sharpen not only your mind, but the quality of your communication and messages. There cannot be a change without clarity on the difference and impact it will have on the individual, otherwise it will be perceived as change for change's sake and met with resistance and compliance rather than commitment.

Principle 4 – Measure, measure and measure

Really simple. How will you measure the success of the change? How will we know that it has taken hold and the needle is being moved in the right direction? Every process in flight was measured and always communicated.

Principle 5 – Feedback, learning and action

Building a commitment to change doesn't happen immediately. In some cases it doesn't happen at all! But it cannot be enough to roll out or communicate a change and expect it to happen. This is where listening, enablement and follow ups come into play. What is working in relation to the change, how is it being executed, are there things to improve and do differently? Change is fluid and dynamic, so being on top of what is working, and what isn't, is incredibly important. Cut through the noise in the system, gather factual evidence and then act.

A key aspect which runs through all the principles is the change plan itself. Let's use an example to highlight the point. It is the start of the fiscal year, and we are kicking off the goal setting process. It is too easy to think that it's something that we do every year, people know what it is, etc.

For every key process being communicated, we would highly recommend a clear plan that details all the key milestones, activities, messages, timelines, channels and owners. Despite this being a process that will be understood by many, this is a renewal of their commitment to the process, so stating the importance, what it means to everyone, must be front and centre.

The plan will likely be multifaceted and would follow some of the principles that we included in Chapter 3. You would expect to see refresher sessions for leaders, for example, on some of the best practices when it comes to setting and cascading goals. Above all, don't assume. If you want people to be committed to something, then your chances will only be enhanced if they can see and feel your commitment too!

We are curious and always open to learning. Managing change and building a commitment is a perennial challenge that we will never achieve mastery over, but we love hearing the thoughts and ideas of others, and the principles that were shared with me on that day have been a staple of my approach when it comes to change and influencing the commitment of one person or many.

Resistance and fatigue

We use the term 'hard yards' quite regularly when discussing change. What we mean by that term, which is commonly associated with sport, is that making progress at times feels very difficult, quite slow, and making any progress feels like walking in treacle.

You may know the film *Any Given Sunday* starring Al Pacino as an American football coach. The film is famous for this speech that he gave to his team at half time in a crucial game. It was all about making the hard inches, which obviously add up to yards!

> I don't know what to say, really. Three minutes till the biggest battle of our professional lives all comes down to today... You find out life's this game of inches. So is football. Because in either game, life or football, the margin for error is so small... The inches we need are everywhere around us... On this team, we fight for that inch.

It's a great film, and a great metaphor. Experiencing resistance is reality, and it is about just making those initial hard inches and yards to make a breakthrough. Of course, there will be times when the inches and yards are not so difficult and there isn't much resistance, but based on our collective experience, resistance should be anticipated so that no assumptions are made at any point.

Now, while this chapter is very much focused on how to understand change at a human level and to build commitment, it would be wrong not to look at it also from the perspective of the person who is leading the change. Meeting resistance or getting pushback is tough. It can dent your confidence, but it is also very tiring.

As John Amaechi shared on the *Human Factor* podcast, 'You need to fill your cup.'[6] Irrespective of whether you are a leader managing people or a leader managing a change, make sure you fill your cup and not just that of others. Always take care of yourself and surround yourself with a great support network of people.

In Chapter 2 we shared the following quote from Eric Tinch, and we wanted to repeat it again:

> I keep going back to the mission at hand and whenever I am just completely exhausted myself, or if I look at the team and I can tell that they're getting a little bit worn, especially if it's a multi-year transformation that you're driving, I'll take everyone back to the mission. **This is why we are here. This is why it matters.** It sounds so simple.

This is why it is so important to stay true to what you are setting out to achieve. Believe in the merits of the change and own it. It does require courage for sure, and you will be met with resistance, but don't be perturbed. Go back to the mission and the reason why you are doing it.

In conclusion

Irrespective of what you are looking to do within an organization, it will require asking someone to do something differently. We make no apology for focusing significantly on change. The ability to effectively get approval for a change, manage the change and get commitment from a critical mass of people will literally make or break the success of the change.

Too often we will see a change focus on perhaps a new solution and what the new solution can do, but we don't hear what it will mean to the individual. We need to spend more time understanding the differences in us as people, what motivates us and how the change will make a difference to their life and is something that they can really get behind.

Tips and tricks

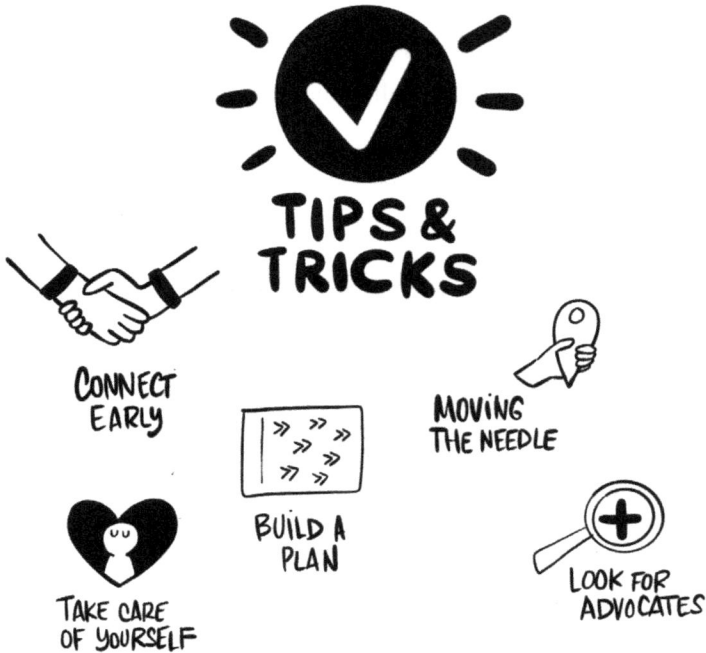

TIPS & TRICKS

CONNECT EARLY

MOVING THE NEEDLE

BUILD A PLAN

TAKE CARE OF YOURSELF

LOOK FOR ADVOCATES

1 Connect with stakeholders early. Share your ideas, get feedback, see if there is an accord or not. Early sponsorship is an amazing help.

2 Build a plan that clearly shows all the activities that will happen, when and by whom.

3 Be clear on how you will measure and communicate success. Moving the needle is the key ingredient in engendering commitment.

4 Look for your advocates across the business. Who is willing to champion and tell your story?

5 Always take care of yourself. It's hard work and you will face resistance.

Notes

1 N Nohria and M Beer (2000) Cracking the Code of Change, *Harvard Business Review*, https://hbr.org/2000/05/cracking-the-code-of-change#:~:text=Here (archived at https://perma.cc/7GJH-3WLV)

2 EKR Foundation (2018) EKR Foundation, www.ekrfoundation.org/ (archived at https://perma.cc/NDP6-PBMA)

3 *The Human Factor* podcast Ep 37: Influencing the C-Suite | *The Human Factor Podcast* by SAP, https://podcast.opensap.info/the-human-factor/2023/11/17/the-human-factor-podcast-ep-37-influencing-the-c-suite/ (archived at https://perma.cc/6B65-LKV5)

4 *The Human Factor* podcast Ep 3: Is Technology the Catalyst for a Transformation? | *The Human Factor Podcast* by SAP, https://podcast.opensap.info/the-human-factor/2021/06/17/the-human-factor-ep-3-is-technology-the-catalyst-for-a-transformation/ (archived at https://perma.cc/W7Z5-M34B)

5 *The Human Factor* podcast Ep 43: Performance through Art | *The Human Factor Podcast* by SAP, https://podcast.opensap.info/the-human-factor/2024/04/18/the-human-factor-ep-43-performance-through-art/ (archived at https://perma.cc/V27H-RM8Q)

6 *The Human Factor* podcast Ep 11: The Relativity of Success – Finding Your Inner Giant | *The Human Factor Podcast* by SAP, https://podcast.opensap.info/the-human-factor/2022/01/18/the-human-factor-ep-11-the-relativity-of-success-finding-your-inner-giant/ (archived at https://perma.cc/X2WP-BUUD)

EVp is the window into the soul of the organization

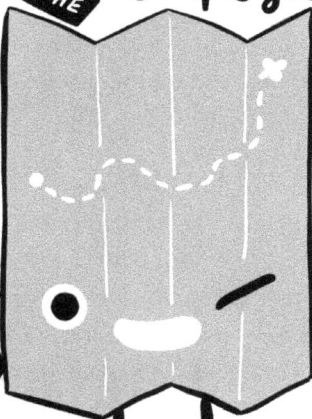

The employee value proposition (EVP)

7

Introduction

One of the perennial challenges that an organization will face every day is the attraction of talent. Throughout the book, we have examined the manifestation of our experiences at work, but what gets us there in the first place? Over the last 50 years, we have seen fluctuations in the supply of talent in the external marketplace, and there is an argument that the concept of the employee value proposition (EVP) was more commonplace 20 or 30 years ago. However, when we started to see a surplus of talent in the marketplace, it perhaps went out of vogue.

When we think about attraction today, it is very different to 20 years ago. We have seen the rise of the contingent workforce, the gig economy; what people look for in work is different, where people work is different, and of course technology has exploded beyond recognition to provide a huge amount of flexibility in how, where and when we work. Therefore, how does your organization stand out in the talent market? The term 'war for talent' has existed for years and years, but over the next decade, with a shrinking talent pool, you could argue that it will become even more fierce.

We were joined on *The Human Factor* podcast by Laura Leyland, and it was a great conversation about the principles of attraction.[1] Laura and her sister Emily started their own business, Fresh Perspective Resourcing, to help organizations be successful with this perennial challenge of attracting talent. Laura and the whole team at Fresh have brought a real energy, focus and purpose to this challenge, but many of the principles are aligned to the fundamentals. 'Clarity', 'pace', 'urgency', 'authentic' and 'innovative' were some of the words spoken during our conversation.

What stuck with me, however, from the conversation with Laura and validated my own thinking was the importance of the EVP. If you want someone to consider joining your business, then what can they expect? What kind of organization are you, how clear and compelling is your purpose, what is your philosophical approach to growth and development? If that isn't clear in your external communication as part of a recruitment process or campaign, then how can someone make an informed decision on whether to join your organization or not?

This chapter will dig into this important topic and again explore it from multiple angles. But first, let's start at the beginning and explore the notion of what a value proposition is. We will begin by looking through the lens of a consumer.

What is a value proposition?

Before we truly dive into the heart of this chapter, it's important to dissect what some of these words mean, as one of our main objectives in writing this book and setting up the podcast was to challenge assumptions. A value proposition is:

> a statement which identifies clear, measurable and demonstrable benefits consumers get when buying a particular product or service. It should convince consumers that this product or service is better than others on the market. This proposition can lead to a competitive advantage when consumers pick that particular product or service over other competitors because they perceive greater value (Wikipedia).

Let's pick that statement apart. As a modern-day consumer, we are provided with a wealth of options and choices. Whether it is the supermarket we use, a restaurant that we eat in or a particular brand of clothes, we are making decisions and choices. What is that based on? In our opinion a proposition is a statement which identifies clear, measurable, and demonstrable benefits consumers get when buying a product or service.

In Chapter 1 on strategy, we shared the view of Michael Porter that a strategy is a proposition that is better than or differentiated from the market. The proposition is a statement or commitment to deliver something. There is an intent, but when we look back at the quote above from Wikipedia, there is a crucial point – the last line: 'when consumers pick that particular product or service over competitors because they perceive greater value'. The key word is 'perceive'. It is a perception. To every individual perception is reality, but that will vary from person to person.

Later in the same article, we read:

> The phrase 'value proposition' (VP) is credited to Michael Lanning and Edward Michaels, who first used the term in a 1988 staff paper for the consulting firm McKinsey & Co. In the paper, which was titled 'A business is a value delivery system', the authors define value proposition as 'a clear, simple statement of the benefits, both tangible and intangible, that the company will provide, along with the approximate price it will charge each customer segment for those benefits'.

Let's look at this from the perspective of a consumer. Understanding the proposition of an organization is important. Whether the proposition is a product or a service, we want to understand the meaning and purpose behind it, the intent, and the proposed outcome or benefit to us as a consumer. We will address this notion of 'value and benefit' a little later in this chapter, but for us there is a defining point in all of this – do we believe it?

Do we believe that proposition? Does it do what it says on the tin? Does it deliver what was promised at the outset? We all have those moments where we will have an experience of some kind, and our response is, 'That wasn't value for money', or 'That is nowhere near as good as what was expected or what we believe was promised.' This is why the articulation of a proposition, and the perceived value, is so incredibly important.

Let me provide a personal example. I remember listening to a podcast episode about Five Guys, a business started in the US by five members of a family. Their proposition is simple – they make burgers, hotdogs, fries and shakes. There are thousands of ways to have their burger, with up to 15 optional toppings, but that is the proposition. The items are all cooked to order and fresh. Their brand and proposition have grown through word of mouth; there is no marketing machine.

I will visit a Five Guys perhaps two or three times a year, but I know what to expect, I know how the proposition works, and every time I visit the product is as good as the last time. The burger is more expensive than other fast-food retailers, but the quality of the food removes that barrier. I will pay more for this product and experience.

Prior to the pandemic, Five Guys UK wanted to introduce a home delivery option. The founding family members came to the UK and stayed in a variety of locations to receive a delivered order. They wanted to ensure the product was not compromised by being delivered and would only sign off this change to the proposition if they felt the quality was the same. I loved that. Their conviction and commitment to meeting the expectation of the consumer was clear to see.

When it comes to Five Guys, I believe them. I have belief in the simplicity of their proposition and belief in the product that I know will be produced for me. Due to that level of belief, I can form a perception of value. I firmly believe that 'value' is a very personal thing. I believe when I visit Five Guys, I am getting great value for my money. That is my perception. Someone else may have a completely different point of view. The notion of 'value' is multifaceted – in some instances it is an emotive feeling; in others it is very much financial.

In Chapter 5 on the predisposition of a human being, I mentioned Catrin and Osian from Crwst who appeared on our podcast.[2] They are based in my hometown and whenever I am home, I will visit. I will book a table well in advance to ensure I can visit. I know what the experience will be. I know how good the product will be. We asked Osian and Catrin how important the consistency of the experience and the product is, and I loved Osian's answer:

> We have a gentleman who calls in every day for a coffee and doughnut, and I will absolutely ensure that the experience and product is the same. There cannot be a dip or change in quality.

It's all about that commitment and care. A deep conviction to meeting the commitment. When that happens, you realize a level of belief and advocacy in your customer base. From that you get customer retention and loyalty. That is the bedrock of any business, but it goes without saying that you cannot rest on your laurels. The foot must be kept on the pedal, the finger on the pulse, because if the standards drop and the experience changes, then suddenly belief will dissipate, and you will lose customers and talent.

That is the crux of this chapter. Attracting talent is hard enough, but keeping hold of talent is even harder. When someone joins your organization, they will come with an expectation of what is to come. That is the proposition. It will be all the things they heard and were told during the recruitment process, and now comes the moment of truth. The reality.

So, let's pivot from the lens of a consumer to the lens of an employee. What does an EVP consist of, and how does it influence both the attraction and retention of talent?

What is an EVP?

In essence, it is very similar to the value proposition that we have just covered. We are making a decision to consider or join an organization based on a stated proposition which we hope will result in expectations being met and personal objectives being achieved. That is obviously very simplistic, but, when you boil it down, putting the remuneration to one side for the moment, the hope is that you are joining an organization which delivers on its commitment, and you enjoy being part of it.

What is it?

- The EVP is part of employer branding, in that it is one of the ways companies attract the skills and employees they desire. It is how they market and communicate their company to prospective talent, and how they retain them in a very competitive job market. It is intended to communicate the values and culture of the organization, which is important.

- A successful EVP when done well can really help to build a happier, more committed and productive workforce who feel aligned to the purpose of the organization. It may also have the side benefit of improving the company's perception in the eyes of consumers.

What should it include?

- It should bring to life the philosophy of the organization in relation to performance, career development and learning.

- It should articulate the values, the behaviours and the experience that ultimately delivers on the proposition.

- It should be clear for the person joining the organization what is expected of them.

What does it mean to the individual and the organization?

- It should detail what is expected of any employee. It is the beginning of a psychological contract between the employee and the organization where all parties are clear on what is expected of them.

What does an EVP mean to the employee?

We have always made it our business to understand the context in which we all work and live. It doesn't stand still. We know we are saying that throughout the book, but the world of attraction has changed significantly. The current generation have gone through two financial crises and a pandemic. Is the focus of the current generation the same as previous generations – the desire to buy a house, be settled in an area, etc – or is there now a greater desire for new experiences, to be mobile and transient in their thinking?

This is what we need to understand and be able to respond to. This is why businesses need to be agile in the design of EVPs and constantly refresh them to reflect the evolution of the organization and society.

What people are looking for from work is changing. Now, people have always wanted interesting work, a good work-life balance, fair pay, a good relationship with colleagues and managers, etc – it's just that, in the past, their expectation of getting these things was less. The increased competition for talent these days means they are more able to demand what they want, and with the amount of information they can access online they can shop around between what different employers are offering. They can also see from online sources (Glassdoor, Fishbowl) which EVPs are authentic and which are just words. When you layer on top the changing demographics and shortage of certain skills/talent it is competitive, so you need to stand out.

One of my favourite TED Talks was produced in 2014 by Rainer Strack on the 2030 workforce crisis.[3] Since joining Boston Consulting Group in 1994, Rainer Strack has led projects on strategy, process optimization, culture, organization, transformation, change, talent and human resources management in many industries. From 1996 to 1998 he was based in BCG's office in Boston as a BCG Ambassador. In 2001, he was elected Partner & Managing Director, and in 2008, Senior Partner & Managing Director. In 2008 he was also appointed as one of the first BCG Fellows by BCG's CEO.

Rainer has built and led BCG's work in HR globally for ten years. He was the head of the People & Organization practice in Europe, the Middle East and Africa for more than ten years and served as lead for the Social Impact practice in Germany. In 2001, he received the Erich Gutenberg Award for the development and implementation of new HR and customer-controlling concepts.

Using demographic data, the BCG study Rainer discussed was able to show the shortfall in talent leading up to 2030.[4] With an ageing population leaving the workforce, birth rates clearly show the shortfall. Technology and AI will play a big role in taking on some of the workload, but not all of it. We will see a need for new skills emerging.

The study also highlighted two other important pieces of data. Looking at over 200,000 global job seekers, it validated the view that the future workforce is both transient and open to working experiences all over the world. This isn't a surprise, but it will lead to shortfalls within countries. The study also highlighted what is important to people when it comes to work, and this brings us back to the EVP.

The top four items that people are looking for were as follows:

1 appreciation for your work

2 good relationship with colleagues

3 good work-life balance

4 good relationships with leaders

Attractive fixed salary was 8th on the list.

Those items are very much cultural and, thinking back to Chapter 5, *The predisposition of a human being*, they speak to our motivation as people. The challenge therefore for organizations is to design and articulate a proposition that brings to life the culture of the organization. Is it attractive to candidates? Does it truly reflect the commitment being made? Does it enable people to make an informed decision as to whether they believe they will thrive or not?

Let's consider personalization for a moment. Is it possible for organizations to have flexibility in the EVP to offer different benefits and working conditions to different groups of employees? For example, different options on pensions and critical illness cover for older generations; or hybrid and/or flex hours working for employees who want to work during school hours (and not in school holidays) or who have other 'within normal work hours' commitments. Using the Five Guys analogy, you have the core burger at the centre, but 14 options on the fillings to personalize your experience. It is certainly something we expect to see more and more as organizations get creative to attract and retain talent.

A recruitment decision is not only made by the organization. It is made by both parties. The culture of the organization and the EVP is put to the test through the selection process, the onboarding process and without a doubt over the course of the first six to nine months of employment. Using the famous phrase 'Does it do what it says on the tin?' – we are constantly making that evaluation and judgement.

That is the challenge. There is an argument that new employees now won't wait for three, six or nine months to evaluate. We don't consider this to be a generational issue either. We have said it many times in the book, but as consumers we have high expectations, not as much patience and we are not afraid to make a quick judgement.

During our conversation on *The Human Factor* podcast with Sally Winston on 'The value of voice', Sally believed the honeymoon period is now over. Sally Winston is the Experience Management (XM) Strategy Lead at Qualtrics for EMEA, APJ, and LATAM. She oversees a team of XM experts responsible for the development of strategies designed to enhance customer and employee experience (CX and EX) as well as broader XM initiatives. Sally believes that judgement will be made almost immediately, so those first few days are super important. There is an argument that organizations need to be listening intently especially in those first few days. It's a time to lean into the EVP and ensure that the new joiner perceives the organization to be living up to it in that early period and correct any misalignments (i.e. things that can be fixed).

Let's drill down into more detail and look at the elements we believe truly influence our connection to an organization and provide the foundation and framework to execute and underpin this thing called the EVP.

Building connection, belonging, engagement and advocacy

Let's go back to something we covered earlier in this chapter: the word 'belief'. Deep down when you believe in something, it has a huge impact on your feeling or perception of belonging or connecting. We get a sense of trust and hope that what we expect is going to happen will happen. As a consumer, this is tested every day through our interactions, but when it comes to our place of work, the importance and strength of that connection is super important.

Take the simple view that when an organization attracts someone to their organization, they want them to do well, feel connected/engaged and hopefully stay with the organization for a long period of time. Is fostering a sense of belonging therefore an unrealistic aspiration? It's a fair question and we don't doubt how difficult it is to achieve when dealing with a critical mass of people, but whenever we have led a team, it has been our aspiration. We want people to feel like they belong and are an integral member of the organization.

The word 'belonging' can mean different things to different people, but we will often hear people say it is about having an affinity with a place, a situation or group of people. For us this is the reason that the EVP is so important in the first place. It is the window into the soul of the organization and can engender that feeling of 'I want to be a part of that' or 'It's a place that I would really like to work.' Starting to build that affinity is very much the starting point. However, to truly create that feeling of belonging, we believe there are several aspects that determine whether someone feels as if they belong or not.

Based on all our conversations through the podcast, we have been pulling together some of the key themes and conclusions, and the model below very much depicts what we have taken away and reflected upon. We concluded that the absence of any one of the four areas below will impact on the perception of 'belonging'.

In the chapter on strategy, we covered the importance of a *purposeful* strategy to employees today. Do they believe the work has meaning, that the organization lives up to its commitment? Having the capability to execute tasks is now a hygiene factor. We have been ridiculously spoilt in this era of smartphones and iPads. The ability to execute tasks in work is often not commensurate with the experience at home/outside work and consequently causes enormous frustration.

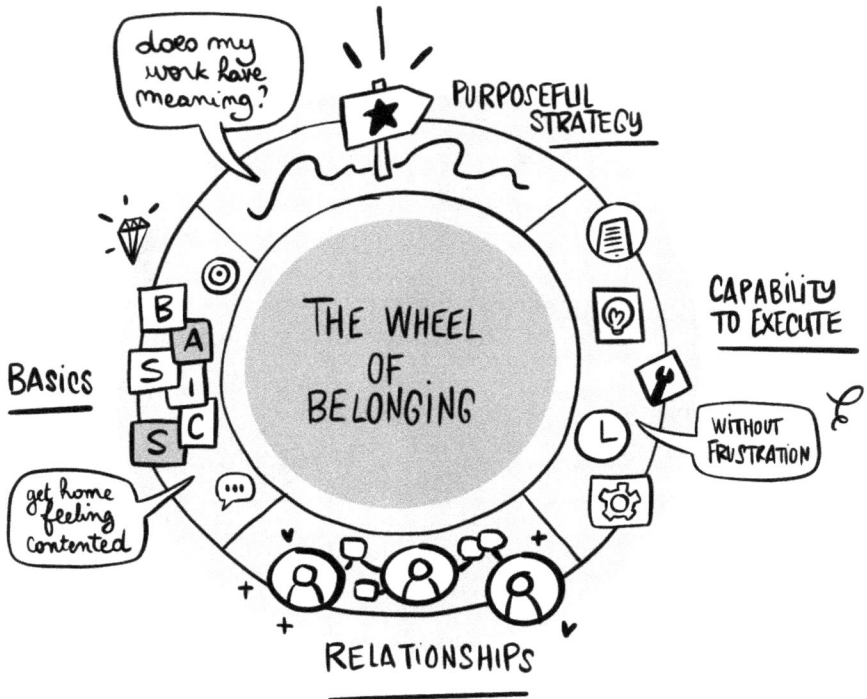

'The basics' has been one of the most common themes on the podcast, and rightly has a chapter to itself, but to summarize what we mean: it's the processes and actions that enable a person to come to work each day and go home feeling contented. Clarity on goals, clear feedback, recognition, access to learning. These are the basics, and they really matter to human beings.

Finally, relationships. We know from the chapter on the predisposition of a human being that affiliation is one of our unconscious motives. There is a need to maintain close, friendly relationships, as we know that relationships energize people. In this instance, we believe it very much concerns the relationship with your manager, your team, and key stakeholders who you support. The quality of those relationships has a significant impact on people. While we won't always get along with everyone we work with – that is perfectly understandable – we know that relationships are a significant element of making someone feel like they belong.

Imagine a scenario whereby an individual has joined an organization. On Day 1 the individual is in the building, but nobody is there to meet them, no manager or buddy. They have a desk, but there is no equipment, no phone, and it is like this for the first week. They have no onboarding plan and are largely left to their own devices to work things out. Over the course of the next four weeks, they haven't been set any clear goals and have received no feedback.

That is quite an extreme example, but imagine if that was the scenario. How long do you think it would take for that individual to become disengaged and disillusioned? 'Not very long' is the answer and arguably within the first week when expectations and hope are at the highest.

We have talked about what an EVP is, and how it can create a sense of belonging, but how do we measure the effectiveness of it? Measuring the effectiveness of the EVP is very much a combination of multiple factors. During the podcast we started using the term 'organizational health' to describe this point. Like us as people, when doctors measure our health, they look at a range of indicators to indicate if we are healthy or not. We believe the metaphor applies in the same way to an organization.

Delivering and measuring the EVP

Effective EVPs are woven and intertwined into all aspects of the employee lifecycle and proposition. If a key component of the EVP is behaviours and values, for example, we will often see them playing a key role in the selection process. We would expect to see elements of the EVP woven into the onboarding process, bringing to life the proposition and commitment of the organization. Throughout the employee lifecycle, we would expect to see the EVP woven into the various processes that underpin performance, reward, learning and talent.

As we have mentioned on several occasions, the execution of these processes is critical and intrinsic to the connection and motivation of the individual. This is where the role of the leader becomes so important. Understanding the purpose behind the process, ensuring flawless execution, standing in the conversation with the individual, supporting and challenging in equal measure and ensuring follow-up. Delivering the EVP requires total commitment. There can be no lip service. The moment that happens, the 'belief' will start to slip away.

A personal story from my wife Jayne Esau. Once a year, Jayne would alert me to the fact her performance review was happening, and would I help with her self-assessment? I did this for a couple of years, absolutely no problem, until one year she informed me the night before that her review was the next day and I asked why she hadn't asked for my help. Her reply: 'They don't look at it and there is never any follow up, so why bother?' There was no evidence to suggest it was anything but a process for process's sake. When you then multiply that across hundreds and thousands of people, you can see the problem.

There shouldn't be a process in flight which has no measurement. If we go back to the concept of 'organizational health', we believe identifying the critical KPIs across a range of processes will provide a balanced view of the health of the organization. The concept of a balanced scorecard is not new; far from it. The question that needs to be asked is: are the KPIs being captured and measured effective, or not?

It is common for organizations to measure the effectiveness of processes such as recruitment (time to fill, time to hire), learning (% compliance v learning paths), goal setting (% alignment to strategy), succession (% succession bench strength and readiness), turnover %, absence %, and many more, but can you create KPIs that align directly to the EVP? During our conversation with Will Lankston from Timpson, Will shared that colleagues are asked to rate their happiness out of 10 on a weekly basis.[5] This metric is held so dear by Timpson. In a business of very few KPIs, this one really matters and is followed up immediately if a score is reported below 8.5. In other organizations the measurement may well be an engagement score of some ilk, and this is an area that continues to evolve.

Employee engagement has been a popular metric for some time. It is seen as a unique indicator of how the organization is 'feeling'. It often carries a significant amount of organizational credibility and is heavily socialized. The frequency of measuring engagement can vary too, and this links back to the chapter on listening and how effective is the organization at understanding and listening to the sentiment of the organization. As the saying goes, the 'proof of the pudding' is in the eating, and this is very much the case with measuring engagement.

The skill today with listening and looking to measure the effectiveness of a proposition is in the questions being asked. The questions should be directly related to the process or processes as well as the relationship with leadership/peers, and really get to the heart of the matter. It should be all about effectiveness, but at a level that provides confidence in the data and confidence that it carries meaning.

We want to refer to the conversation we had on *The Human Factor* podcast with Helen Willetts, Director of Internal Communications, BT Group.[6] Her role at BT has been one of internally showcasing the best of BT Group, but also tells a story of modernization of one of Britain's most trusted companies, taking its 100,000 people on the journey.

To do this, Helen and team set out a new internal communications mission, 'to create a community of advocates for BT Group'.[7] It was underpinned by a ton of hard work and innovation from her team that has seen an impressive 6 percentage point increase in all three key advocacy measures from its 100,000 people. We very much see advocacy as a proactive action whereby someone speaks, recommends, champions or defends a cause. BT is committed to creating an amazing experience for all employees. They recognize that some people will move on, but when they do, they will hopefully still be advocates. They will champion the brand, the product and it being a great place to work.

Therefore, does that almost imply that advocacy as a measurement is the holy grail of KPIs to measure your EVP? Not just belonging and being happy but feeling proud and wanting to champion the organization; very much like a net promoter score.

In conclusion

We will often hear an EVP referred to as the North Star, helping to guide the direction of the organization and the experience of its employees. In this chapter we wanted to explore what that proposition ultimately means and how it engenders belonging, value and connection in the employee. Ultimately, much of it comes down to the execution of the proposition and the level of belonging, hope and belief that it generates. That is the challenge. The goal, very much in line with a customer net promoter score, is the level of advocacy that can be generated.

Having individuals with a high level of advocacy in your organization is the ultimate win-win scenario. The end customer benefits from an increased level of service; the individual is somewhere they want to be and be a part of. We recognize that achieving advocacy isn't easy, but the investment in people is one of the biggest that any organization will make and ultimately the key question is: 'Why wouldn't you wish for that to be the aspiration?'

Tips and tricks

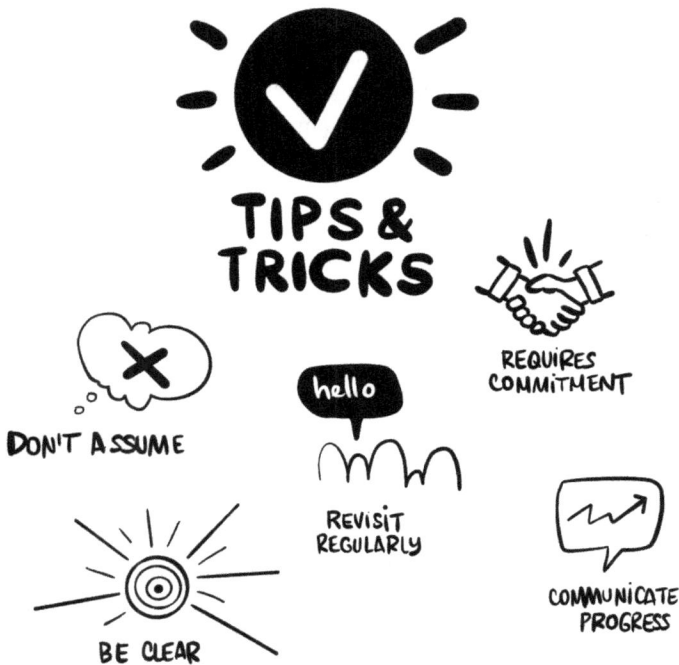

1 Don't assume that people know what your organization is and what you do. To stand out in the market, that needs to be crystal clear.

2 Be clear on what your EVP aims to achieve and how it will be achieved. Sounds obvious, but that isn't always the case!

3 An EVP requires a commitment across the whole organization and needs to be understood by all concerned to ensure a flawless execution – it can involve significant change.

4 Revisit your EVP at regular intervals to ensure relevancy and effectiveness.

5 Communicate progress and wins – super-important as it creates impetus and momentum. This in turn raises confidence and the level of belief in individuals.

Notes

1 *The Human Factor* podcast Ep 24: The Art of Attraction | *The Human Factor Podcast* by SAP, https://podcast.opensap.info/the-human-factor/ 2022/11/18/the-human-factor-podcast-ep-24-the-art-of-attraction/ (archived at https://perma.cc/96FM-V5XU)

2 *The Human Factor* podcast Ep 46: The Power of Brand Advocacy with Catrin and Osian Jones | *The Human Factor Podcast* by SAP, https://podcast. opensap.info/the-human-factor/2024/07/18/the-human-factor-podcast-ep-46- the-power-of-brand-advocacy-with-catrin-and-osian-jones/ (archived at https://perma.cc/2TBZ-2E6K)

3 R Strack (2014) Rainer Strack: The surprising workforce crisis of 2030 – and how to start solving it now, YouTube, www.youtube.com/watch?v=ux1GxExRUUY (archived at https://perma.cc/7RMF-XH7Z)

4 BCG Global (2014) The Global Workforce Crisis: $10 Trillion at Risk, www.bcg.com/publications/2014/people-organization-human-resources-global- workforce-crisis (archived at https://perma.cc/UCL9-3756)

5 *The Human Factor* podcast Ep 41: The Happy Organization | *The Human Factor Podcast* by SAP, https://podcast.opensap.info/the-human-factor/2024/03/13/ the-human-factor-podcast-ep-41-the-happy-organisation/ (archived at https:// perma.cc/6XJZ-32PX)

6 *The Human Factor* podcast Ep 39: The Art of Communication | *The Human Factor Podcast* by SAP, https://podcast.opensap.info/the-human-factor/2024/01/18/ the-human-factor-podcast-ep-39-the-art-of-communication/ (archived at https:// perma.cc/7743-27Z2)

7 BT (2022) Our purpose and values, www.bt.com, www.bt.com/about/bt/our- company/our-purpose-and-values (archived at https://perma.cc/4CKK-6FBD)

The relativity of success

8

Introduction

Let's turn our attention now to success. What is success? Easy, right? We either succeed or we don't, and it's a binary concept. Not really. There are degrees of success, and what we will explore in this chapter is all aspects of what success means.

How do we define the term 'success'? What are some examples of success that, on face value, might not be perceived by others as success? How do we measure success? How can we attribute a value to it and, having achieved it, how can we sustain it on an ongoing basis?

What we also need to discuss is how success can be relative rather than binary. How can one person's success be another person's failure when they are the same outcome achieved?

We will explore life goals vs work goals. Can the two co-exist, and can we achieve one without the other? Can the success of the organization influence personal success and performance, and consequently, is it possible to succeed when the organization is failing?

When we think we have failed, are there things we may have succeeded in that are overshadowed? And how should we react to perceived failure - firstly to those giving us feedback, and secondly to ourselves when reflecting upon outcomes?

As we always do, we will wrap up the chapter with some tips and tricks on success for consideration, both at home and at work.

What is success?

We will start by setting a common understanding of what the word 'success' means. The dictionary definition is 'the achievement of a goal'. And we are already off to the races in terms of meaning different things to different people at different times. When we use a phrase such as 'the accomplishment of a goal', then it all depends on what that goal was. Some 'goals' are harder than others. Some have more impact or resonance. Some affect individuals and others affect groups. As we progress in life, it may also be that our own definition of success changes and evolves.

When I (Simon) began my career in consulting, one of my own perceptions of success was to become a partner in a large consulting firm. I saw it as the primary goal of my career. It would therefore be what would drive my behaviour and aspirations. It was a very logical aspiration and I suspect quite common in the industry. That said, I wasn't clear to myself why I wanted to be a partner. Did I really understand what it meant? Did I really want it, or was it what I thought I was supposed to try and be?

As I progressed in my career, it became apparent that I was probably not going to succeed. I wasn't going to make partner. In the meantime, I had a very rewarding and satisfying career, where I learnt a lot, I grew as an individual, I travelled the world and was well-rewarded. By all other metrics, my career was successful – but I wasn't going to make partner. Was I success or a failure? My perception of my time in consulting was a mixture of success and failure. I had provided for my family. I had seen the world. I had a very comfortable life. But I would also beat myself up. I didn't make partner. When I left consulting, it felt an unachieved ambition (and to someone who is very competitive by nature, that was hard to accept).

FOR A GROUP? — DIFFICULTY LEVEL?

WHAT IS THE AIM?

FOR AN INDIVIDUAL? — IMPACT?

But I also then changed my perspective. After years of running in the proverbial rat race in the pursuit of partnership, I also operated under significant stress, either organizationally imposed or self-imposed. Now that I am out of that rat race for now, I am more relaxed, healthier and enjoy work more. I can reflect that my time within consulting was very successful and allows me to continue to be successful. This is because my definition of success has now changed. I want to enjoy work. I want to enjoy what I do every day and I want to share knowledge and experience with others. But I also want to enjoy time outside work with family and friends.

For me, being a partner would have led to prestige, recognition, and, of course, would have been financially rewarding. But I now feel I have those things anyway. Well, maybe not the financial riches, but riches of another kind – serenity, calmness, satisfaction and comfort in my own skin. And for me, at this stage of my life, that's success.

Relative success

As mentioned at the start of the chapter, success is not binary. It is relative to who we are, what we are trying to achieve, what the original aim/purpose was and whether we are happy with what we did.

My co-author, Michael, frames this well with a personal anecdote. Usain Bolt can run the 100m in less than 10 seconds and is phenomenal. My colleague can probably do the same distance in maybe 30 seconds. If he were to train and train, he could feasibly get that under 25 seconds, and for him, that would be success. He is nowhere near challenging the standard set by Bolt, but his success is personal to him and represents a significant improvement on performance. It is therefore relative to him, his starting point, his objective and his ability.

FAST *BOLT*

OR

MiCHAEL **SLOW**

Let us look at Hollywood for an example, in particular the film *Cool Runnings*. The story follows the Jamaican bobsleigh team, loosely based upon the 1988 Winter Olympics. Our story follows the paths of four athletes who have suffered in their attempts to qualify for other sports, primarily track events. They decide that the only way to go to the Olympics is to try an event that will ensure they reach Calgary. They track down a disgraced coach and set off for Canada.

It becomes clear they are considered a laughing stock and they are given no hope. However, they train, and try to find their own identity, all the while bonding and becoming a team. They crash in their final downhill race. But in line with their newfound team ethic, and emboldened by the Olympic spirit, they carry their sled across the line and finish. The epilogue then tells us that they returned home to be greeted as heroes and returned to the Olympics four years later as equals.

The team failed to win, or even place in the medals. However, they succeeded in many ways – they reached the Olympics, they bonded as a team, they represented their country, and they showed the spirit of the Olympics. They earned the respect of their competitors and the praise of their country when they returned. By every metric other than the primary one when entering a race, they succeeded.

There are many other similar examples. Another example of Olympics-influenced success was the story of Eddie 'The Eagle' Edwards. Michael Edwards was an English ski jumper who competed in the 1998 Winter Olympics in Calgary. He came last in both events he competed in, but, like the Jamaicans in the bobsleigh, showed the spirit of the competition. In the closing ceremony, the President of the Organizing Committee, Frank King, addressed the competitors and observed: 'You have broken world records and you have established personal bests. Some of you have even soared like an eagle.'

Edwards went from famously losing to being considered a success when he returned to the UK and enjoyed a career from his infamy. He even became an Olympic torchbearer for the 2010 Olympics in Vancouver.

Finally, in a different sport, but still at the Olympics, Eric Moussambani (Eric the Eel as he was named by the media) created his place in history. Eric was a swimmer, representing Equatorial Guinea at the summer 2000

Olympics in Sydney. Prior to the competition, he had never even seen an Olympic-sized 50m swimming pool, and qualified through a wild card given to encourage developing countries.

In his heat, he set an unprecedented slow time, but incredibly won the heat as his two competitors in the heat were disqualified. To set this win into context, though, his time was more than twice the time set by the eventual competition winner, and Eric struggled to even finish his heat. He unfortunately didn't advance in the competition due to his time.

How did Eric succeed. He only took up swimming eight months before the Olympics, and practised in a local lake and then a small 12m hotel pool. He not only represented his country at the Olympics (and it's a very small number of people that can claim this achievement), but he also actually won his heat. In 2012 he went on to become the coach of the national swimming squad of Equatorial Guinea.

Sport is filled with examples such as the ones above. Just getting to the start line is success for some. For others, like Usain Bolt, Michael Johnson, the USA dream team basketball team, and many others, nothing short of victory is success. Anything less than first place is failure.

This is what we mean when we say success is relative. But how can we measure success and start to put a value on it?

SUCCESS
is
relative
START

Measuring success

We want to put a measurement behind success. Sometimes, success is binary – we achieved, or we didn't. But sometimes, success is to achieve an improvement. How do we know whether something has been improved?

We need to establish a baseline so that we can then compare the outcome with the start point. Not only can we then say whether something has improved, but we can assign a qualitive value to that improvement – was it a good improvement or a disappointing improvement? And so, when we then come to evaluate if the improvement is a success or not, we can also set some definition of a target by which the improvement can be compared. Is success a 5 per cent improvement, 10 per cent, 50 per cent?

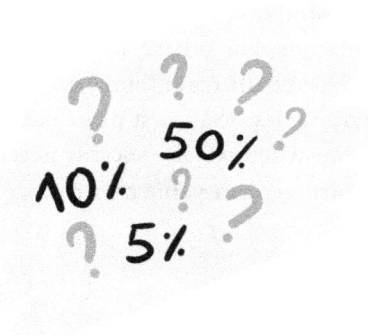

When we started the chapter, we talked about my co-author and his 100m sprint time. For him, cutting five seconds from a sprint time is a tremendous success, but it is only possible to evaluate it as such because we know what the baseline was. If we had no baseline, and then he ran that 25 second 100m distance, how can we know if that is good for him or not?

When we bring this into the world of work, it becomes very important to measure. We need to establish if performance is improving or reducing, whether that is for an individual, a department, or an entire company. Here we are interested in not only the snapshot 'in the moment' view of success, but also how that performance is trending.

But again, we need to understand relativity in the context of success. A high performing individual has consistently achieved high performance over, let's say, two to three years, and is promoted as a result. Is it reasonable for the organization to expect that high performance to continue unabated? Or would we expect a degree of development was then needed in the new role? Could there even be a dip in performance as the individual acclimatizes to the new objectives and behaviours needed? But does the dip in performance mean they are less successful?

How we evaluate their success needs to be relative to their new role, their new targets and their relative inexperience when we compare them to role peers who may have been in that role for several years already.

Sustaining success

As we have discussed so far, success can be defined clearly, or can also be something that is more personal. Ben Affleck won an Oscar at the age of 25 for best original screenplay in *Good Will Hunting* along with his co-writer, Matt Damon. At 25, he had achieved the pinnacle of defined success in the film industry.

When interviewed about how it felt to win, he likened it to a car crash with regards to it being almost hallucinatory and everything being in slow motion. He talked about how he didn't know what to expect or what was expected of him. He mentioned it was difficult to appreciate so early in his career, and that personal appreciation of his success came later in life. He then achieved his second Oscar for Best Picture for *Argo* in 2013, some 15 years later. What drives a person to achieve success and then to keep achieving success again and again? How can success be sustained?

What we have seen in our conversations with people who have been successful is that they share common traits, or 'ingredients', which include the following:

- There is always room for improvement, regardless of the initial outcome.

- Having personal standards and maintaining those standards underpin successful outcomes.

- Celebrate success, but then put it aside. Start again with focus and clarity.

- Self-awareness and reflection are very important when trying to understand areas for improvement and growth.

Success through failure

Can you learn from failure and turn that into success? I subscribe to the belief that I learn and grow more from failure than I do from success. I learn what didn't work, and hopefully learn what I need to do next time to succeed. I also firmly believe that sometimes success has the potential to hide areas for improvement. If we succeed, do we analyse our performance as closely as when we fail?

In Episode 34 of *The Human Factor*, we wanted to ask this question and dig into the mindset that drives this sustainability.[1] Our guest was Maggie Alphonsi OBE. Maggie is the face of international women's rugby and arguably one of the best-known names in women's team sports on the planet. Before announcing her international retirement in 2014, she represented her country an impressive 74 times, scored 28 tries, won a World Cup and helped England win a record-breaking seven consecutive Six Nations crowns.

Through her England rugby career, she has become a household name but also a media professional, and since retiring, she has commentated on live rugby matches and featured in a diverse array of media outlets, from Stella Magazine to BBC's *Children in Need* and *The One Show*.

Our conversation was a fascinating insight into a high-performance, high-achievement athlete, who had achieved success at the pinnacle of her sport. We covered many aspects of standards, ingredients of success and sustainability, including:

- how standards are sustained and reinforced, and by whom
- ensuring inclusivity – tapping into the individual capabilities of each person
- the impact of misalignment, productivity dips and a lowering of standards
- the importance of 'multiple leaders' in driving dynamic teams
- the ingredients required to drive a climate of growth
- creating alignment to a common goal and achieving it
- creating 'team spirit'

One of her observations around driving successful outcomes was to ensure buy-in to the culture and the values of the organization: 'You have to really emphasize what does it mean to represent that logo or that brand or whatever your organization is and what does it truly mean.'

However, Maggie and the England Team did not win the World Cup at their first attempt. They were losing finalists in 2010 to a powerful New Zealand Team. By most of our standards, that would still be a success – to reach a World Cup Final. Maggie talked about how the team reflected on how they could improve in the 2014 competition, and one of the key areas of improvement was for the team to evolve from having one clear leader, to being a team of leaders:

Try and create 15 leaders on the field so they can all be accountable for their decisions and direct themselves... I think that's absolutely brilliant and that's how I see the best teams.

Maggie spoke to us about establishing and then maintaining standards. About the importance of being comfortable with being uncomfortable, and about having an increased awareness of self. She talked about understanding what someone's personal driver is – what makes that person get up every day, and tapping into that to ensure continuity even after initial success.

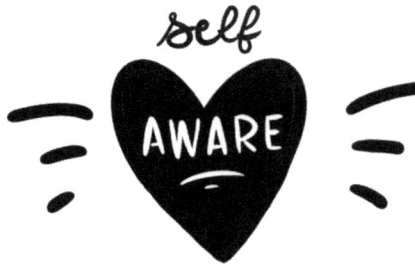

The ability to be self-aware is so critical to sustaining success. The people we have spoken with all have that common trait of self-awareness. They are able to recognize success, but also to analyse how they can build upon it and improve. To learn from failure and use that to help achieve success going forwards. But what happens when doubt in ourselves starts to creep in? How can we look inwards and be more aware of ourselves to help steady the ship?

When doubt creeps in

When assessing our personal and professional successes, listening to ourselves is an essential skill. In another episode of the podcast series (Episode 28 for those keeping track), we spoke with Glenn Bracey.[2] Glenn is the founder of Future Vision Training and is a wellness and performance coach. We spoke with Glenn around the topic of 'awareness of self'. Listening to ourselves is a crucial link to success.

Glenn frames this at the beginning of our conversation as follows: 'The more conscious you are in recognizing your aspects of self and the differences between your psychological self and your aware self... the less pain and suffering you're going to have in your life.'

He goes on to define our psychological self and our aware self as follows:

> The psychological self includes our thoughts. It includes our emotions and particularly our hidden fears. It includes our ego. It includes our biases. It includes our emotions and our feelings. It includes our psychological behaviour.
>
> The psychological self is duplicitous – it will tell you in one breath or one moment or one day how good you are, how successful you are. Have always been, how lovable you are, how wanted you are and in the next moment it will tell you the complete opposite.
>
> Our aware self is simply the awareness of all of the things that we notice about our psychological self. So my aware self has the ability to be able to watch my thoughts and notice them and see how they serve me. Watch my emotions. Recognize ego welling up in me and watch the fears. It would be able to sit with those fears in such a way that it realizes that most of my fears are unfounded.'

Many of us have experienced imposter syndrome at some time in our lives. The National Library of Medicine describes this as 'a behavioural health phenomenon described as self-doubt of intellect, skills, or accomplishments among high-achieving individuals'.[3] This can be attributed to listening to ourselves negatively, allowing that demon on our shoulder to whisper in our ear to create doubt.

We touched on this with Glenn in some detail, as we both have felt this doubt in our past and, to some degree, our present. His advice was:

Our psychological self is searching for all the things that our aware self has already got, and all I need to do is learn how to stay with my aware self a little bit more, and then imposter syndrome fades.

By more actively listening to our aware self, we can improve our sense of success, and thus our personal and professional wellbeing.

What other factors can influence success? Sometimes there are external factors that can have either a positive or a negative impact on the ability to deliver success. Can we be nurtured to succeed, and can we be held back from success depending on the culture of the organization?

The impact of culture on success

We have discussed culture already throughout this book. How though can culture influence success? It's obvious to state, but a healthy positive culture can nurture and encourage success, and a negative or toxic culture can have the opposite effect. Let's explore both perspectives.

Within an organization, a positive culture can create the environment for success. A culture that allows for experimentation and expression, and

one that rewards success without criticizing failure encourages positive behaviours from the workforce. The freedom to experiment allows people to try out ideas, new ways of working, to innovate. If this is underpinned with a culture that rewards success and doesn't criticize failure, then those new ideas and innovations can evolve and grow. We can learn from failure to try again.

The Purpose, Approach, Mindset framework we highlighted in Chapter 2 was an innovation that was conceived, built and delivered within the culture of SAP. The freedom to explore an idea, combined with positive support to enable it to be built and deployed, was employee behaviour that is actively encouraged. We are very proud of the framework and from thousands of entries, it was one of three finalists for the Hasso Plattner Founders' Award in 2022.

The Hasso Plattner Founders' Award is SAP's highest honour for employee recognition and achievement, paying homage to the entrepreneurial spirit of the company's founders. Conceived to spotlight remarkable inventions and solutions that substantially impact the business, the award breeds an environment where innovation thrives.

The award evaluates innovations against the five core cultural values of SAP, namely:

- Tell it like it is.
- Stay curious.
- Embrace differences.
- Keep promises.
- Build bridges.

The organization culture at SAP not only allows for innovation and new ideas, but also rewards, recognizes and actively promotes this as success.

But what happens when a culture is more restrictive? When your boss or supervisor is always finding fault or concentrating on the negatives in your work? When the fear of failure is crippling? When the overwhelming feeling is that it's all going wrong and there is no value in trying? This negativity is an incredibly hard culture in which to succeed, and succeed in a sustainable manner. It affects our emotional wellbeing, our self-esteem and our motivation as individuals. In recent times we have seen new lexicons appearing, such as 'quiet quitting', describing the outcome culture can have on success if toxic.

We have explored how culture can influence success, but what about age? Does age affect our expectations and perceptions of success? As we get older, do we re-evaluate what success even means to us?

Does age influence our perception of success?

When we were young, we all had dreams of success; astronaut, ballerina, sports star, chef, film star and so on. For many of us though, those were pipe dreams. Reality often plays a different hand for us, and we pursue more realistic careers through our lives. As we get older, we tend to reflect more. Is our life fulfilling? Do we enjoy our work? Have we succeeded so far?

Mid-life can be a very unsettling time for some. That feeling that time is moving on. That our working lives are finite and potentially approaching an end point. It's not uncommon for us as humans to suffer from a mid-life crisis as we realize we will never fulfil our dream of being a sports star, break through into Hollywood films or reach space.

Fortunately, a mid-life crisis is not as common as we might think, typically affecting 20 per cent or less of adults.[4] For some, mid-life can be very liberating also. It's a chance to redefine what success will look life in the second half of life. For many, the pursuit of money, love, fame begin to recede, and life goals become more orientated around giving back, mentoring, nurturing and finding tranquillity. It's not uncommon for people to challenge the constraints that they have lived by in their earlier years.

We enjoyed a very reflective episode on the podcast (Episode 30) with Gabby Logan.[5] Gabby is one of the UK's leading broadcasters and has recently been recognized with an MBE. The honour is for services to sports broadcast and promoting women in sport.

A former international gymnast, Gabby began her broadcasting career in radio in 1992 and joined Sky Sports in 1996 where she quickly established herself as one of their key presenters. In 2004 Gabby hosted *Sport Relief* for the BBC, before joining the corporation in 2007.

A prolific writer, she's been a columnist for *The Times* and has previously written for *The Independent*, *The Guardian*, *Glamour* and *Stylist* magazine, and more recently has entered the ever-growing podcast world, launching her chart-topping *The Mid•Point with Gabby Logan*, now in its sixth series.[6] Gabby's candid debut memoir *The First Half* hit shelves in October 2022.[7]

During our conversation, we reflected on reaching middle age and what it meant. Gabby talked about many of her reflections and summarized her perspective now. She reflected: 'What can I do in my life that I've previously felt was out of bounds?'

This revision of what success will look like in middle age can be liberating. As consequence of failure decreases, so our perception of possibility changes. We approach challenges with more freedom and realism, and therefore the potential for successful outcomes can increase. No longer the lofty goals of superstardom; now success goals are more grounded and realistic.

the appreciation of what we do

For Gabby, this was summarized as follows:

> I've got an appreciation of what I do, and I really am in the moment.

We, your illustrious co-authors, were privileged to be invited to be the inaugural guests on a new podcast show, *Life's 2nd Act: A journey into finding direction and purpose*, hosted by Simon Burgess.[8] Simon asked us for our feelings about middle age, and how we reflected on reaching this point of our lives and careers. We both thoroughly enjoyed the conversation, but also the chance to stop and reflect. To consider where we were in our lives, what we felt were our successes that had been achieved and what was still to achieve.

This chapter has been moulded by those reflections. Our own thoughts on what success means. How failure can help us become successful, and about how our very perception of success going forwards has evolved from when we first dreamed.

(For the record, I wanted to be a professional footballer and then, later in life, a professional ten pin bowler.)

In conclusion

One person's success is another person's failure, even when the outcome is the same. We started this chapter with the premise that not all success is equal. It is driven by the baseline. In fact, success could even be maintaining the status quo or making a loss. Certainly, during the pandemic breaking even or managing losses was an important consideration for many businesses, biding their time until lockdowns were lifted and more 'normal' service could be resumed. In those times, success was simply continuing to exist.

But it's not just achievement of success that we have considered in our thoughts in this chapter. It's also about sustaining that success. If we succeed in a sales function, for example, we could find that the following year's targets are elevated and thus the baseline has changed. Maintaining that success has thus become harder, even without taking into consideration any other conditions.

Tips and tricks

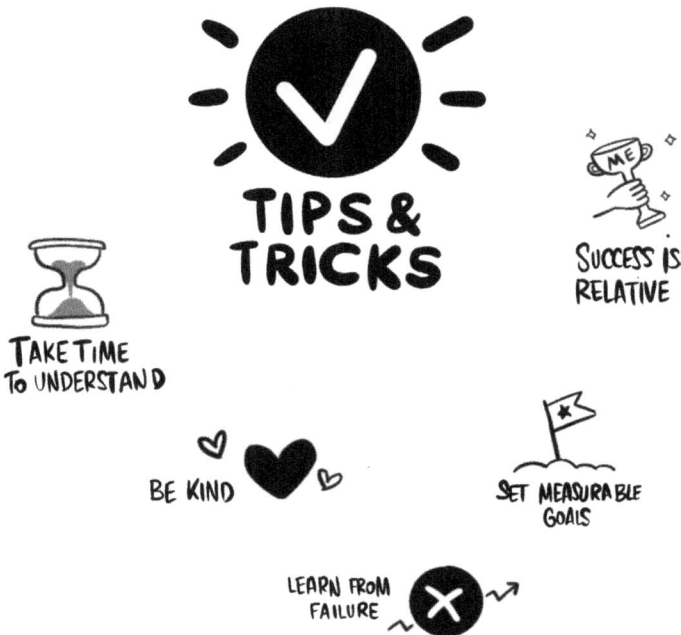

1 Take the time to really understand what drives you as this will help define what success looks like for you.

2 Be kind to yourself when success is not instant.

3 Learn from failure and be resilient enough to try again.

4 Set goals that can be measured and regularly evaluate progress against them.

5 Success is relative. Don't be defined by the success of others. Define your own success and celebrate when you achieve it.

Notes

1 *The Human Factor* podcast Ep 34: The Ingredients of Success | *The Human Factor Podcast* by SAP, https://podcast.opensap.info/the-human-factor/2023/08/18/the-human-factor-podcast-ep-34-the-ingredients-of-success/ (archived at https://perma.cc/QM7N-8RA8)

2 *The Human Factor* podcast Ep 28: Understanding Self | *The Human Factor Podcast* by SAP, https://podcast.opensap.info/the-human-factor/2023/02/28/the-human-factor-podcast-ep-28-understanding-self/ (archived at https://perma.cc/2ZPE-GWRC)

3 M R Huecker, J Shreffler, P T McKeny and D Davis (2023) Imposter phenomenon, PubMed, www.ncbi.nlm.nih.gov/books/NBK585058/ (archived at https://perma.cc/43V2-SN85)

4 S Reid (2022) Midlife Crisis, HelpGuide.org, www.helpguide.org/articles/aging-issues/midlife-crisis.htm (archived at https://perma.cc/TB8K-S8N2)

5 *The Human Factor* podcast Ep 30: They Think It's All Over, It's Only Just Begun | *The Human Factor Podcast* by SAP, https://podcast.opensap.info/the-human-factor/2023/04/18/the-human-factor-podcast-ep-30-they-think-its-all-over-its-only-just-begun/ (archived at https://perma.cc/88EA-MTJ3)

6 *The Mid•Point with Gabby Logan* on Apple Podcasts, https://podcasts.apple.com/gb/podcast/the-mid-point-with-gabby-logan/id1527545442 (archived at https://perma.cc/XRD3-5Q24)

7 G Logan (2022) *The First Half*, Piatkus Books

8 Getting out your comfort zone and life in your 50s | Life's 2nd Act: A journey into finding direction and purpose, https://lifes2ndact.podbean.com/e/get-out-your-comfort-zone-bring-on-later-life/ (archived at https://perma.cc/7RWF-RNZH)

ENGAGEMENT
IS A  OF
Commitment

Human experience, engagement and advocacy

9

Introduction

We have deliberately not titled this chapter 'Employee experience, engagement and advocacy'. This is because, as can be seen throughout this book, we want to explore all those human factors that influence us as employees, but also those that influence us outside work. Therefore, we will look at human experience and human engagement as a wider focus.

We have experiences all the time. Sometimes that experience is new and sometimes it is a repeated one. However, we are potentially influenced by that experience each time, perhaps in different ways. Whether it's a trip to a shop, a stay in a hotel, a visit to the cinema/theatre or a trip to the bank, we are having these human experiences all the time. Sometimes, we have a positive or negative experience, but it's also true that the experience doesn't stand out as special. When we go into work, we might have similar feedback – sometimes the day goes well, sometimes not and maybe most of the time it's neutral or unremarkable.

As humans, we are typically very receptive to experiences. They influence us to want to repeat or avoid the interaction in future. We have seen an increase in requests for feedback in recent years: 'How was your stay?' 'How did we do?' 'Would you visit again?' As consumers, our opinions matter. The same can be said when we are employees at work. Our opinions matter. They can influence whether we are happy at work or unhappy, and of course, if we are unhappy, whether we are then likely to leave. We will explore this in more detail throughout this chapter.

These experiences also drive our level of engagement. We will look to define what engagement means and how our experiences influence our levels of engagement. What happens when our engagement is high, and what are the consequences of low engagement?

Finally, we will also discuss advocacy. Creating advocacy is key to any business, whether from consumers or its own employees, as this generates loyalty and sustainability. What creates advocacy, and how is it sustained? Why is it so important, and how do we place a value on it?

We will draw upon our findings and discussions from other chapters in this book, for example the chapters on the predisposition of a human being (Chapter 5) and listening, insights and feedback (Chapter 12). We will reflect on some of conversations from *The Human Factor* podcast series, such as with organizational psychologist Caitlynn Sendra. We will also touch base with conversations we have had with Jason Averbook and Bentley Motors, amongst others.

To start, let's go back to basics and establish a common definition of what we mean by human experience, engagement and advocacy.

Human experience

Defining 'experience' is going to be tricky, but probably largely unnecessary. Difficult because it can mean many things. Unnecessary because we all really know what 'experience' means. What we are interested in is what happens when we experience something. It usually triggers an emotion or reaction. We often think of experiences as good or bad, positive or negative. We will also of course encounter experiences which don't invoke much of a reaction, either positively or negatively. These could be activities that are often repeated, and therefore the experience is already known (maybe emptying the dishwasher), or they could be activities that haven't grabbed our emotions ('That film left me feeling empty of feeling').

As humans, we generally strive for the experiences that leave us feeling positive. Sometimes, though, we must go through experiences that we know will trigger emotions in us that we don't want to go through. Attending a funeral, for example. We know we will feel sad, but we know that it's important nonetheless. Other times, we will not know what the experience will bring, and that in itself triggers emotions – fear, anticipation, excitement, etc.

Let's go back to the types of experience we mentioned in the Introduction – the trip to the bank or visiting a shop. Here, our experience is very broad. What is the ambience of the shop? How helpful and friendly were the staff? Did they have what I wanted? Was the price acceptable? All these factors contribute to the overall view of the experience and, as humans, we will often feel different views on the experience depending on who we are and what our expectations were. Hence, the experience can be personalized, and also feel personal.

So, what happens when we go to work? Our experiences at work can have profound impacts on our working lives, but also on us as individuals. When someone asks if we have a positive work experience, we are likely evaluating against several parameters. For example, is my work experience:

- safe?
- healthy?
- rewarding?
- interesting?
- fruitful?
- seamless?
- supportive?

Our feelings about the experience are contingent on different elements – the physical work environment, the culture, and any digital tools being used. All must work in harmony to create a positive workplace experience.

We are often invited in to work with companies who are considering implementing new technology for their HR capability. The company may be considering spending thousands, if not hundreds of thousands or sometimes millions on their new technology. Many times, this also means going through a significant due diligence exercise on the technologies available in the market as well as extensive evaluation processes.

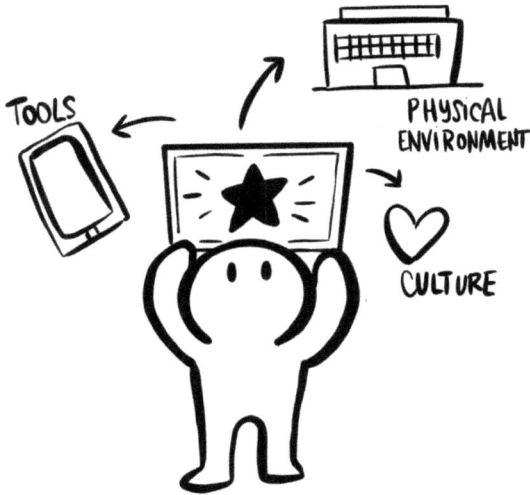

However, what is sometimes surprising is that the HR team in the company have not re-evaluated their underlying processes and ways of working. Often the list of requirements needed for the new system to be evaluated against are the same processes as before, with a few extra features thrown in. Typically, one of the evaluation criteria for the new system is then 'user experience'. This is problematic for a number of reasons.

Firstly, without changing the underlying processes, the overall experience will be little different to before. Technology can bring improvement, but if the foundational processes and ways of working are unnecessarily complex or inefficient, then this will continue regardless of the technology solution chosen. The overall experience may get a facelift, but is unlikely to be a significant improvement.

Secondly, modern cloud-based solutions are constantly re-inventing their user experience. These systems can innovate at pace, and keeping the user interface modern, efficient, and appealing is a never-ending task, a bit like painting the Forth Road bridge. Once you have completed a user interface refresh across the whole solution, you start again with new additions and changes. Therefore, to make the user interface a critical selection criterion, when it could easily change inside a year, is flawed in its perceived value.

Very early in the book, in Chapter 2 on the case for change, we introduced Bentley Motors. Bentley had to go through a significant transformation. There was huge disruption in the motor industry with the shift towards electrification. Geopolitical drivers were also emerging as the Chinese motor industry began to accelerate, for example.[1] To remain as one of the premium luxury car makers in the global market, they had to reskill and reshape their workforce, not only to transition away from the internal combustion engine to electric engines, but also to make their daily processes more efficient.

A major part of their project was to protect their excellent culture in the workforce. They took the decision to implement SAP SuccessFactors for their new HR solution and embarked on a transformation journey. Their learnings were many, and they shared these with us in a conversation centred around the attraction and retention of talent.

One of their key learnings was to ensure that whenever they transformed a process:

We need to constantly remind ourselves, working in HR, that there's a human being on the end of every process.

They recognized that the experience had to encompass not only new technology, but that the processes themselves needed transforming to ensure that the resulting outcome was one that would not only be efficient, but consumable by the user.

In a later episode of *The Human Factor*, we talked with Dr Caitlynn Sendra.[2] Caitlynn is an Employee Experience (EX) Product Specialist at SAP. Her academic background is as an industrial and organizational psychologist. In our conversation, we wanted to explore what gives a user experience impact. How do some technology solutions thrive and become 'sticky' and others fall by the wayside, unloved and unused? We approached this topic from a human perspective, and Caitlynn was clear: 'Humans will adopt any new technology that fulfils an immediate need that they have, and they perceive it as being useful and easy to use.'

This reminded me of a story that we tell on many occasions to illustrate this point. A colleague purchased a smart watch. It was shiny new technology, and he was keen to experience what it could offer. A week later, he had taken it off and never put it back on. The issue was not the watch. The design was great, the features were many. The issue was that he had no immediate need that the watch fulfilled over and above a normal watch. So, while easy to use, and undoubtably useful to many people, the watch didn't meet the personal expectations of a positive experience.

Caitlynn encouraged anyone who was designing a solution, for any audience: 'Take a step back and think about the human need that's driving your technology that you are creating.' Without this step, we could just be designing a watch that will never be used by Michael.

Another key consideration when we talk about experience is standardization versus personalization. If we make the experience the same for everyone, we make the process of providing that experience efficient, and ideally cost-effective. The issue with standardization is that it can sometimes leave the experience feeling a little sterile. It lacks the ability to feel personal, or special to me. Humans like individuality. We see this all the time in life – the choice of car, how we decorate the home we live in, the clothes we wear. These are all statements of personalization, and they define our style and taste. The same can be observed in how we process information and undertake tasks. Some people are highly creative, some very detail-orientated.

So, when we look at experiences, why then should we expect universal approval for a standardized experience? What we have seen time and time again is that people want to be able to personalize the experience. This can come with a potential cost either to the supplier/employer or the individual. But this can have a significant impact on the resulting feedback about the experience. Chapter 5 included some of our conversation with Cirque du Soleil and the design of their company processes. Their underlying philosophy was 'one size fits none'. People should not be treated the same, and should not expect a one size fits all experience while working at the company.

Our user experience at work is changing. Cloud based solutions, such as SAP SuccessFactors, are collaborating with other technology companies so that the experience can be improved. The phrase 'meet me where I am at' describes a user sentiment principle that articulates a changing paradigm in modern systems: being able to perform activities inside one system without leaving the system you are in.

For example, since the pandemic, organizations are now using collaboration tools like Microsoft Teams more and more in their daily lives – video conferencing, chatting, collaborating across multiple geographies. 'Meet me where I am at' means I am in MS Teams, but I need to do something that is hosted in another system, let's say recording some upcoming vacation. The collaboration between SAP and Microsoft now allows the user to record their holiday from within Teams, meaning the user does not have to log into a different system, find the capability, record the information and then return to what they were doing. It can all be done within Teams.

This experience then eliminates the disruption, and captures the information needed, while integrating it across the two systems behind the scenes and, importantly, invisibly to the user. In the past, this would have required significant cost and effort from the IT department – building the integration and ensuring it was robust and reliable, even when the solutions were constantly changing with new features. However, because the integration is productized and provided by a cross-vendor collaboration, even this work is not needed, as it is a vendor responsibility.

This means that our user experiences at work will transition to cross-process, cross-functional, cross-product, and even cross-vendor. This dramatically improves our experience at work. Now, the finance clerk who needs to raise a requisition to recruit a new team member can undertake the process without worrying about gaps in the processes and systems.

The other major development currently underway is the addition of artificial intelligence into our working lives. In our previous example, our finance clerk is not necessarily familiar with company recruitment rules and processes. In fact, our clerk might have never hired someone previously. To them, this can be a scary process, full of opportunity to get lost or make mistakes which could have significant impact on the outcome.

The emergence of AI will provide guidance, content and direction to the process, which are all there to improve the user experience. Completing the recruitment requisition, creating a job description, scheduling interviews, suggesting interview questions, creating a job offer and finally onboarding a new team member are all activities that can be supported by AI to help the user through the right steps, and to suggest content that can be used.

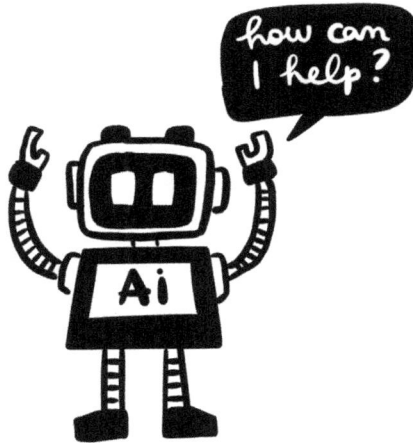

In 2024, SAP announced an acquisition of WalkMe.[3] WalkMe was founded in 2011 as a tool to support guidance and navigation help to system users. It has evolved now to become an embedded help and guidance tool to help infrequent users through the process complexities of their organization.

So, what we now have is cross-functional, cross-solution integrated capabilities, with AI overlaid to provide content and direction, and embedded navigational help. That scary user experience is now something that not only is easier to understand and complete successfully, but also supports someone who may only run that process infrequently. We can anticipate a future where even inputting our data through a keyboard could become more of a rarity. Voice driven AI, operating with natural language, could become our default user experience at work, as we are already seeing this develop at pace in our home lives with tools such as Alexa, Siri and Google Assistant.

Why does the experience matter so much, whether at work or in our personal lives? What does a positive or negative experience then lead to? Usually it's a form of engagement. We are either engaged with the experience or disengaged. We need to now look at why being engaged is important and what its impact can be.

What is engagement, and why is it so important?

Engagement is a measure of commitment. If I am engaged in a process, I am committed to its successful outcome, and if I am engaged in my job, I am committed to helping my company achieve its goals.

There are many schools of thought on engagement, and while we will explore the topic it's probable that we will only scratch the surface. Our goal here is not to dissect how to achieve engagement, but to observe the consequences of getting it right or getting it wrong. Because the consequence is significant.

Workplaces have always had their share of disengaged workers. More recently, we have attributed phrases to try and encapsulate this, including 'quiet quitting'. A disengaged worker can however become a multiplier for trouble. They can create toxicity in a workplace very quickly and affect other people.

But do we need to like our job to be effective? There is considerable research into that very question – does employee happiness have an impact on productivity? A 2019 study by Oxford University, in collaboration with British Telecom, found a conclusive link between the two.[4] They estimated that there was a 13 per cent improvement in productivity in people that were happy. Here we can make a link between happiness and engaged. If I am engaged in what I am doing, I am likely to be happy. If I am happy, I am more productive.

But there are also other words we can start to link with being engaged. 'Commitment' is one of those. If we can move from compliance to commitment, we are now in the realms of strategic value. If I am compliant with a process, whatever that process may be, then I am doing it because I have to. If I can be engaged with the experience such that I am now committed to the process, then I am doing the process because I want to and I will seek to ensure a successful outcome.

When we design our processes, and we create a positive experience for our employees, we improve their engagement in those processes. When we have engaged employees, we improve their commitment to the processes. And when we have commitment, we can realize strategic benefits such as increases in productivity and improvements in retention.

Have a look at the following diagram as a model of execution and impact.

In any organization, there will be a large number of transactional processes. While they don't really excite us, being able to execute them flawlessly and efficiently is the goal. When that doesn't happen, and it is hard for managers and employees to get processes executed or processed, and HR teams are keying in data multiple times in multiple systems, this would be categorized as 'doables without efficiency'.

This is not a great place to be. It means the organization as a whole is working hard to execute important work that is crucial to the running of the organization, but it doesn't necessarily add huge value to the bottom line. The goal for any organization is to be functioning as efficiently as possible, leveraging all digital capability possible to reduce the manual and heavy burden and to be classified as 'transactional excellence'.

When the classification is the bottom right, it means that the more strategic processes on the right of the model don't receive the focus, attention and rigour they require. We will then hear that people are executing the experience because they must, so this execution is then classified as 'HR initiatives for HR's sake' and engenders compliance.

Therefore, we can now see the challenge in front of us and why the engagement of the workforce in the process is so crucial. It cannot just be rolling out a process or telling people to complete this new system – the change needs to be explained, managed, trained, reinforced, coached so you get to that point where people want to be engaged in the process, and see the immediate value to them. This is the classification in the top right-hand box 'deliverables with a business and customer return' – the ultimate win-win for organization and employee where commitment is engendered.

If we overlay typical business benefit areas that can be improved by my proposed change, depending on where we are on the operational vs strategic scale, we can move from doing things well, to doing the right things well. Our change has both a high business impact but is also focused on a strategic area for our business. Ideally this could have a direct correlation to customer improvement and/or profitability.

But engagement isn't limited to just processes and/or new systems. It's reflective of many other factors, including but not limited to:

- Do I get on well with my manager?
- Do I understand and embrace the organization's vision and philosophy (see our Chapter 4 on the importance of philosophy)?
- Is the culture right for me (we have had a number of discussions so far on the importance and fluidity of culture)?
- Do I have clarity on my role and objectives within the organization?
- What is my relationship like with my peers and colleagues? What about my relationships outside the organization – like suppliers and customers? Is that also a series of healthy relationships?
- Do I have satisfaction in what my role provides to the organization?
- Can I grow in my role and in myself, or am I trapped under a limiting ceiling?
- Do I feel that my contribution is both welcomed and valued?
- How am I treated when I succeed and when I fail? Am I treated fairly, with respect and encouragement, or am I punished?

All these factors will contribute to my engagement with the company I work for. All are driven by experiences I have (or don't have). Some will be weighted differently in terms of importance – this is what makes us individuals (and so fascinating to observe).

So now we understand the positive and negative impacts on experience and engagement. What does this then lead to? Advocacy.

Why do we seek advocacy?

Advocacy is powerful. If I can engage my employees to such a point where they become advocates for the company, I now have a very strong value proposition. The same can be said for making our customers advocates. This makes them not only loyal, but typically they are also vocal in that loyalty.

Recalling another of our colleagues' anecdotes (and I love telling anecdotes to reinforce the point being made), he loves doughnuts. In particular, he loves doughnuts made by Crwst. Crwst is a café in Cardigan in West Wales. They started in 2018, and have since expanded to additional premises, and supply 20 local shops and restaurants. Most notably, they now have their products on the shelves at Harrods and Selfridges.

But our colleague doesn't just like their doughnuts; he is an advocate for them, telling others about how great they are. His voice, and many others, have helped Crwst establish a reputation for excellence, which is built on customer loyalty (for example, they were named in the World Pastry Awards 2024, compiled by La Liste).[5]

But our colleague's journey to that excellent doughnut is a result of many factors. Clearly the doughnuts themselves have to be pretty good (and they so are). But they also need to be consistent every time. Our experience of them has to be both positive and sustainable. We then, to stretch the analogy a little, become engaged with the doughnut and subsequently an advocate of it.

We talked with Osian and Catrin Jones from Crwst in an episode of *The Human Factor*, and discussed how the experience their customers have is paramount in how they operate.[6] They create brand advocacy by ensuring consistently high standards that are repeatable. They have a workforce that is engaged and committed to that shared vision.

However, when they first started, it wasn't always this way. Osian talked with us about how inconstancies crept into recipe execution, resulting in variations of outcome and taste. They had to consciously commit to ensuring consistency, writing everything down in detail, measuring ingredients with precision, and making quality checks at the pass before the food was sent to the table. For their vision, consistency was key to ensure that the experience they delivered was maintained to a high, sustainable standard.

We also talked about their engaged employees that work in Crwst. That engagement manifests itself in staff that contribute to menu design, recipe changes and new business ideas for consideration. That shared passion then translates ultimately to customer satisfaction and advocacy.

In Chapter 7 we introduced Helen Willetts from British Telecom (BT). Helen is the Director for Internal Communications at BT and in Episode 39 of *The Human Factor* she talked with us on the topic of managing the message.[7] During the conversation, Helen shared with us that BT had transitioned from measuring engagement to measuring advocacy, as they believed this was a stronger barometer of success for their workforce.

In her eyes, 'Are you proud to work for BT?' was a passive measure of engagement and they wanted to go further in their analysis. Helen and the team at BT set out to create a community of advocates for BT Group. They introduced three measures for advocacy:

1 Would you recommend BT as a place to work?
2 Would you recommend BT's products and services?
3 Would you recommend BT for its role in society?

Helen believed that these metrics were more effective as a measure of advocacy as they lead to action – recommending, rather than just being proud. When the metrics were introduced, they noticed initially that while the pride measure was very high (and that is easy to accept given the heritage and stature of a company like BT), there was a 20 per cent shortfall of advocacy compared to pride.

What this meant was that the feeling of engagement was very good within the organization, but wasn't leading to the desired level of action of promoting the company to others outside the organization, and thus this became a key improvement area for them when building and managing their communication strategy. As a result of the hard work delivered by the team, there has been an impressive 6 percentage point increase in all three advocacy measures across their 100,000-strong workforce.

In conclusion

Our journey in this chapter has taken us from positive experiences to engaged consumers, and ultimately to advocates. People are increasingly vocal about their experiences. We are encouraged to provide our feedback in all walks of life, whether that is our view on being able to complete a micro transaction with our bank to whether we enjoyed our summer holiday. Social media has seen an explosion in people providing feedback on their experiences, and people generally are not shy in speaking their minds.

At work, though, it still seems to be the exception for employees to be asked for feedback about processes, systems, company direction and other topics more frequently than in an annual engagement survey. While an annual process is an opportunity to check how engaged our workforce really is, it often doesn't capture sufficient detail and feedback about those significant moments that matter. What did I think about the hiring process? Why not ask me just after I have been hired, when the process is fresh in my memory and giving the company the information in a timeframe where improvements and changes can be actioned more immediately?

But we strove in this chapter to connect experience to engagement and then to advocacy. What is the so-what of these connections? If our experience is poor, we are likely to disengage and we will never become advocates. If our experience is positive, we will engage with it, and, as seen, likely be more productive. We already discussed the impacts on productivity, but we should extend that to improvements to employee wellbeing, levels of absenteeism and retention rates. It's not just that we might be productive if engaged; it's that we will impact on many other key areas of a healthy organization.

Gallup, a global analytics and advisory organization, runs an annual survey to investigate country rates of employee engagement, and the results are not encouraging.[8] If we look at the results for the UK in 2023, the survey shows that approximately 18 per cent of the employee workforce are actively disengaged, approximately 79 per cent of the workforce are not engaged, and a miserly 9.9 per cent are actively engaged.

These numbers are not just low, they are catastrophic, and represent a ticking time bomb for UK organizations looking to build sustainable, prosperous growth. And this does seem to be even more of a local problem. When we look at the global average, at least 23 per cent of the workforce is engaged (still a very low number of course, but 2.5 times higher than the UK).

If we turn that engagement into advocacy, we add the power of our voices to improve our company brand. As we said within the chapter – happy employees are productive employees. Productive and engaged employees will help drive sustainable business. They will also spread the word and advocate our company to our customers.

Why would we not want that?

Tips and tricks

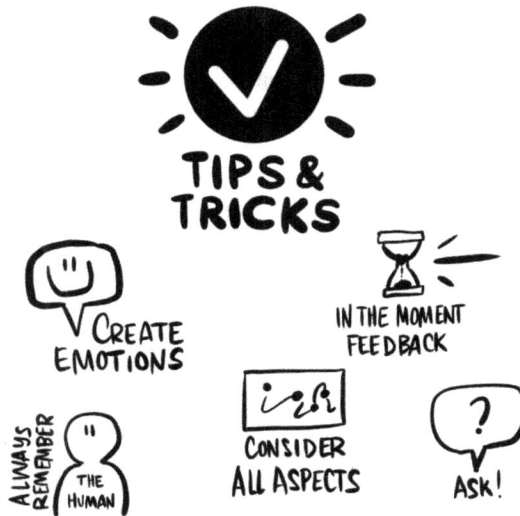

1 Experiences create emotions. What emotion are you aiming for when you introduce a new change into your organization?

2 Ask for more regular in-the-moment feedback to gain real insight into how the experience is being perceived.

3 Consider all aspects of engagement, rather than just focusing on individual processes or systems.

4 Experiences, engagement and advocacy are driven by human factors. Always remember the human when improvements are sought.

5 Don't assume your employees are engaged if they are quiet. Ask, listen and act before poor engagement turns toxic.

Notes

1 O Edwards (2024) How will Chinese automotive expansion affect UK market? Grant Thornton UK LLP, www.grantthornton.co.uk/insights/how-will-chinese-automotive-expansion-affect-uk-market (archived at https://perma.cc/YQP7-FY3R)

2 *The Human Factor* podcast Ep 16: Designing a User Experience That Has an Impact | *The Human Factor Podcast* by SAP, https://podcast.opensap.info/the-human-factor/2022/05/18/the-human-factor-episode-16-designing-a-user-experience-that-has-an-impactguest-speaker-caitlynn-sendra/ (archived at https://perma.cc/7S45-L6AR)

3 AP News (2024) Software giant SAP agrees to buy WalkMe for $1.5 billion cash, https://apnews.com/article/sap-acquires-walkme-digital-adoption-platform-aeca9d28c2498efecaf62960b90c9947 (archived at https://perma.cc/VNZ3-PU8A)

4 C Bellet, J-E de Neve and G Ward (2019) Does Employee Happiness have an Impact on Productivity? *SSRN Electronic Journal*, http://dx.doi.org/10.2139/ssrn.3470734 (archived at https://perma.cc/P836-WDMH)

5 A Houghton (2024) World Pastry Awards 2024: Full list of UK winning bakeries and pastry shops, Time Out, www.timeout.com/uk/news/world-pastry-awards-2024-full-list-of-uk-winning-bakeries-and-pastry-shops-061824 (archived at https://perma.cc/5VRE-WAQ5)

6 *The Human Factor* podcast Ep 46: The Power of Brand Advocacy with Catrin and Osian Jones | *The Human Factor Podcast* by SAP, https://podcast.opensap.info/the-human-factor/2024/07/18/the-human-factor-podcast-ep-46-the-power-of-brand-advocacy-with-catrin-and-osian-jones/ (archived at https://perma.cc/Q5PA-U8FX)

7 *The Human Factor* podcast Ep 39: The Art of Communication | *The Human Factor Podcast* by SAP, https://podcast.opensap.info/the-human-factor/2024/01/18/the-human-factor-podcast-ep-39-the-art-of-communication/ (archived at https://perma.cc/X8U6-YZED)

8 Gallup (n.d.) Indicator: Employee Engagement, www.gallup.com/394373/indicator-employee-engagement.aspx#:~:text=In%202023%2C%20the%20percentage%20of (archived at https://perma.cc/2TKF-D4UB)

LEADERSHIP

CARRIES a GREAT

Responsibility

BUT IS ALSO A

PRIVILEGE

The role of the   10
leader

Introduction

As we mentioned in Chapter 5, *The predisposition of a human being*, if you do a search on the internet for human motivation you will find many different theories and opinions. When you consider the discipline of leadership, I think it's safe to say the list will be even longer. It is a discipline that has been debated, discussed, pulled apart and put back together so many times. We have no desire to compare the merits of the many theories, but we will pose some questions which we believe are influencing the philosophy of leadership today.

As we have done with all the other chapters and very much in line with the podcast, our goal is to ground our subjects and not leave them too open ended, and we will do the same with leadership. As a discipline, it is very much an 'art and a science' but at its roots we believe are some foundational aspects which when done correctly can lead to the attainment of desired outcomes. The question as always, however, is: what are those outcomes, and do they constitute success? We will explore this.

Therefore, we will again be leveraging McClelland's work at Harvard University, but also referencing the work of Litwin and Stringer and Daniel Goleman. McClelland's study on human motivation plays a huge role in helping someone to better understand 'self'.[1] When you then start to apply different motivational profiles to different scenarios, it's possible to observe the different behaviours exhibited, and this very much was the focus of Daniel Goleman's research on emotional intelligence and managerial styles.[2, 3, 4]

Litwin and Stringer's research then centred on the manifestation of those behaviours in terms of outcomes both for the individual and the organization. We will be leveraging their research as the basis of this chapter and helping us to convey and communicate what we believe is a fabulous depiction of the foundational elements on which a leader role is built.

To avoid any confusion or doubt throughout this chapter (and indeed the rest of the book) for us a leader is a person who manages people, irrespective of level in the organization. It could be a first line manager or a senior director. We appreciate naming conventions vary organization by organization, some using 'manager' and some using 'leader'.

The purpose of leadership

Before we dive into the actual role of a leader, we think it's important to reflect on the purpose of leadership. For us in simple terms, it's often a couple of things: the design and creation of a strategy or plan, and then the execution of that strategy. We accept there are many scenarios where teams can exist without a manager or leader present, and this is the case with self-directed teams.

We also accept if we take the world of sport, that a team may have several 'leaders' within the team who push others and drive standards, and this was a big takeaway from our conversation on the *Human Factor* podcast with Maggie Alphonsi, who we discussed in Chapter 8 on the relativity of success. She talked about the World Cup winning team she was a member of having many leaders, instead of just one. It meant more responsibility was taken on the pitch, more accountability for decision-making. It wasn't just sitting with the coach in the stand and perhaps the team captain.

When we think of a team, we often think of a RACI model: who is **R**esponsible, who is **A**ccountable, who is **C**onsulted and who is **I**nformed? At the end of the day, there should only be one person who has the A. There can be multiple people who are responsible; again, when we think about the context of team sport, the players are responsible for their performance and achieving the desired outcome. However, when it comes to results it is the manager, leader or coach who is accountable.

Therefore, in our view the purpose of leadership is having an individual who is leading a team of people and truly leveraging their skills, capabilities, ambitions and experiences to achieve a desired outcome. They are creating the climate and conditions for people to be their best every day, where ideas and innovation can be cultivated and explored.

It is crucial to remember, and it will become evident throughout the chapter, that team members have high expectations of leaders, and of course leaders don't only exist in the workplace. We have leaders in society, sports teams and even pub quiz teams (those leaders who tell you off for shouting out the answers). Team members will want direction, challenge and to feel motivated to come to work every day. More on that a little later.

Sounds simple! Of course, it isn't, hence why leadership is often considered to be an art and a science. It requires wisdom, patience, curiosity, resilience, strength, character, inspiration, trust, honesty, collaboration, respect, and the list goes on. It requires you to know your 'self' and truly understand the people working in your team: their motivation, their aspirations, their interests, their backgrounds and of course that will be different for each person. Their needs as people will be different and how they prefer to work will be different.

It is also contextual, and situations will sometimes dictate the leadership style and approach. For example, it is not uncommon to see leaders parachuted into a struggling business unit to initiate a recovery plan. In a sporting context a manager may take over a team struggling with results and facing relegation. In both of those cases a judgement must be taken on the most appropriate and effective style and approach to achieve the desired improvements.

A little later in the chapter we will touch on philosophy in the context of leadership, because there are many different approaches and styles when it comes to leadership. When I think about leadership styles and philosophies, I often go back to my school days and my teachers. In their own way, they were leaders of a class and they all had different ways of achieving what was ultimately the same goal. I knew which classes I liked more, I knew which ones I hated and others which were productive but not necessarily enjoyable.

First, let's get back to some foundations of leadership and how it shows up in behaviour and manifests in terms of outcomes.

The four-circle model

For this section of the chapter, we are going to build on Chapter 5 and the research of David McClelland, Litwin and Stringer, and Daniel Goleman.

Over the course of multiple decades, the names mentioned above and many others have devoted their lives to build a better and accurate understanding of who we are, how it influences our behaviour and also other outcomes in terms of performance, engagement, retention and so on. During their collective research at Harvard, carrying out hours upon hours of research, many conclusions and outcomes were surfaced. We will be utilizing the four-circle model in this chapter to show causation between motives and climate.

One simulation that was run proved to be inspired. It involved the establishment of three teams with three different leaders, all with different motivational profiles and philosophies. In each team were workers who were being paid to participate in the simulation, and this is a very important point. Each team was provided with the same brief. The simulation ran over several days to enable the individual leaders to work with their teams and attempt to accomplish the brief. It also allowed the researchers to video and observe the behaviour displayed by the leaders and the impact of those behaviours on the workers in their teams.

What was striking about that research was the observed impact after only a handful of days due to the behaviour of the leader. One of the teams thrived, achieved the task and prospered. One team just had fun and partied but with no real execution or output. Quite quickly, boredom kicked in which led to significant disengagement and demotivation. The last team quit, which was quite a development. Despite being paid and rewarded for their efforts, they walked out as they could no longer tolerate the behaviour of the leader.

This research formed the basis of a four-circle model which correlated the motivational profile of the individual to the 'organizational climate' experienced by the team. This is where the power really lies in the research – it is the causal impact of a person's motivation when it manifests in behaviour. Having worked with and applied this research for over 20 years, it has been the bedrock of much of my work. I found that it didn't matter if I was working with a leader in Europe, Asia or North America, the research was impactful, applicable, relatable, and actionable, which is the crucial element. Leaders were able to develop clear action plans, coping strategies and adjustments.

Note – the tables below contain definitions used by myself as part of our leadership development programme. They are entirely based on the work of the researchers mentioned, but it is acknowledged that these labels over time will be adapted and updated.

Let's look at the model and examine the components and how they all hang together.

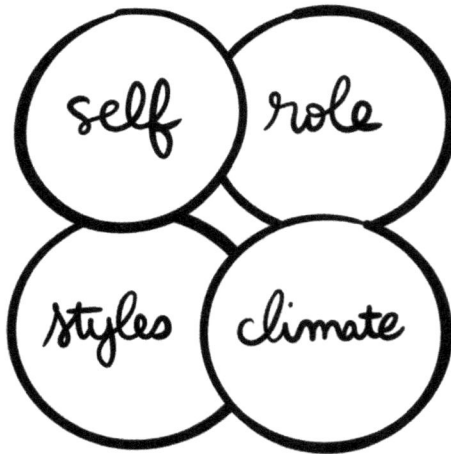

Self

In Chapter 5, *The predisposition of a human being*, we focused extensively on self, breaking down the composition into all the layers using the analogy of an iceberg. At the very bottom are the non-conscious motives. An individual will possess all three motivations to a lesser or larger degree. Often one motivation will be more dominant than others. Gaining an insight or taking the time to understand who we are provides us with the best opportunity to maximize our motivation, orient our behaviour and, in the words of McClelland, avoid the chasing of rainbows that are not for us.

Please refer back to Chapter 5 to read about the motives and their descriptions.

Role

This is where the work of McClelland and others broadened out. A reminder that the role of the leader is to maximize and influence the contribution of their team. A question that was asked on a regular basis was 'Is there an optimal profile for a leader?', and we found this to be a difficult and possibly dangerous question. Instead, we would encourage leaders to think about what the role of a leader entailed and the motives they believed were most appropriate.

It is also important to note the difference between motive and capability. We can all demonstrate what would be considered motive-related behaviours, even if they don't come naturally from a motive perspective. The motives denote where our energy is coming from and influence our thoughts and our behaviour. It means the behaviour comes more naturally.

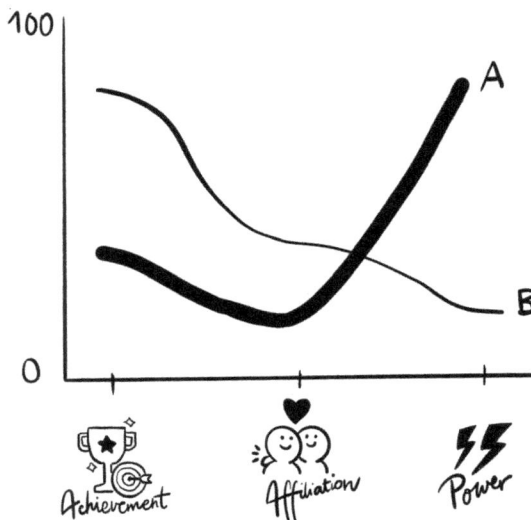

The graph is simply providing a visual of differing profiles. Profile A is showing someone who is high on power, low on affiliation and moderate on achievement. Profile B is almost the reverse, higher on achievement, moderate on affiliation and lower on power.

Before reading on, let's take a pause and pose a couple of questions. *If we think about the role of a leader for a moment, what do we believe the motive profile could look like, and what would be most appropriate for a leader role?*

Think about teams you have worked in. *What was the boss doing that made the job enjoyable/satisfying?*

Of the three motives how would you rank their importance in a leader's role?

In the tips and tricks at the end of Chapter 5 we asked you to discuss the motives with someone you trust. Have you had any further insights into what your own motive profile might look like?

Below is some further insight on the motives and some of the conclusions that were drawn from groups of leaders that we worked with:

- **Achievement**: A leader role is different to being an individual contributor. You are not 'doing the job' – you are leading the team, therefore someone who is high on achievement could be tempted to get their head down and 'do the job', neglecting their role as a team leader. It can also lead to behaviours that are more compliant than committed in nature, or you might see the leader taking over if they felt the task was not being completed to their liking or standard.

- **Affiliation**: In the context of the workplace, you don't want or need leaders focusing their motivation solely on building relationships and having a concern for being liked. We will cover this in more detail a little later in the chapter, but is leadership about being liked? Is being popular important? This isn't about being unkind or not treating people with respect, it is about recognizing the optimal profile for a leader role. Someone who is high on affiliation could struggle quite significantly to be effective in a leadership role because their focus is primarily on relationship building and not on achieving outcomes.

- **Power** – the role of the leader is to influence, coach, facilitate, challenge, support and develop their teams. The emphasis when tapping into this motivation should be on engendering commitment through coaching and positive influence, but this motivation arguably tests us more than the others as the absence of self-control can lead to behaviour being demonstrated that is not only inappropriate, but also destructive. This brings me back to the experience of school, and the teachers who used their power motive more effectively than others. I recall one teacher who just barked instructions, controlling behaviour by raising his voice and often shouting. You did as you were told, and you spoke when you were spoken to. Some people could operate in or tolerate that situation. I then recall a teacher who was full of encouragement, engaging, always offering an insight or piece of advice. They had very high standards and didn't stand for any messing about, but they also welcomed humour and a bit of spirit. A real focus to help you to achieve your results and to give you confidence.

When we then apply self to the motive profile of a leader, we can start to identify possible gaps or adjustments in areas where we might not be as strong or naturally energized towards. For example, a leader who is not high on power and does not enjoy influencing people. They will potentially face scenarios where difficult decisions need to be communicated, organizational changes that need to be implemented and where they are likely to face some resistance. How can a leader in this scenario build a plan to ensure that doesn't happen and they are able to deliver those tasks?

Another example, if the leader is higher on achievement, they may gain pleasure by doing some of the day job. In that scenario, they become a pseudo individual contributor. This can result in them potentially taking over tasks or inserting themselves into the flow of work, and it can diminish the confidence and contribution of the individual.

Irrespective of profile, understanding and managing our motivation enables us to better orient and direct our behaviour, particularly in situations which perhaps are not as energizing or enjoyable. It can identify where support or coaching is required.

It's important to be honest with ourselves. To assess and identify the behaviours which are working well and those which are perhaps not achieving a desired outcome. The reality is this: we are behaving every second of every day (verbally and non-verbally) and it is impacting our people and our direct reports either in a way that we wish or perhaps not.

Let's look at some of the prominent managerial styles (behaviours) that were deduced through the research.

Styles

The manifestation of behaviour. This is how a leader will show up in front of their team. The research concluded that there were six dominant styles, three of which were considered more long-term and three that were short-term.[5, 6] Let's look at the six styles in Table 10.1.

The skill of a leader is to demonstrate balance, adjusting and selecting the appropriate style for the situation you are in. That is the root of how we select behaviour, apply judgement and of course self-control.

Table 10.1

Style	Primary objective	
Coercive (short-term)	Immediate compliance	• Gives lots of directives. • Expects immediate compliance. • Controls tightly. • Relies on negative, corrective feedback. • Motivates by stating the negative consequences of non-compliance.
Democratic (short-term)	Building commitment and generating new ideas	• Trusts that employees can develop the appropriate direction for themselves and the organization. • Invites employees to participate in the development of decisions. • Holds many meetings and listens to employee concerns. • Rewards adequate performance and rarely gives negative feedback.
Pacesetting (short-term)	Accomplishing tasks to high standards of excellence	• Leads by example. • Has high standards and expects others to know the rationale behind what is being modelled. • Is apprehensive about delegating. • Takes responsibility away if high performance is not forthcoming. • Has little sympathy for poor performance. • Rescues the situation or gives detailed task instruction when employees experience difficulties. • Sees coordination with others only as it impacts immediate task.
Authoritative (long-term)	Providing long term vision an direction	• Develops and articulates a clear vision. • Solicits employee perspective on the vision. • Sees selling the vision as key. • Persuades employees by explaining the 'whys' in terms of employees or the organization's long term interests. • Sets standards and monitors performance in relation to the larger vision. • Uses a balance of positive 'did well' and negative 'do differently' feedback to motivate.

(*continued*)

Table 10.1   (Continued)

Style	Primary objective	
Affiliative (long-term)	Creating harmony	• Is most concerned with promoting friendly interactions.
		• Places more emphasis on addressing employees' personal needs than on goals or standards.
		• Pays attention to and cares for 'the whole person'; stresses things that keep people happy.
		• Avoids performance-related confrontations.
		• Rewards personal characteristics more than job performance.
Coaching (long-term)	Long-term professional development of others	• Helps employees identify their unique strengths and weaknesses.
		• Encourages employees to establish long-range development goals.
		• Reaches agreement with employees on the manager's and employee's roles in the development process
		• Provides ongoing instructions as well as feedback.
		• May trade off immediate standards of performance for long-term development.

Behaviour = Function (Person × Situation)

Behaviour is a function of the person and the situation you are in. Behaviour is not automatic, it is selected.

As an example, in a highly pressurized top-class kitchen you would expect to see a lot of the coercive style being displayed as orders come into the kitchen and need to be delivered on time to the pass and out to the customer. Highly appropriate. However, out of service when new dishes are being created, or new chefs are being brought into the team, you would hope to see some of the other styles being displayed.

This is where the art and science of leadership really comes into play. It's about deploying and using the right style/behaviour at the right time, and highly effective leaders are dipping in and out of those styles fluidly at many junctures in a day. It's important to note there is no right or wrong with any of the styles, but it's about considering the impact if they become overused or not appropriate to the situation you are in. It's about judgement and balance to achieve optimal outcomes.

So, let's look at outcomes and the fourth circle in the model. The ultimate acid test and the measurement of the manifestation of those behaviours.

Climate

This is what Litwin and Stringer called 'organizational climate'. The definition of climate is 'What does it feel like to work here?' so the emphasis is very much on feeling; whereas culture is 'How are things done here?'

Climate very much aligns to the quote sometimes attributed to Maya Angelou: 'People will forget what you said, people will forget what you did, but people will never forget how you made them feel.' During the simulations they were able to identify the dimensions that made up this thing called climate. There are six dimensions, as shown in Table 10.2.

Whenever we reflect on the climate dimensions, it's like staring at a jigsaw puzzle and seeing so many parts come together. We know as an individual that we bring with us to work a predisposition. We know that we have motivations that we need to satisfy to go home and say that we had a good day. The behaviour of a leader can have a significant impact as we have now seen through the styles being used and then how that impacts on climate. Reflecting on Chapter 5, it is important to note that team members are not alike, everyone is different and motivated by different things.

Therefore, we know for some that being autonomous, feeling empowered and trusted to get on with a job is important. However, what does it feel like if you have a leader who only displays short-term styles with a mixture of coercive and pacesetting behaviours being displayed every day, and essentially micro-managing all aspects of your performance? How would that feel?

Imagine you are an individual who is very achievement-orientated but your leader only demonstrates long-term styles. You spend a lot of time visioning, which is great as we know that clarity is crucial, and a fair amount of time on the affiliative style building relationships, team building, blue sky sessions; however you don't ever really get to execution. You talk a lot about what you are going to do, but you don't get it done. How do you think that scenario would feel?

Table 10.2

Climate dimension	Definition
Flexibility	• The feeling that employees have about constraints in the workplace • The degree to which they feel there are no unnecessary rules, procedures, policies and practices that interfere with task accomplishment • The feeling that new ideas are easy to get accepted
Responsibility	• The feeling that employees have a lot of authority delegated to them • The degree to which they can run their jobs without having to check everything with their manager/leader • The degree to which they feel fully accountable for the outcome
Standards	• The emphasis that employees feel management puts on improving performance and doing one's best • The degree to which people feel that challenging but attainable goals are set for both the organization and its employees • The extent to which mediocrity is not tolerated
Rewards	• The degree to which employees feel that they are being recognized and rewarded for good work • The degree to which recognition is directly and differentially related to levels of performance • The degree to which people know where they stand in terms of performance
Clarity	• The feeling that everyone knows what is expected of them • The feeling that everyone understands how those expectations relate to the larger goals and objectives of the organization
Team commitment	• The feeling that people are proud to belong to the organization • The feeling that people will provide extra effort when needed • The feeling that people trust that everyone is working toward a common objective

Leadership is very much about intent and impact. It requires an individual to apply judgement and skill to every situation to ensure the desired outcome is being achieved. We know from the research that the achievement of high climate scores can lead to higher levels of performance, discretional effort and engagement.

Through our careers we will have worked in many teams and under many managers, and I will often ask people what was the most successful team or where they felt the most engaged. Often they will have one or two examples, and when I ask 'What made that difference?', it was the skill of the leader to bring people along and all of the climate dimensions being met.

Let's go back to my example of being in school and reflect on the styles and dimensions for a moment. When I think of the classes I loved and thrived in, the teacher demonstrated a range of the styles. You were encouraged to speak, to think and to participate. The teacher would brilliantly work from some of the more long-term styles into some of the more short-term styles without you noticing. You would get the bigger picture, but then translate into something you could action and execute. As a result, the climate was great. It was a classroom I wanted to be in. I knew what I was doing, I had feedback, I was coached, I was trusted to get on with my work, I could ask a silly question without fear, and I felt that my peers felt the same as me. There was no one heckling or messing about at the back!

The research that we have referenced in this chapter is as applicable today as it was 70 years ago. It perfectly demonstrates how our human motivation influences our behaviour and ultimately from a leadership perspective influences what it feels like for people working in your team.

Let's now add some further colour by exploring some of the other decisions and considerations that a leader is faced with.

Leadership and philosophy

We dedicated a whole chapter to philosophy. We consider it to be that important. As mentioned earlier in this chapter, there are different ways of achieving the same outcome. A philosophy is a 'belief' in doing something in a certain way. Using my analogy of my schoolteachers, they all had a different philosophy on how to teach their classes. That was quite clear. At the end of the day, they wanted as many of their pupils as possible to succeed and achieve great results. How they went about achieving that every single day was different. That was their decision, but did they ensure that pupils wanted to be in the class and, when they were there, wanted to learn?

Ultimately, it is about judgement. There are no leaders without followers. As we have discussed in this chapter it is all about balance, so let's consider some scenarios and philosophical debates:

- *Does a leader need to be liked to be successful?*
  The short answer is no. Would it be preferable? Without doubt, but being liked does not guarantee success and as we have mentioned already, being overly concerned with being liked can get in the way of leading the team.

- *Does leadership need compassion? Does compassion make you a better leader?*
  For us, absolutely. It is an essential element of being a leader. Compassion is about creating an environment where people feel psychologically safe, supported and challenged. Making decisions that have the best interest of your team at heart.

- *Is leadership all about the result and nothing else?*
  Not in our opinion. It would be an unsustainable approach to win at any cost. Leadership requires followers and a focus on results, and nothing else is unlikely to be tolerated or accepted today.

- *Does a leader need to engender belief and hope in their teams?*
  Without a doubt. As organizations strive to create a feeling of belonging and seek to build advocacy, leaders have a fundamental role in the execution of the business strategy and the employee lifecycle/experience. Through consistent actions, leaders can help to build a feeling of 'hope and belief' through the consistency of their behaviours and the quality of their communication and ability to connect, collaborate and inspire.

- *Does a leader need to have close, friendly relationships to be successful?*
  Being respected is super important as a leader. Being able to nurture and develop relationships can only help create that followership, trust, and support from within the team and wider organization.

- *Is a leader accountable for the development of the individuals in their team?* This question often surfaces much debate, and we believe it to be a classic example of philosophy. I was once told: 'Your career is far too important to trust it to someone else', and I agree. Every individual should take accountability and ownership for their development, but of course the leader can play a pivotal role in supporting, challenging, and providing timely and actionable feedback.

These kinds of questions are extremely common when discussing the role of a leader and very much lie at the heart of philosophy. Do you believe in leading in a certain way because you believe it to be the right way for you? We often reflect on the conversation that we had on the *Human Factor* podcast with John Amaechi.[7] John is an organizational psychologist and founder of APS Intelligence. John was awarded an OBE for services to sport and the voluntary sector, a chartered scientist, elected Fellow of the Royal Society for Public Health, bestselling *New York Times* author and Research Fellow at the University of East London.

John had some wonderful insights and views, and I took away two points that resonated with me. Firstly, a leader needs to take care of themselves. As we have covered in this chapter, the expectations and demands can be high. They need to 'fill their cup', and I took this to mean energy, space, knowledge, experience, wisdom. Look after your health but also invest in your future, keep learning, be curious, develop your leadership approach and philosophy. Standing still as a leader isn't an option.

Secondly, and it aligns to the point about compassion: a leader can be challenging and compassionate. Compassion doesn't mean being soft. John shared that feedback is enshrined in his organization, and he believes that it is possible to provide some tough feedback in a compassionate way. The focus is on helping the individual to be better, and not on setting out to 'wound' them.

Every leader has their own style, whether that is conscious or sub-conscious. We have had the privilege to work with many leaders and have also coached and mentored many leaders. We don't believe there to be a right or wrong approach, but we would always advise leaders about 'intent and impact'. Think always about what you are looking to achieve and then use the best approach to achieve the outcome.

I was very fortunate early in my career to spend time working with my dad, Robert Esau. He was a leader in the retail industry managing large groups of people. We would often talk about his philosophical approach to leadership and managing people, and he was very clear on his philosophy. When I sit back and reflect, it was all about balance and delivering on the climate dimensions.

He would tell me often the following piece of advice which has never been forgotten:

> Popularity does not win prizes. If your only concern is being liked, you will likely fail. You need people to respect the decisions you make and the direction you are taking them.

He was very fair. He knew his team. If someone needed help, he would always be available to help. Clarity and standards were everything. Upon going into one of the stores, he would always look at the cleanliness of the floor. It was his barometer of standards. If the floor was dirty, it told him that standards were not being maintained in other areas, and he was often right. He believed greatly in personal accountability. His team were accountable for their performance and their development. He was a great coach, would give great advice but you were accountable.

Even though I was his son, I felt his strictness, but it taught me the importance of setting and maintaining standards. For me he was the epitome of balance and taught me lessons that I still apply to this day.

In conclusion

As we mentioned in the introduction, we wanted to ground this important topic. The danger sometimes when discussing leadership is it becomes a little too abstract and perhaps overly theoretical. We have used multiple pieces of research to create the baseline and provide a link between human motivation and the impact that it has on the climate that is created for our teams. However, as I mentioned earlier in the chapter, leadership is also contextual, and therefore the skill of any leader is to adopt the appropriate style and philosophy for that situation or team.

We recognize it is absolutely an art and a science. Being able to apply judgement and make effective decisions very much lie at the heart. Being able to marry your intent with your desired outcome. It is about under-standing self to be able to better orient behaviour and manage thoughts. Being able to adapt to different people, different situations, and using the styles most appropriate for the situation.

In our conclusion we would highlight three fundamental points:

1 Being able to deal with a changing world is going to be so important. The expectations of the workforce are changing, and how people will work will be different. It might be virtual, hybrid or something completely different. Know your people, what makes them tick. Be flexible, agile and adapt as necessary.

2 The basics matter greatly. A leader needs a strong foundation and base to build on. The team needs that solid foundation too. Clarity, standards, feedback, recognition and empowerment really matter to people and have a significant impact on the climate being created.

3 Belonging, belief and hope. There are no leaders without followers. Be clear on your philosophy and approach. Be consistent with your actions and behaviours. Inspire the people working in your team. Be kind, be compassionate but also challenge your team. Focus on the end goals, bring people with you, and help them to be successful.

Leadership carries a great responsibility but is also a privilege. We genuinely believe there is no greater gift than helping someone to grow, develop and progress. Helping a group of people to deliver on their goals and enjoy being part of that environment: nothing beats it.

Tips and tricks

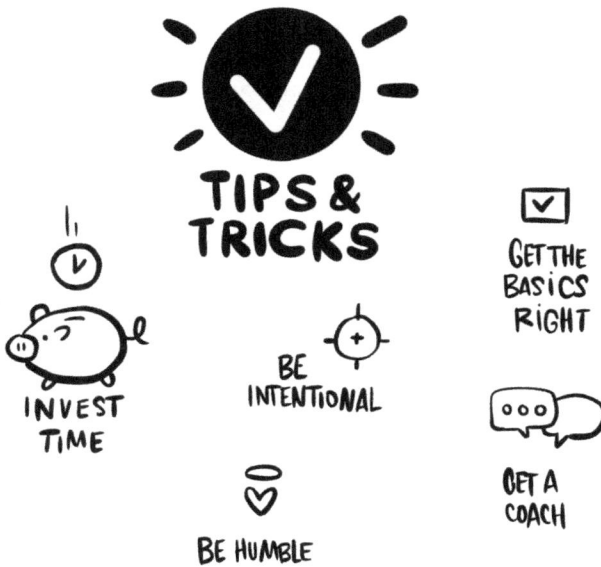

1 Invest the time in understanding yourself. There is no greater investment you can make than in yourself.

2 Be intentional. Develop your own philosophy and style that best suits who you are and your strengths.

3 Get a coach or mentor. It could be a peer or a friend, but have someone who you can share experiences or challenges with. It can be lonely as a leader and having someone to give advice can be super helpful.

4 Be humble. We are all learning. It's OK to make mistakes.

5 Clarity, standards and recognition are the foundation of effective leadership. These are the basic fundamentals that we need to get right every day.

Notes

1 Harvard University (2019) David McClelland, https://psychology.fas.harvard. edu/people/david-mcclelland (archived at https://perma.cc/8X4K-W3AR)

2 Mind Tools (2022) Six Emotional Leadership Styles, http://www.mindtools. com (archived at https://perma.cc/J43F-D4ZZ), www.mindtools.com/as8cal8/ six-emotional-leadership-styles (archived at https://perma.cc/KZ4X-GRXP)

3 M Shamian-Ellen and P Leatt (2002) Emotional Intelligence – How Well Do We Know Ourselves and How We Relate to Others? *Healthcare Quarterly*, **6** (1), pp. 36–41, https://doi.org/10.12927/hcq.2002.16653 (archived at https://perma. cc/E3VW-QB7N)

4 H Sims and W LaFollette (2006) An assessment of the Litwin and Stringer Organization Climate Questionnaire, *Personnel Psychology*, **28**, pp. 19–38, https://doi.org/10.1111/j.1744-6570.1975.tb00388.x (archived at https://perma.cc/9DU7-WUZH)

5 D Goleman (1998) Leadership that gets results, https://dta0yqvfnusiq. cloudfront.net/slsglobal/2015/11/Leadership-that-Gets-results.pdf (archived at https://perma.cc/4NN2-S53V)

6 R Knight (2024) 6 Common Leadership Styles and How to Decide Which to Use When, *Harvard Business Review*, https://hbr.org/2024/04/6-common-leadership-styles-and-how-to-decide-which-to-use-when (archived at https://perma.cc/3WPQ-AJ3C)

7 *The Human Factor* podcast Ep 11: The Relativity of Success – Finding Your Inner Giant | *The Human Factor Podcast* by SAP, https://podcast.opensap.info/ the-human-factor/2022/01/18/the-human-factor-ep-11-the-relativity-of-success-finding-your-inner-giant/ (archived at https://perma.cc/K38Z-AEX9)

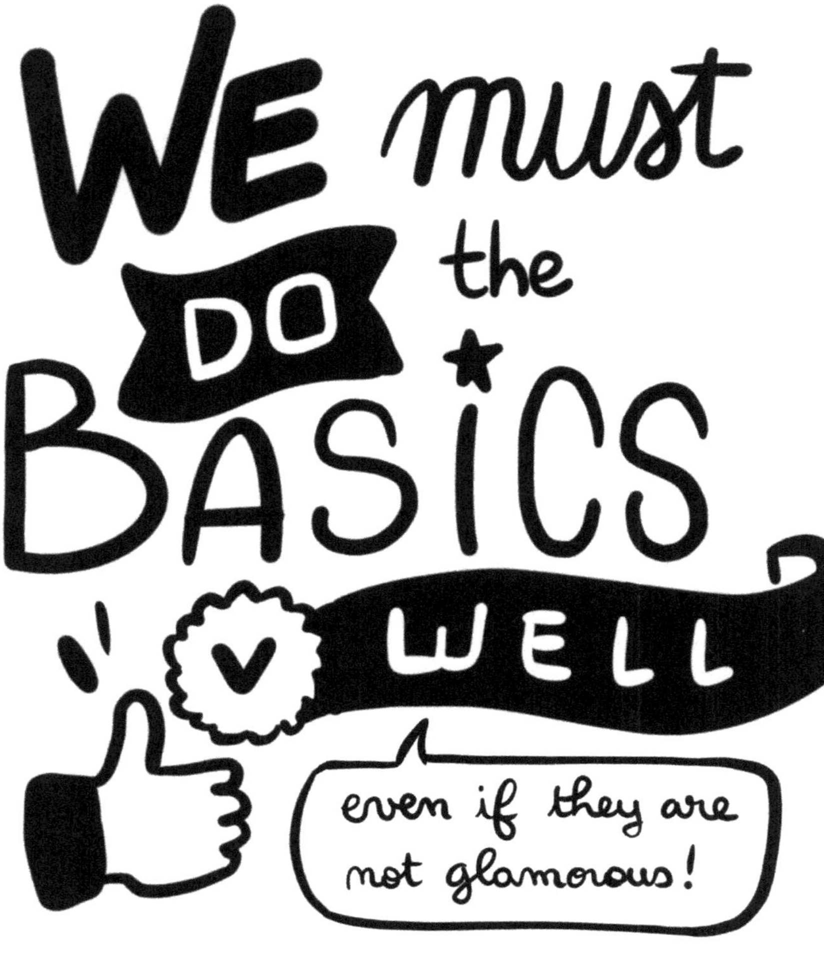
WE must
DO the
BASICS
WELL
even if they are
not glamorous!

Executing the basics brilliantly 11

Introduction

Throughout many of our conversations on the podcast, and in customer meetings we have had in our careers, there is one phrase that has consistently emerged – we must do the basics well. In this chapter, we will explore what the basics are, and why they matter so much. What happens when the basics are not in place? How can the organization thrive with well-established foundations?

We will explore the basics from three dimensions – the foundations of human motivation, making the basics a way of life at work and sustainability at a team level. We will draw upon many of the topics in other chapters in this book and look at the impact that basics can have on areas such as culture, change, technology and leadership.

The other observation we have is that conversations about getting the basics right can apply just as much to startups as to mature organizations. We have been privileged to meet with many companies and organizations that are household names, yet have had a flawed ability to execute. Fortunately, going back to basics is a fix that can be achieved and measurably established.

We will begin by establishing what we mean by 'the basics'.

What do we mean by 'the basics'?

We all know what the basics are. We don't need a dictionary definition of what the word means. So why would we be writing a whole chapter on this topic? The issue with the basics is that they are not glamorous. Who wants to read the manual when they buy a new toy or piece of equipment? We want to leap right in there and try it out, right? We might then miss things or have gaps in our understanding. When we learn to drive a car, we don't start in the outside lane of the motorway. We start gently by learning what all the controls do and ease ourselves into it. We must understand the basic principles of operating the car safely, or we will likely have a crash at some future point. Cutting corners is always likely to lead to future issues.

But 'the basics' can also mean different things depending on the context in which it is used:

- If I am going to learn a new skill, I need to learn the basics first to establish a good grounding of competence before going on to learn more advanced capability.
- When creating a budget, we need to ensure we have enough of the basics so that we can deliver what we need.
- 'We need to go back to basics and start delivering on our promises to customers.'

In the simplest terms, then, it's those elements that are central and fundamental principles of something.

Our easiest example is that of building a house. Our new build must have robust foundations, walls, a roof, and so on. These are the basics of any house and yet, if done badly, this can lead to serious issues. Issues with the foundations have far wider consequences than, say, issues with kitchen worktops.

If done well, it can be true that the basics are not as immediately visible as other areas. And herein lies some of the challenge when discussing the basics. They aren't exciting. The basics don't grab the emotions as much as the proverbial 'whistles and bells' that can distract us. When we see a sports person pull off some super-human skill, we don't see the hours and hours of drills and training that has been put in to establish the basic skills. This dedication to establishing those basic skills allows them to flourish and create those pieces of brilliance. When we eat a wonderful plate of smoked haddock soufflé, do we credit the roux that was needed to make it? So why do we wonder why organizational requests for funding to improve the basics sometimes struggle to secure approval?

We need to drill down into some examples so that we can explore the impact of getting the basics right (and wrong). We will start by looking at basics from an individual perspective.

The foundations of human motivation

When we look at ourselves as individuals, what do we mean by getting the basics right? Of course, that depends on context and is determined by what we are doing. In Chapter 2 we discussed changing a golf swing. If we look at the swing, it should be a simple operation, but in reality, it is complex. There are many parts to it – how we hold the club. How we stand. Where we stand in relation to the ball. How we swing the club. How the ball is lying and so on. As we then chart a route around the golf course, with the intention of making the least number of shots possible, it's clear there are many complexities to navigate. So, what do we mean in this example by the basics?

In this context, the basics include holding the club with the correct grip, getting the right stance, positioning the club and stance correctly in relation to the ball's position and lie. It's those fundamentals that give us the best chance of making a clean connection with the ball and hitting it in the right direction. It is stripping away some of the more complex aspects of the game (drawing and fading the ball, the amount of spin on the ball and so on). If we just play the round in this very basic way, we won't set course records, but we will hopefully eliminate basic errors that can destroy a good score.

We can apply this logic to most activities we undertake as individuals – can we strip back what we are doing to the most basic elements so that we can ensure those elements are done correctly? This is because they create the foundations for success or failure. Done well, they allow us to fulfil what we are trying to achieve and can lead to further improvements by building on these basics.

Done badly though, problems will occur and re-occur on a regular basis. If we are driving a manual car, and we don't have the basic skills needed to change gear correctly, our ability to drive the car is fundamentally compromised until we can correct this issue. One of our basic skills is preventing us from fulfilling our objective.

Identifying basic issues and opportunities for improvement is sometime difficult, and often it is others that will observe issues. Sometimes it is obvious – for example, many of us are not good golfers. Our basic skills are shaky and there are many things that could be fixed with time and some training. However, sometimes it might not be so obvious that something being done is incorrect due to a basic failing (for example, gripping the golf club incorrectly), and identifying a root cause can prove difficult unless external guidance is given.

What we do see though is when things are going wrong, there is value in 'going back to the basics' to try and correct the problems. Stripping away any complexities with the intention of simplifying what we do, and trying to ensure the foundations are performed correctly. Golfers around the world can be heard constantly muttering to themselves 'get the basics right' as they thrash around the golf course in the vain hope that they can put together a great round of golf – getting the basics right is easier said than done. But it is the right place to start.

When we go to work, getting the basics right is just as important. We need to therefore move on to what getting the basics right at an organizational level means.

Making the basics a way of life at work

Right back in Chapter 1, we looked at the business design model. We explored how our business strategy performance is driven by the operating model we have in place – how are our processes performing, what structures we have in place, do we have the right people, and is our technology fit for purpose.

We have been in many meetings with organizations that aspire to create world-class operations, underpinned by ambitious strategies, yet there have been fundamental gaps in processes, people, structures and/or technologies. The basics were not running well, yet the organizations were looking to develop capabilities without addressing these gaps.

When we look at the basics in an organization, it can mean many things, and again, context is everything. At a fundamental level, though, we need to have people with the right skills in the right place at the right time, we need to pay people correctly, our data needs to be accurate so that our reporting is reliable, and our processes should drive the right outcomes.

There are many more 'basics' that need to be in place for a sustainable business of course, and we won't have the time to cover them all. What we have seen though is that successful organizations are executing these basics brilliantly. We have spoken with many people and organizations in our podcast conversations that verify the importance of doing the basics well as a foundation for success. It has been one of those recurring themes in the conversations.

GIVE CLARITY

In Chapter 5 we introduced Will Lankston, the Managing Director of Timpson Direct. Will discussed how Timpson operated and the underlying principles that led to their success. He told us how they had stripped back the behaviours they expected from their workforce to two basic elements – look the part and put the money in the till. For him and for Timpson, if that was done right, then the business will grow. Clearly, their business is far more complex than that, but if those basic elements are correct, then every other aspect can operate with confidence. If one or both of those two elements are not working well, then it's hard to see how the business can thrive.

He also shared how they measure employee satisfaction, and again, it reflects that simple approach. Each week, every employee is asked if they are happy. This happiness index is the key metric for workforce reporting. Interventions are triggered if responses are below a certain point, but the importance of asking the question regularly and looking at the responses is part of their DNA. James Timpson discusses this further and many other aspects on how Timpson operates in the excellent book *The*

Happy Index: Lessons in upside-down management.[1] It's well worth a read to understand what practices Timpson has implemented.

When we combine the individual and the organizational views on getting the basics right, there can be misalignments and these misalignments can cause dissatisfaction. An individual is likely to want and need feedback on their job performance. The regularity of this feedback may change depending on the individual, but some feedback is typically desired by everyone. However, an organization may not have a structured approach to feedback and this could lead to situations where individuals have gone long periods without receiving any. Here the basic needs of the individual are not being met.

As an organization, we need to ensure that we have basic processes in place – to give clarity to our people about what is expected from them in terms of goals and objectives, and to give regular feedback on how our people were performing against those expectations. In this example, once these basics are established, they need then to become core to how the organization operates. Core to the way of life for the organization, rather than seen as a process that must be gone through because it's that time of the year and HR are telling us to do reviews.

We have advised and worked in organizations where giving feedback was not part of the way of life for the organization. It was a process to be done. Too many times, we've heard and seen colleagues disengage with the process because it is seen as a box-ticking exercise and not as a core part of how the organization operates. Yet we know that receiving feedback is a basic need for the individual. In that case, the organization may be operating a performance review process, but it is not executing it brilliantly. It also could be that the organization does not have the philosophy or culture of feedback. Both of these elements are also needed to ensure sustainable processes are in place to provide this to its workforce. It is likely not giving it the importance that individuals attribute to it.

It also could be that the processes are correct, but that the people operating the processes (typically the managers/supervisors) are not implementing it correctly and that governance is not in place to identify that. Here, the process may be correct, but is not being operated as a core way of life for the organization. The consequence of not operating this basic process brilliantly and as a core way of operating is that there will be a breakdown in employee engagement and potentially a breakdown in trust between the employee and the organization, which can lead ultimately to resignations and departures.

There are many other areas of working for organizations that can cause dissatisfaction when we discuss basics. Employees can get very frustrated with processes that are inefficient (or broken) and/or with technology that hinders rather than helps. These frustrations can be attributable therefore to not having the basics in place and operating brilliantly.

Many organizations embark on projects to 'go digital'. These projects are typically to address paper-based or manual processes and tools. By going digital, filing cabinets for employee records can be removed, paper-based processes can be moved online with self service capabilities, and manual workarounds can be remedied by integration and automation. These digital projects then are addressing the basics and leaning into technology usage to support the future way of working.

But these digital projects should not be seen as one-offs. When we discussed what being digital meant with Jason Averbook, we also clarified a very important point.[2] Jason, at the time, was CEO of Leapgen which was subsequently acquired by Mercer in 2023. In the conversation, we established with Jason that it was not enough to simply 'go digital'. Organizations then had to 'be digital'.

> Being digital means I'm constantly improving. I'm treating my digital
> capabilities like a pet, not like a rock. I have to walk it daily. Water it daily.
> Clean up after it daily. Pet it daily.

This is also true for the basics. It's not enough to establish the basics, but the basics need to be constantly measured and monitored to ensure they remain relevant, appropriate and being operated brilliantly. It's back to our sports example of doing drills each day in between matches. That reinforcement of execution, but also at the necessary high standard. The desire to avoid complacency setting in in our daily life. The execution of basics brilliantly therefore must become the new way of life for an organization, rather than seen as an activity done once that can then can be forgotten about.

Jason then went on to talk with us about the way forwards for HR in organizations, about how HR can be transformed and how it can innovate. He astutely observed:

> Let's shift from focusing on getting people connected to building
> connections with people.

However, this aspiration needs the basics to be operating brilliantly. People need to be connected. Without that basic principle, then, we can't shift our focus to building and/or maintaining connections.

We will discuss later in this book, in Chapter 14, about the role of technology in execution. We will examine the importance of how technology must provide a completeness of capability, but also a connected capability. We will also examine the importance of our data being correct and complete. These areas can also be considered as the basics. If our technology stack is not fit for purpose, then our organization and people can't operate efficiently.

A very typical issue that surfaces in meetings with organizations is that technology has evolved over time through functionality being amended or supplemented when requirements have changed. We have heard often that the system has progressively changed through its lifetime in operation. What is not so common is whether that technology is re-assessed as still the right tool for the job or set up and configured correctly. It is often difficult for organizations to go back and evaluate the technology against the basic requirements that it should be meeting.

Even when organizations seek a new solution, and go through the process of defining their requirements, too often these requirement lists are built based upon legacy ways of working and legacy processes. The opportunity to go back to basics and challenge ways of working and processes, and therefore requirements, is sometimes skipped, and then the technology project fails to deliver all the benefits needed.

We can see therefore how operating the basics brilliantly can liberate an organization and support delivery excellence. We have also seen how not operating those basics well can significantly hinder an organization.

We have explored the basics from an individual perspective and from an organizational perspective. What about the impact of the basics on and in a team?

Sustainability at a team level

We will explore many of the dynamics of team structures later in Chapter 15 of the book, with a whole chapter dedicated to that topic. However, as we have explored the basics from individual and organizational perspectives, it would be remiss not to cover the team perspective here.

Teams can be very successful. However, sustainable team success is built upon doing the basics brilliantly. It is highly unlikely that success can be repeated without robust foundations in place and being operated well. This is true whether it is a sports team, a team at work, a face-to-face team, a remote or dynamic team or a new or established team.

We see many examples of team success, and there are often discussions and explorations of why these teams have succeeded. Doing the basics brilliantly will probably not be the headline reason for the success. However, when we look at why teams fail, it is more often than not the case that the basics are not in place or are being done poorly.

Doing the basics is not glamorous. They aren't headline grabbers. We explored this earlier in the chapter. However, they are critical. We know the value of sports teams doing practice drills over and over again until they become second nature. The term muscle memory has evolved to articulate doing repetitive drills of the basics until they become that way of life. So, just like we observed in organizations doing the basics as a way of life, so too we need to see this in team structures.

But just as we observed in organizations, we need to ensure that the basics also undergo regular review to ensure relevancy. However, another basic when looking at teams is character.

We have met with several people from elite sport, such as Maggie Alphonsi, Russell Martin, Paul McVeigh and Paul Gustard. All spoke about the importance of the basics, but in our conversation with Paul Gustard we went into depth about what he looks for in new players.[3] His point of view was that character was more important than technical skill. Technical skills can be taught and developed, but character is more defining on impact on the team. Paul's view in recruitment was:

Person before the player.

If the person's character and personality are a good fit, then the recruiter has more confidence. For Paul, these were the basics that he was looking at and assessing, as well of course as an assessment of their technical skills. For him, if the person was a good person at a basic personal level, then they would be a good fit for the team. The characteristics that mattered included being supportive to others, a good communicator and respectful of team standards. If a player has good technical skills, but these basic characteristics are not in place, it can lead to poor habits at an individual level or, worse, a drop in team performance.

Team dynamics and culture can be very influenced by the basics. If we are in a team and observe other team members not doing the basics properly, it can cause toxicity in the group. 'Why do I have to do something if that other person doesn't?' We have seen public fallouts in sports teams when some of the basics are not being observed by all – being late for team meetings, being distracted by mobiles in meetings, not providing updates or input when needed, and many other examples. These basics matter because they define a standard for the team by which to operate.

What is interesting to observe in a team dynamic is who takes accountability for maintenance of standards in the team. In the world of sport, and one of the most successful football teams in England, Roy Keane was the team captain for Manchester United. His personality was such that 'good enough' was not good enough. He detested disorder and was a strong advocate for getting the basics executed well. He ensured that these basic standards in the team were respected and not allowed to degrade. If he observed someone not giving their best or exhibiting a behaviour that dipped below the expected standard, he would give feedback to the player and seek a commitment for improvement.

We spoke about Maggie Alphonsi in Chapter 8 on the relativity of success. When we talked with Maggie, she talked with us about her team becoming and being a team full of leaders, with everyone taking accountability for the team performance and maintenance of standards (i.e. the basics). If we apply that now back to a work environment, who in your team is accountable for ensuring standards are maintained and the basics are performed well? The team manager? The person with the loudest voice? The reality is that it should be everyone.

In 2024 we saw INEOS acquire a 27.7 per cent stake in Manchester United.[4] INEOS already have had great success in the world of professional cycling. In that sport, they made their reputation based on executing the basics brilliantly, and then making incremental gains in performance, no matter how small. It is believed that they intend to take a similar approach with the football operations at United.

In June 2024, they announced a £50m investment in upgrading the facilities in the Carrington Training Ground where the first team trains.[5] One of the teams' famous alumni players, Gary Neville, has been vocal for several years that it is difficult to achieve elite level performance on the pitch if the basics are not in place off the pitch, including the stadium and training ground facilities. It is becoming clear that INEOS agree, and are taking steps to remedy this. They will take this methodology into the way the team trains as well, and this is being led by Sir David Brailsford, who is widely credited with making British Cycling a superpower in the sport when he was performance director.

In conclusion

Whether we look at the basics from an individual, organizational or team perspective, there is a consensus that they must be done well to ensure sustainable success. It's clear to see that when the basics start to slip, then so does performance and outcome.

Tips and tricks

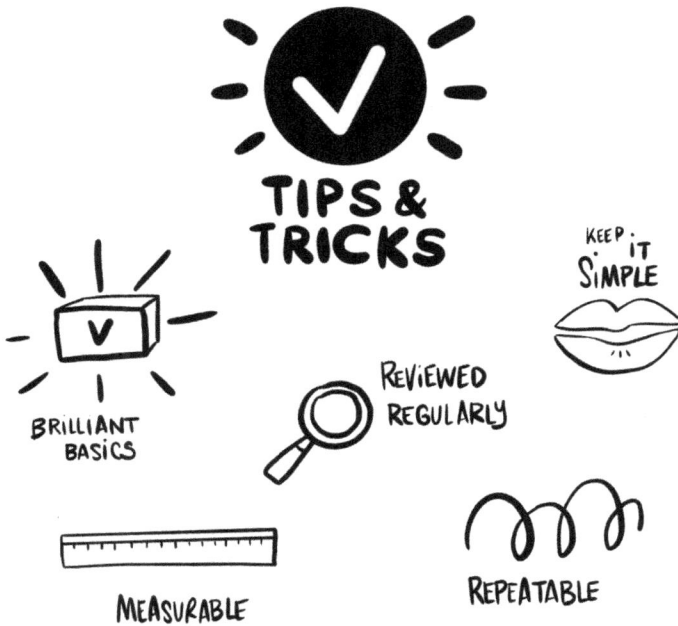

TIPS & TRICKS

KEEP IT SIMPLE

BRILLIANT BASICS

REVIEWED REGULARLY

MEASURABLE

REPEATABLE

1 Sustainable success requires doing the basics brilliantly.

2 The basics should be reviewed on a regular basis to ensure relevancy and execution continue to be at the expected standard.

3 Basics should be simple. Complexity can lead to confusion and/or the inability to execute.

4 Basics need to be repeatable.

5 Basics should be measurable to ensure they can be monitored regularly and consistently.

Notes

1   J Timpson (2024) *The Happy Index: Lessons in upside-down management*, HarperCollins UK

2   *The Human Factor* podcast Ep 13: The Future World of Work | *The Human Factor Podcast* by SAP, https://podcast.opensap.info/the-human-factor/2022/03/18/the-human-factor-ep-13-the-future-world-of-workguest-jason-averbook-ceo-of-leapgen/ (archived at https://perma.cc/V9XZ-EMVM)

3   *The Human Factor* podcast Ep 20: The Dynamics of Teams with Paul Gustard | *The Human Factor Podcast* by SAP, https://podcast.opensap.info/the-human-factor/2022/08/18/the-human-factor-ep-20-the-dynamics-of-teams-with-paul-gustard (archived at https://perma.cc/4DEN-5ASF)

4   Sky Sports (2024) Sir Jim Ratcliffe completes deal to buy Manchester United minority stake, www.skysports.com/football/news/11667/13071401/sir-jim-ratcliffe-completes-deal-to-buy-manchester-united-minority-stake (archived at https://perma.cc/RVP6-DND8)

5   T Marshall (2024) INEOS have made their first major transfer move with £50m Man United decision, *Manchester Evening News*, www.manchestereveningnews.co.uk/sport/football/ineos-made-first-major-transfer-29355177 (archived at https://perma.cc/8SW7-6AGC)

FEEDBACK

are the
BEDROCK
of
GROWTH

INSIGHTS

LISTENING

Listening, insights and feedback

Introduction

We debated whether to create individual chapters for each of these topics, but they are so inextricably linked, we decided to keep them together and consolidate into one chapter – this one. We hope we do them justice!

Listening, insights and feedback – on the surface we think they are labels that are well understood at an intellectual level, yet we have observed through *The Human Factor* podcast and our experiences of working within many organizations that they are often absent within the cultural fabric of organizations and not necessarily behaviours exhibited on a day-to-day basis. This often leads to the view that they are assumed and will just happen automatically. They are seen as events rather than a cultural way of life, and consequently just don't happen. Our aim is to bring some different perspectives and food for thought, and put some context around them.

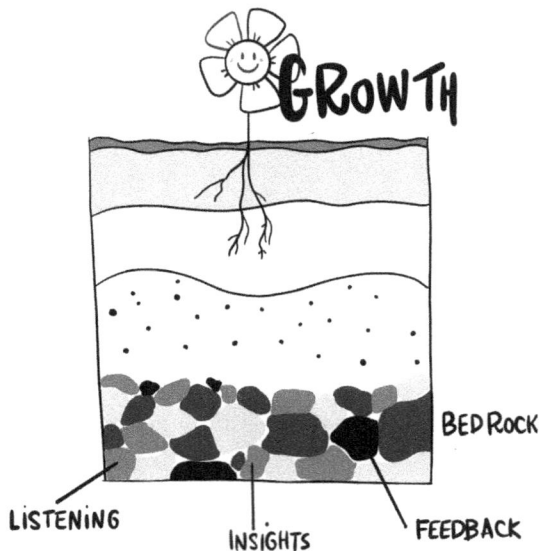

In this chapter, we are going to really dig into listening, insights and feedback individually, but also collectively. Together they are so important to an individual human being and to an organization but often they are taken too literally. Ultimately – the 'so what' of listening, insights and feedback – in our opinion they are the bedrock of growth and progression. Whether that progression is individual, or at scale across an organization, the principle is the same. Standing still isn't an option, so how do we improve, how do we adjust to feedback, performance gaps and much more?

In Chapter 5 we looked at 'The predisposition of a human being' which is very much directed at self, appreciating the many different aspects of us as human beings and what we bring with us every day in and out of work. We intertwined the importance of listening and feedback through many parts of that chapter also.

What is listening?

There are many different definitions of listening, so let's look at Wikipedia for their definition: 'Listening is giving attention to a sound. When listening, a person hears what others are saying and tries to understand what it means. Listening involves complex affective, cognitive, and behavioural processes.'

I am more than used to telling my daughters: 'You weren't listening', and they would say, 'But we heard you, Dad.' I would reply, 'But did you understand what I said?' and the answer was often 'No.' Only recently we had a conversation about the difference between listening and hearing, and the way I explained it to them was very simple – listening requires a commitment. It's not automatic and doesn't happen by accident. You must want to listen, and you need to be committed to wanting to understand. These are important principles, and this was evident in Chapter 5 looking at the predisposition of a human being.

LISTENING requires a COMMITMENT

When you scale this to the organization level, the principles are the same. Is there a commitment to listen and understand what is happening within the organization? The importance of listening has grown significantly in recent times, and it would be wise to question and query why.

The word 'experience' has become synonymous with listening. Now, that is nothing new. Businesses like hotels, for example, have been asking for feedback on your stay for years and wanting to understand how your 'experience' was, but now we are asked those questions all the time in different ways and via different channels.

In our opinion, it links back to the rise of consumerization and the impact on our behaviour, our expectations, and our decreasing amount of patience.

Firstly, what do we mean by consumerization, and what impact has this had? Over the last 20+ years, with the introduction of smart phones, we have seen a shift in how we behave as consumers. Everything is at our fingertips, and it has altered so many things – how we shop, communicate, transact, learn, socialize and connect with other people. We design and curate how we do things, how we execute tasks, and it is providing us with so much choice. We have significantly more autonomy, we can self-serve via the web or indeed in physical locations without having to engage in stores with a member of staff. It's something we have become accustomed to and now expect.

In terms of disruption and changing the fabric of our lives, the smartphone must stand out as one of the biggest disruptors in recent times.

So, what has been the impact? Well, when we think about businesses who are looking to attract and retain their customers, they have a different challenge now. As the majority of shopping has moved online, the relationship with the customer is different. The physical in-store experience for many consumers has disappeared, so how can the business connect with you and understand your thoughts, your preferences and opinions? By listening. It is common practice today to be asked to complete a survey at the end of a transaction or answer a short survey on our phones. Businesses are desperate to know how we are feeling and if we are happy or not. Did we have a good 'experience' – that word again, which we examined in more detail during Chapter 7 on the employee value proposition (EVP).

We spoke with Helen Willetts, Director of Internal Communications, British Telecom Group about the 'Art and science of internal communications'.[1] The conversation provided a fascinating insight into Helen's principles, philosophy and approach to communicating with people. BT Group has transformed significantly since the days of landline telephones, with a now 100,000+ strong workforce. They are committed to delivering a fabulous experience for all colleagues and listening is an integral part of that process.

As part of their listening strategy, Helen shared that BT Group are looking to understand and measure 'advocacy', and this makes a huge amount of sense. Advocacy we believe is what all businesses should be striving for – will your customers and employees proactively champion you? Do they believe in who you are, your proposition, your product, your service, the quality of the experience – is it something that they will advocate?

We believe this is why listening today has become super important. We have so much choice – do we have the same level of loyalty, and have we become more demanding as consumers and colleagues? As consumers and colleagues, have we become more fickle and less tolerant of a perceived bad experience? Arguably yes. When we think of the work context, we have so many experiences in any one given day. What happens when they don't meet an expectation, or they become too difficult? It is something to ponder.

There are many other reasons why listening is important, but we have always been guided by the context in which we live. Through the podcast we are seeking to understand at that moment what something means today, because it doesn't stand still. As we progress through this chapter, we will use this foundation setting on listening to shape the other elements – insights and feedback. At this point in the chapter the listening is one way – but what happens when it is bi-directional?

Listening and insights

It's all good and well doing a lot of listening, but what are you going to do with it? This is the 'so what', and we are going to look at this from within an organizational context and build upon the insights shared on the *Human Factor* podcast by Helen Willetts, but also our conversations with David Perring, Director of Research for Fosway Group.

Fosway Group is an HR industry analyst based in the UK, focused on next gen HR, talent and learning. Founded in 1996, businesses across Europe trust HR Insights from Fosway Group for their next level research and analysis of HR, Talent and Learning systems. David has been a HR professional for over 30 years. Over that time, he has always been at the forefront of innovation and has retained a strong sense of optimism, energy and passion for transforming organizational learning and performance. Similarly with Dr Sascha Härtel, who is the Head of Performance, Coordination Science at TSG 1899 Hoffenheim, a football club in Germany. He is also responsible for performance diagnostics at Adler Mannheim (a professional German ice hockey team) and Rhein-Neckar-Löwen (a professional German handball team).

So how do we convert our listening into insights? The starting point must be the questions that are being asked. It goes back to the initial point of understanding. What are you looking to understand, what are the real points of relevance that you are seeking an opinion on? Insights are more than data. An insight is telling us something. It's not just a raw piece of data, it has some meaning or consequence.

the questions you ask are important

This was extremely apparent in the conversation with Sascha.[2] Sascha started our conversation by providing the context of the competitive environment that Hoffenheim operates within, and the importance of having the capability to capture data that truly informs decision making. We will be covering more on this in Chapter 14 on the role of technology, but Sascha reinforced something that we had discussed previously on the podcast, that the questions you ask are important. It cannot be a case of listening for listening sake and doing nothing with it. Working backwards from your desired outcomes, constructing questions that your audience can respond to, will provide you with the raw data you are hoping to receive.

In the context of Hoffenheim, the audience is the players, and gaining their commitment to provide the data is so important. It enriches the picture that Hoffenheim have on each player and improves the 1-2-1 dialogue with each player on their performance, their recovery and their training schedule. The same principle applies in other industries.

Our conversation with David provided a similar sentiment.[3] He talked about 'experiential flow' and using insights to engage with the organization and individual through feedback loops. Engaging individuals with insights and feedback to enhance a process or performance. Ultimately there are different dynamics at play with this kind of 'loop' – you need a commitment or a willingness from people to share their voice as part of the listening. It then requires a commitment from all parties to the follow up – the 'so what' – and a commitment from managers and leaders to engage their teams in the experiential flow.

Frequency of listening + having a finger on the pulse

As we keep saying, the objective is to make something better. Really simple. Nobody has total mastery, we can always improve or be better at something. Standing still isn't an option, but unless there is a commitment to listen, to understand, to make sense and translate into meaningful insights, then nothing will change or improve. The finger really does need to be always on the pulse. There are differences in opinion on frequency, and it depends on the questions being asked but asking people a few times a year to answer some questions in a survey is unlikely to keep that organization ahead of the curve, and opportunities to improve things will be missed.

Therefore, making insights available throughout the organization should be common practice. Provide managers and leaders with access to key information at the right time to make important decisions in business operations. It can also be used at a senior level to inform and influence strategic and mission critical decisions. When this is done well, it becomes a positive virtuous circle. We listen, we improve. We listen again, we improve again. Without listening, how do we know if intended improvements are effective?

Insights and intelligence

So far, so good. We have established the context of why listening is so important both from a consumer and organization perspective. We have a solid foundation of a clear listening strategy, and in the example of TSG 1899 Hoffenheim we learnt about the importance of gaining commitment from the players in the process. We know the questions we want to ask people; we know the data that needs to be collected. We also have mechanisms to turn that data into meaningful insights that can be shared at first line manager level to support that 'experiential flow and loop'.

I would describe the above as the formal approach to listening and insights. You ask, you receive, you process and you act – a nice linear flow and process. The world in which we live, however, does not run on just linear and structured processes. What about the unstructured? Those pieces of information which have been gleaned in confidence or perhaps within a circle of trust conversation? I'm sure we have all watched enough crime or spy movies to know that information is often sourced from multiple sources and not always through official channels. We call this intelligence.

In the same way that insights are more than just data, intelligence is the same. This is where things really become an art and a science. We have made the point that frequency of listening and having a finger on the pulse is important, and it's for the simple reason that things don't stay the same, and unless we are aware, we can't act.

I often recall a personal experience of working in the coal industry. I was privileged to spend some time underground on the coal face. I recall being shown one day the ceiling of a tunnel that had dipped dramatically overnight. It was remarked to me that: 'Mother nature decided to make her presence felt overnight', and now there was a massive drop in the ceiling. It posed a health and safety risk, and without action could have disastrous consequences. The final comment was: 'You need to have your finger on the pulse down here.' A great analogy, and a sentiment that very much underpins our argument.

As humans we are living and breathing every day. We have good days and not great days. We go through a myriad of experiences every day. Again, some good and others not so much. We are open to temptation (who isn't!) and in a work context may have unfulfilled ambitions or underappreciated skills. We experience boredom, we change our minds on things. This is life. This is what happens.

Let's scale that scenario back to the organization. That scenario may be playing out across multiple people in different roles. In Chapter 13 we will discuss the role of the mentor. We believe they play a fundamental role in the acquisition and sharing of intelligence regarding individuals.

We said at the outset of the chapter that the 'so what' is the progression and growth of individuals and organizations – right people, right place, right skills, feeling connected, engaged, valued and recognized. That is the goal, but we know that every day that is at risk, and we don't always know about it.

NURTURING PEOPLE IS A way of life

Nurturing and developing people and organizations is a way of life. It simply cannot be an event carried out once or twice a year. As mentioned above, if I feel that my skills are under appreciated or feel unfulfilled and not getting noticed, then I may look elsewhere. In the organization's eyes, however, I may be seen as emerging talent, high potential, and my leaving would be viewed as high impact. All round – not a great scenario, but not uncommon at all.

This is where the importance of dialogue and listening formally and informally really kicks in. Listening to not only what is being said in 1-2-1s, but also what isn't. Focus on the person and how they are feeling, their energy, focus, level of connection – it's amazing what we can learn and find out. This is intelligence gathering, applying our judgement and 'sensing' when something perhaps isn't quite right. Using that intelligence to check in with others, validate any possible assumptions being made or confirm initial judgements or hypotheses.

Retention is a challenge for everyone, whether it is the business looking to retain existing customers and add new ones, or an organization that is super committed to the retention and growth of talent. The sharing of intelligence when scaled can prevent risk to the organization – imagine if a key talent was about to leave without any warning and the organization wasn't able to react? They didn't have any succession lined up and had no strategy to convince the individual to stay, because it was too late.

I have sat in meetings after a key talent has decided to leave, and the first question is often, 'Why didn't we know they were thinking of leaving?' At that point it is often too late, but it's a great example of not having a finger on the pulse, keeping the organization informed, alleviating potential risk and securing the commitment and advocacy of the individual.

As we move to the last section of this chapter, the emphasis now shifts again. While feedback lies at the heart of organizational listening, the process for individuals is often very different and brings with it many personal and cultural challenges.

Feedback and growth

For many people, giving and receiving feedback is daunting. It can present opportunities for conflict, exposure of weaknesses and disagreement. As we have covered in this chapter, we are asked to provide feedback probably every day in some way shape or form. It could be within the organization we work, or by the person who served you at your table in the restaurant. We are not averse to giving feedback, but as they say context is everything, and when it concerns us, the psychology of the process changes. The microscope is now on us, and unfortunately when you have been the recipient of some feedback in your career which was delivered in a way that was cruel, unhelpful and personal, it can leave a mark.

At an organizational and personal level, feedback is a critical process. It should encourage growth, development, learning and recognition. Nobody has mastery and standing still isn't an option, so how do we listen, understand, learn, and act. Feedback featured in Chapter 10 on the role of the leader, and there is no doubt that leaders play a pivotal role in any feedback process, but we will provide a different point of view regarding where ownership lies.

Feedback is generally defined as reactions to the performance of either a person or a product. The purpose of feedback is to provide input which can be used as a basis for improvement.

Building a culture of feedback is difficult and takes time. We have experienced this ourselves at SAP. In the UK, we didn't always have processes in place by which feedback could be provided, and only when we changed did we see a corresponding improvement in performance. We continue to separate performance from financial reward, so that the feedback can focus on improvement and growth rather than be distracted by pay changes.

We sat down with Michiel Verhoeven and John Amaechi, OBE in Episode 11 of *The Human Factor*.[4] We wanted to discuss feedback and the relativity of success. Michael Verhoeven was SAP UK & Ireland Managing Director in 2022, responsible for one of the largest SAP market units. John Amaechi is an Organizational Psychologist and the founder of Amaechi Performance Systems, also known as APS Intelligence. APS Intelligence is a company that provides coaching, advisory, training and speaking services for organizations looking to create a high-performance workplace culture.

In the conversation, Michiel described the difficulties of establishing a feedback culture into SAP UK & Ireland, but also why it was important to do so. When Michiel took on the role, he made three primary observations:

1 The organization needed to serve customers and employees better, by ensuring it kept its promises.

2 The perception internally was that opportunities came through personal networks rather than through observation of performance.

3 The organization needed its workforce to adopt an aspirational culture of growth to support its strategy to become a cloud software company.

This meant SAP UK & Ireland needed to listen to its customers and employees, but also provide feedback of progress against these drivers. To achieve this meant identifying behaviours that were desirable and then using feedback to assess and drive change.

> What are the behaviours that we want? And then we did workshops on a very regular basis on giving and receiving feedback. The other thing we did was listening actively, not just speaking to be the smartest in the room but listening actively. We put together a program me where these people felt acknowledged, recognized as important beyond the goals of their jobs.

John had many tips and anecdotes on giving feedback, but what struck us the most was that feedback did not need to be cruel. It's a sentiment we absolutely agree with, as even the most difficult feedback can be delivered in a way that makes it clear that you believe in the potential of the individual.

John recounted a situation of being about to give feedback to someone. He was upset at a piece of work that had been done. However, he took the time to reflect and realized that he may have given the feedback in an angry and potentially unproductive manner. He felt it was about wanting to make himself feel better in that moment, and often the way that many of us feel better is by wounding others.

We also spoke with Caroline Goyder on the *Human Factor* podcast.[5] Caroline is an author and a voice coach. She has three bestselling books:

- *The Star Qualities: How to sparkle with confidence in all aspects of your life* (2009)
- *Gravitas: Communicate with confidence, influence and authority* (2014)
- *Find Your Voice: The secret to talking with confidence in any situation* (2020)

Caroline first came to our attention when we saw a TED Talk she delivered on 'The surprising secret to speaking with confidence'; an impactful presentation which now has over 10 million views.[6] She talked with us about 'Finding your voice', but this included listening and providing feedback as part of that discussion.

As part of the conversation, we were talking about developing confidence to help with speaking, but Caroline astutely observed that we not only have to find our voice, but also our ears. We must help people with feedback:

You've got to celebrate people before you give them refinements. When we slow down and think about giving feedback, step into the other person's shoes.

We discussed advice I had been given by one of my managers, that instead of focusing on negatives and failures, development can be framed as: 'Wouldn't it be better if…?'

wouldn't it be better if?

> The 'even better if' is much easier to take on board. If we don't feel safe, if we feel judged, we close. We stop breathing. We hold our breath. We can't take it on board so absolutely the quality of the feedback you give someone is so powerful to their learning if you do it with kindness.

For us this is where the power of 'labels' can really get in the way of progress. Whether it is feedback or passing on some advice, take away the labels of 'constructive criticism', 'negative feedback', 'positive feedback', 'good', 'bad', 'right', 'wrong'. As Caroline pointed out during our conversation, we close down when we feel we are about to be judged.

well DONE! *next TIME?* *better iF?*

A simple framework for feedback and can be used by anyone could be as follows:

- What did you do well?
- What could you do differently next time?
- Wouldn't it be better if…?

The removal of labels avoids barriers going up. The other crucial tip – unless the feedback is helpful to the person and they can do something with it, then it isn't feedback. The focus is on growth, progression and doing something better. It's not an opportunity to punish, wound or make someone feel bad and you feel better. This all assumes that a person is sitting and waiting for someone to come along and give them feedback – isn't there another way?

Take ownership. The feedback is about you, your performance, behaviour or development. Why wait for someone to come along? Go and ask people. Take control and ownership. Think about the different situations you are in, think about the range of people who you believe can help you with their observations. Avoid any unwanted scenarios of people passing along unsolicited feedback and get ahead of the game. Be your own source of intelligence, get down on the pitch and be active. Don't just sit in the stands and wait. We believe everybody has a role to play in moving things forward – be willing and committed to sharing your voice, your intelligence and your feedback.

In conclusion

At the outset of this chapter, we weren't sure if combining these three topics together would work, but it's clear how they are so closely linked. Listening, understanding, insights and feedback – it's an experiential flow, that is agile, dynamic and essential to moving things forward, whether at an individual level or organization.

It is multifaceted in its nature, but at the heart of it all is progression, growth and learning. Building and nurturing a culture of intelligence and feedback requires a concerted effort from all employees. Developing the right behaviours takes time and reinforcement and, in our opinion, a powerful feedback culture is integral to individual and organizational success.

Tips and tricks

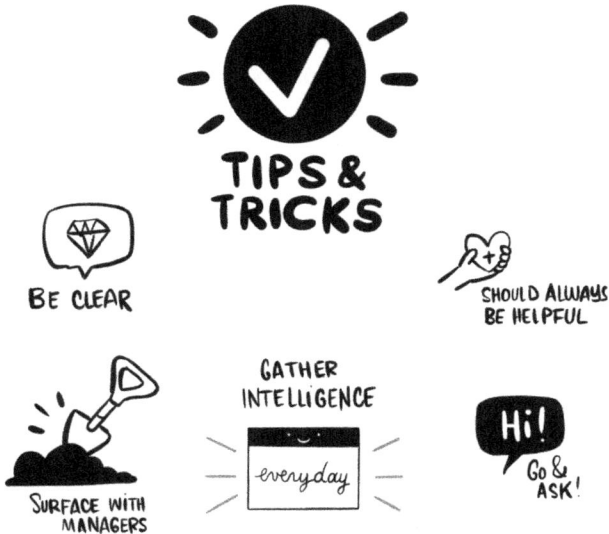

1 Be clear on what you are asking when listening – the design of questions is so important.

2 Surfacing insights with managers and leaders helps to cultivate a culture of learning and growth.

3 Gathering intelligence is an everyday activity and needs to be a way of life and not an event.

4 Feedback should always be helpful to the person. If it isn't, it's not feedback.

5 Take ownership for your feedback, don't wait for others – go and ask!

Notes

1 *The Human Factor* podcast Ep 39: The Art of Communication | *The Human Factor Podcast* by SAP, https://podcast.opensap.info/the-human-factor/2024/01/18/the-human-factor-podcast-ep-39-the-art-of-communication/ (archived at https://perma.cc/T8EY-SS4X)

2 *The Human Factor* podcast Ep 33: Turning Instinct into Insight | *The Human Factor Podcast* by SAP, https://podcast.opensap.info/the-human-factor/2023/07/31/the-human-factor-podcast-ep-33-turning-instinct-into-insight/ (archived at https://perma.cc/TRF5-VWYS)

3 *The Human Factor* podcast Ep 26: Operating in the New Era | *The Human Factor Podcast* by SAP, https://podcast.opensap.info/the-human-factor/2023/01/18/the-human-factor-podcast-ep-26-operating-in-the-new-era/ (archived at https://perma.cc/39M3-GXPB)

4 *The Human Factor* podcast Ep 11: The Relativity of Success – Finding Your Inner Giant | *The Human Factor Podcast* by SAP, https://podcast.opensap.info/the-human-factor/2022/01/18/the-human-factor-ep-11-the-relativity-of-success-finding-your-inner-giant/ (archived at https://perma.cc/8NPA-4FDE)

5 *The Human Factor* podcast Ep 18: Finding Your Voice | *The Human Factor Podcast* by SAP, https://podcast.opensap.info/the-human-factor/2022/06/17/the-human-factor-ep-18-finding-your-voiceguest-caroline-goyder-global-voice-coach-author-and-tedx-speaker/ (archived at https://perma.cc/ATT6-JL6K)

6 C Goyder (2014) The surprising secret to speaking with confidence | Caroline Goyder | TEDxBrixton, YouTube, www.youtube.com/watch?v=a2MR5XbJtXU (archived at https://perma.cc/A4KG-PSJM)

having the RIGHT

PEOPLE with the SKILLS in the ROLES

Nurturing and developing 13

Introduction

It would have been easy to title this chapter 'Nurturing and developing talent', but we have intentionally left 'talent' off the end, as it's something that we believe needs to be discussed and perhaps debated a little. There are many elephants in the room when it comes to the field of development, and what constitutes talent in an organizational context is often one of them.

This chapter is primarily going to focus on the nurturing and development of people in the workplace from a succession and development perspective, but the principles apply generically to how we live our lives every day. Our esteemed colleague and friend James Kelley will always remind us: 'If you are not learning, you are falling behind. Always must make time for sharpening the saw.' He is so right, but what we most admire with James is the rigour and commitment that he applies to his own personal philosophy, and that will be a big theme throughout this chapter.

We will consider the various elements that we believe influence and enable an effective nurturing and development strategy, in particular the identification and classification of employees and accelerating the readiness of people who have been classified as emerging or key talent and are part of a succession process. We will focus heavily on the cultural implications of making this work as a way of life (and not an event) and the importance of a strategically aligned and effective mentoring programme.

Before we dive into the heart of the topic, let's discuss and address a few of those elephants that are often in the room when the words 'development', 'succession' and 'talent' are discussed. We recognize that there are so many philosophical approaches when it comes to development, talent and succession, so let's start there.

A development philosophy

I think we have all heard that infamous quote from Henry Ford: 'The only thing worse than training your employees and having them leave is not training them and having them stay.'[1] It is a classic statement that has been repeated many times and reinforces the point that when it comes to the development of people it is very much a philosophical decision.

One of the perennial challenges facing any organization is having the right people with the right skills in the right roles. The decision for any organization is their recruitment strategy. If we take the quote at the beginning, there are some organizations that are not committed to the internal mobility of their people. Their preference is to look outside to find the right people. Of course, it is absolutely a personal choice, but if we look at any trends data over the last few years, it will clearly show that having the ability to build and develop a career within an organization is very important to people coming into the workforce. This was captured in an SAP research document on the perennial challenges facing organizations. Therefore, does a lack of commitment to developing and promoting from within create a competitive disadvantage for any organization? You could very much argue that it would. If building a career is important (and we recognize that isn't the case for all employees), will people stay if they feel that progression is not available, and therefore what is the point of being there? This is where disengagement and frustration kicks in.

For this chapter, we will focus on an organization that is absolutely committed to the development and promotion of people within the organization. This is when some of the big philosophical decisions will need to be made. Let's consider some of the key questions:

- How deep will the organization go with regards to succession planning?
- Will the organization develop a focused and structured career path model?
- Will individuals be able to 'opt in or out' in terms of their career aspirations?
- How will the organization identify and categorize individuals in relation to aspiration, potential and other criteria?
- Who is accountable for talent development? The individual, the manager, HR?
- What development approach will the organization take to accelerate the readiness of identified talent?

That is not an exhaustive list by any means. There are many more questions, but it clearly shows there are many different approaches and strategies when it comes to the internal development and nurturing of talent. It is very much a philosophical decision and approach to achieve the desired outcome.

A key part of any philosophy is commitment. It is not enough to say something and hope it will happen, and arguably we have seen this across many processes related to talent; for example goal setting and performance reviews. The process exists, but there is no engagement with the process, with low completion/participation. This is a major problem for any organization. The processes that underpin any development or succession planning cannot be viewed as events or moments in time. They must become a way of life.

The nurturing and development of talent is not linear. Quite early in the *Human Factor* podcast series we were joined by Paul McGuinness.[2] Paul represented Manchester United Football Club at Youth and Reserve Team level. From 1992 to 2016 he transitioned into the coaching and development side. He was the Centre of Excellence Director, Assistant Academy Director and Under 18 team coach where he successfully led the Youth Team to win the prestigious FA Youth Cup. During his time at Manchester United he operated under the leadership of Sir Alex Ferguson during the most successful period in their history.

If we take the world of sport and football in particular, the emphasis on nurturing and developing talent is part of the DNA of most clubs. Young players are identified at a very young age and are carefully nurtured through the various age groups. It was fascinating to hear Paul describe the life of a young footballer as a '10-year development programme' and built into that programme are many of the things we will discuss in this chapter. Paul was very clear that development is not linear. We all develop at different speeds; it requires patience at times and not losing faith in someone if they make a mistake. It would be fair to ask if the world of sport can be compared to a more traditional organization, but we believe many of the principles apply, but the main one is that the nurturing and development of talent is inherent in the DNA of the organization and a way of life.

Earlier in my career I was extremely fortunate to work under the CEO leadership of Harriet Green at Premier Farnell. One of our key objectives centred on the identification, development and mobilization of talent across the group. We had a sizeable internal fill rate target as part of the overall recruitment strategy. As CEO, Harriet coached and counselled the HR organization and the Organization Development team on her approach to talent identification and development. She also did the same with her direct reports on the executive team.

The organization needed a mindset shift, and all the processes that enabled and underpinned the talent management programme had to become a way of life. Talent calls were held with individual business leaders every six to eight weeks. Talent actions were discussed and followed up, mentoring relationships reviewed, and talent aspirations shared. Anyone attending those calls were expected to know their talent, to have clarity on all known talent intelligence and to be on top of what was happening. It became a way of life and not an event, due to the organization being able to see progress versus KPIs. The commitment and rigour applied was a great lesson that I have never forgotten.

The other big learning point was the capturing of intelligence, and this lay at the heart of Harriet's philosophy and why the development and nurturing of talent must be a way of life. The world doesn't stand still. In between the execution of various processes, life is still happening. Individuals may get frustrated, they may feel overlooked, they may have their head turned by a recruiter; so much can happen. Many times in this book we have talked about having your finger on the pulse, and this is a case in point. Therefore, how are you gathering your intelligence and insights?

Intelligence and insights

What is 'intelligence'? Is it just a fancy word for data? If we take a dictionary definition, it is 'the ability to learn, understand, and make judgements or have opinions that are based on reason'. The key words for me are 'judgements' and 'opinions'. Nurturing and developing the workforce is an art and a science, and I learnt very early in my career it is without doubt one of the most challenging programmes to lead and manage.

CAPTURE THE INTELLIGENCE

Let's start with the most important question. Who captures the intelligence? While you will of course ask the individual for insights and intelligence, the organization needs to have their viewpoint. It's common to capture talent intelligence within performance processes, but the frequency of those processes is sometimes once, twice, or perhaps four times a year.

Therefore, how do you capture intelligence out of a process cycle? I found this is where absolute clarity on the Responsible, Accountable, Consulted, Informed (RACI) model was really needed, otherwise a vacuum would appear really quickly and, basically, nobody does it. As we write this chapter, it is important to acknowledge there are many ways of capturing intelligence and we are not questioning the variety of methods, merely stating that it needs to happen and there must be some rigour.

Being very candid and reflecting on the last 10 years, I have met with many organizations and I often ask if the organization could search for talent simply and easily. The answer has often been 'No.' I then discover that the organization doesn't have a systemic way of capturing any data, let alone intelligence, and will often just rely on what is known by a few people. This usually kicks up the same people or the 'usual suspects', as I was once told!

What intelligence are we looking at? We would expect organizations to be capturing traditional talent data, for example the experiences that some-one has had, qualifications, language capability, mobility status and much more. In addition, there is the key question of whether someone has the as-piration to progress in the organization. We think it is perfectly OK for someone to 'opt in' or 'opt out'. Not everyone aspires to career growth and promotions; instead looking to perform to a high level and continue to grow and develop within role or job family. If someone does have that aspiration, then a view needs to be taken on that person's potential. Again, there are a variety of ways of assessing this and there are some great practices around talent calibration.

Then there are the talent flags or indicators which include things such as risk of loss, impact of loss, assessment of potential, future leader and many others. The principle behind these indicators is simple and the point was made earlier that individuals who the organization has classed as 'talent' may get tired of waiting for an opportunity or have had their head turned. This is crucial intelligence, especially if the individual is also on the succes-sion plan, highly regarded by the organization that is investing heavily in terms of development activity.

Going back to the point of the RACI, it is imperative to agree who will actively capture this kind of intelligence. Is it the line manager, a HR busi-ness partner, the talent organization? It doesn't matter who is capturing it, as long as it is captured. Ideally it sits with the manager, is recorded and made visible to the organization.

Later in the chapter I will discuss the role of mentors. Without a doubt they can play a pivotal role in assisting in accelerating the developing of talent, but they are also a super source of intelligence from their conversa-tions with mentees. In my experience of running mentoring programmes, mentors are simply invaluable in any organization.

Now that we are starting to capture vital intelligence, how do we approach the succession process?

Effective succession planning

We are not going to debate the various approaches to succession plan-ning, as there are many, but instead focus on some key guidance points and reminders. A clear starting point is the scope of the succession. Very often it will concern the top level of the organization down to a certain grade, with critical roles identified.

During my time at Premier Farnell, we held talent calls every six to eight weeks to discuss progress on talent actions. Those main actions were outputs from the two 'key talent reviews' held per year as an entire group. This was an extremely powerful event attended by our executive team, business leaders, and global HR organization – a full review of the talent landscape, classification of talent, local succession plans, key talent actions and risks. Potential successors for roles were discussed, but also, importantly, a judgement made on their readiness – whether they were ready now, in one to two years or in three to five years.

As we have discussed throughout this chapter, the whole process was fluid and dynamic. There was real creativity in some of the decisions taken, collaboration from business leaders to facilitate the movement of talent (which doesn't always happen) and some great inputs from mentors and business partners who were sharing intelligence and insights on several people, which only aids and adds richness to the discussions.

As the process matured for a certain level of the organization, focus was expanded to search and identify 'emerging talent'. This is a development that I believe yielded some great outcomes for individuals and the organization, and is an important consideration when thinking about not only the attraction of talent, but also retention and growth. In some cases, the time to readiness for certain people was quite long, but that was OK. We found that engaging as many people as possible in the programme paid real dividends. It created a connection, a sense of belonging and being true to the commitments in our EVP.

A challenge that is always presented with succession is impatience. This is why developing a clear strategy for developing talent is so important. Not everyone will be promoted, that isn't reality, and this is especially the case in the world of sport. Manchester United will have 50 or 60 players in their academy. How many will make the breakthrough to the first team? Probably a handful, but there is still a commitment to growing all the players so they can go on and have a great career, even if that is not at Manchester United.

In the business context, there is far more scope for movement, but the reality is still that not everyone will get promoted. Being clear on the guardrails and the guidance for managers is super important.

This is where secondments and project opportunities become important. Opportunities to shadow leaders, attend meetings, but also work on development actions and key areas. It takes real skill to manage the expectations of talent. In their eyes, they are ready now and want it now, and often that is not realistic. Being honest and transparent with development actions is crucial, and this is where mentors play another key role in the development process. Being able to provide feedback and, dare I say, some insights that may not have been shared with the individual previously. This helps to anchor expectations.

Before we get to mentoring, let's get into another vital aspect of nurturing talent, and that is effectively managing their exposure. Let's assume for a second that an organization has a robust programme and is extremely effective at identifying individuals who they believe are talent. These are individuals who have the capacity to progress in the organization. So how will they be developed? What is the strategy and plan to accelerate the readiness and growth of individuals to prepare them for future roles and opportunities in the organization?

One of the most common ways is exposure. Inviting talent to different meetings, opportunities to present, leading a project, working in a different functional area. The reason we are focusing a whole section on exposure is because of the complexities when that exposure doesn't perhaps go as well as hoped.

Managing exposure

One of the reasons we have been so keen to speak with individuals from the world of sport on the podcast is because these topics are almost part and parcel of their daily lives. Let's go back to the conversation with Paul McGuinness at Manchester United Football Club. We asked Paul how they managed exposure with the different age groups, and they did this in a variety of ways. The obvious was to get them playing with the age group above them. They would perhaps encounter players who were faster, stronger and quicker than them. This is an immediate test. How do they cope? Do they go into their shell, or does their character shine through and their competitive streak/resilience shine through?

On a match day, they would perhaps play players in a weaker team against a stronger team to see how they handled adversity. It's all good and well seeing them in a winning environment, but what happens when things are not going your way? How do you react? How do you react to your team members? Doing my research for the book, I learned from Sir Alex Ferguson that he would observe players in games where they were losing, to see their character in a difficult situation. Did they sulk or perhaps stop trying, start to blame others? Or did they roll up their sleeves and keep trying?

I mentioned earlier that talent development is not linear, and talent intelligence relies on a sold opinion and judgement. One of the great skills when assessing talent and working with talent is patience and seeing that potential. Also being able to recognize when a talent perhaps reaches its ceiling, which again happens very often within sport. There are countless stories in football of players released by clubs when they are very young who go on to have a marvellous career. It's not an exact science, and allowing for that development to happen perhaps at a slower pace for someone is important.

We referred to our conversation on the *Human Factor* podcast with Russell Martin in Chapter 4 around his philosophy and approach.[3] When Russell finished his career and moved into coaching, he brought with him a huge amount of sympathy and empathy. He understood how difficult it is to manage the development of talent, and we asked him about his approach to exposure.

He shared with us that he has seen players in his career who have maybe five or 10 appearances to their name, and are no longer playing. It's something that really frustrated him because he knew the players would have had ability, but did someone have the patience to realize that before making a quick judgement? He absolutely got that managing exposure required time, patience and support. He shared something interesting that very much applies to the business world too.

During the Covid-19 pandemic, teams played their games in empty stadiums. Russell found that young talent being introduced into the team were able to express themselves and learn about the game. They were expressing themselves. He then noticed the difference when the crowds came back. Now there was 'noise', and a lot of it. Suddenly there was doubt, players were going into their shell, not asking for the ball. Those players still had talent and ability, but now they had to cope with the environment around them. It was now much more than being good at football, and in the business world that 'noise' exists too.

Standing up to present to a senior audience for the first time. Attending a senior meeting and being expected to contribute to the meeting. Standing in front of a board seeking support for an investment. Participating in these kinds of scenarios brings with it a lot of 'noise': inputs from others, contrasting feedback from multiple sources and of course the 'noise' in the mind of the individual. The classic 'what am I doing here?', 'I can't do this', 'My presentation was absolutely awful, I have blown it'.

Managing the exposure and growth of talent is an art and a science, and is a team sport. It needs a framework and guardrails to help people through and across the inevitable bumpy moments, and making sure faith is retained in their ability. The greatest learning in life often comes from mistakes, but for some that is a big challenge. Being able to cope with perceived difficult challenges or how to navigate a complex situation can be tough, and these are great examples of when mentors are an exceptional 'support and challenge' relationship.

The power of mentoring

We were very fortunate to spend some time on the *Human Factor* podcast with Marie Noelle Gagnon from Cirque Du Soleil.[4] I simply loved it when she said, 'I am probably the fruit of many mentors.' I have felt the same. I have been incredibly fortunate to have some wonderful people providing me with guidance, counselling and confidence at various stages of my career. They helped me to make steps I wouldn't have considered, take on challenges that I thought were perhaps beyond me.

Earlier in my career I was responsible for a global mentoring programme. The programme had two clear objectives – to orient and support any new leaders in role or to the organization and to accelerate the readiness of identified talent. Mentors were assigned no more than five mentees at any one time, and mentors included our CEO and all her direct reports. The ownership of the relationship firmly sat with the mentee. They were accountable for driving the cadence and governance of when meetings would occur.

When we consider some of the elements that we have covered in this chapter, namely the accumulation of intelligence, managing exposure, accelerating readiness, and managing risk, the role of the mentor cuts across all those elements. We will often hear people confusing a mentor with a coach or believing they are the same, and in some respects they are, but for us a mentor goes much deeper and can be much more of an influencer.

Let's consider some of those elements in more detail.

Intelligence

Let's look at this as two sides of the coin. On one side, a mentor is not your line manager. A truly effective mentoring relationship is built on transparency and trust. A mentee may share some information with a mentor that they won't share with their line manager. They may be more open about their career aspirations or some challenges they are facing. They may divulge how they are feeling or if they have seen a new opportunity internally or externally. Feeling able to open, share, discuss, debate is the essence of the relationship.

Now when we look on the other side, we start to potentially contradict ourselves when we talk about trust. A mentor is an invaluable source of intelligence. While it can appear that trust is being broken or compromised, a truly effective mentor will share with the organization some invaluable intelligence without compromising or damaging the relationship. This is part and parcel of organizational dynamics, and if that intelligence is warning the organization of a risk related to a person, then it is worth its weight in gold. As we mentioned earlier in the chapter, judgement is a crucial part of intelligence gathering and mentors must always apply judgement.

Managing exposure

We covered exposure earlier in the chapter, but a mentor can play a big role in supporting this activity – whether it is helping a mentee to prepare, dealing with the aftermath if things have not gone well or simply to provide some belief and confidence. When Simon and I think of our mentors, we would love picking their brains, asking them to share how they would approach a situation or how to navigate some resistance.

We are also both great believers in feedback loops, and our mentors were exceptional in helping to process what happened, but doing so by taking all emotion out of it. Focusing on what happened, what went well, what could we do differently next time, for example. Being asked to lead a project or present in front of a board can be scary. Knowing you have that wisdom available to you is phenomenal.

Accelerating readiness and mobility potential

You could argue that managing exposure is the same as accelerating readiness, but there are some differences, and it is linked to managing effective succession. Whether it be operating at a new level in an organization (moving into a director role) or preparing someone for an internal move across geographies, having a mentor who can help prepare a mentee well in advance is another great example of the value of mentoring.

I often recount a conversation that I had with Harriet at Premier Farnell when we were discussing the mentoring programme at its infancy and the role it would play in the forthcoming years. Harriet gave me a scenario whereby she was asking if I wanted to go and lead our business in Guadeloupe, starting next week. The likely answer would be no. However, if I was asked if I would be interested in 12 months' time, I have time to prepare, consider, discuss and plan with my family. This is where Harriet saw real value in the role of the mentor, and it was assisting in our succession plans, helping mentees to be ready, to help visualize what operating in a new geography could look like.

Our mentors were actively engaged in key conversations related to talent. They became sounding boards for ideas and were also asked to test out ideas with identified mentees. This goes back to the Guadeloupe example. Mentors were an immense help in truly assessing mobility aspirations and potential. Their feedback on readiness was super helpful too.

In conclusion

Nurturing and developing people are real skills. It requires a commitment, some clear guardrails, and a rigour. It cannot be viewed as a one-off event, otherwise nothing will happen. If the commitment is there, it must be part of the fabric of the organization and all processes related to the internal mobility of talent need to be aligned and in sync. There are many moving parts, it isn't always linear (in fact rarely is) and co-ordination and powerful facilitation are crucial. The impact, however, for the organization and the individual can be transformative, creating a bond, connection and advocacy which is worth its weight in gold.

Tips and tricks

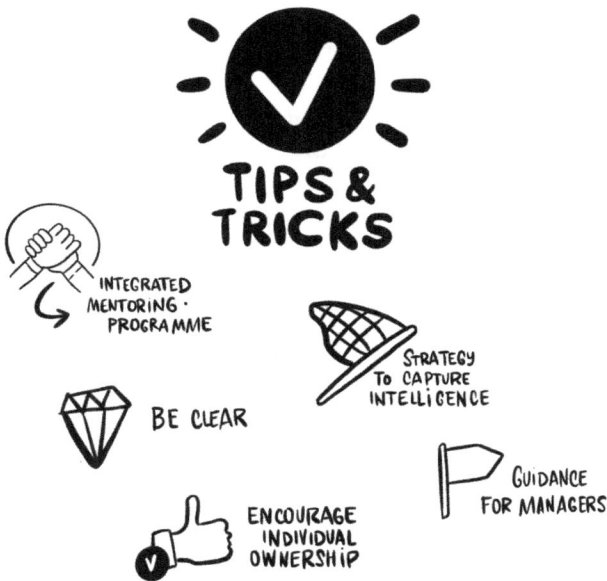

TIPS & TRICKS

INTEGRATED MENTORING · PROGRAMME

STRATEGY TO CAPTURE INTELLIGENCE

BE CLEAR

GUIDANCE FOR MANAGERS

ENCOURAGE INDIVIDUAL OWNERSHIP

1 Be really clear on your strategy for nurturing and developing talent – it sounds obvious, but without one, nothing much happens by accident.

2 Encourage individual ownership – your career is far too important to trust to anyone else.

3 Have a strategy and clear plan for capturing talent data and intelligence – capturing out of process and cycle is super important as life doesn't stand still.

4 Have clear guidance on development options and strategies – this is super important to help line managers when working with their identified talent.

5 Make your mentoring programme, if you have one, an integral part of your overall programme, and not just something that runs alongside.

Notes

1 T Chamorro-Premuzic, S Adler and R B Kaiser (2017) What science says about identifying high-potential employees, *Harvard Business Review*, https://hbr.org/2017/10/what-science-says-about-identifying-high-potential-employees (archived at https://perma.cc/HF6P-N9KX)

2 *The Human Factor* podcast Ep 23: The Nurturing and Development of Talent with Paul McGuinness | *The Human Factor Podcast* by SAP, https://podcast.opensap.info/the-human-factor/2022/10/28/the-human-factor-podcast-ep-23-the-nurturing-and-development-of-talent-with-paul-mcguinness/ (archived at https://perma.cc/78FG-CUAZ)

3 *The Human Factor* podcast Ep 15: The Power of Philosophy | *The Human Factor Podcast* by SAP, https://podcast.opensap.info/the-human-factor/2022/04/13/the-human-factor-ep-15-the-power-of-philosophyguest-russell-martin-head-coach-swansea-city-football-club/ (archived at https://perma.cc/P5SV-RESY)

4 *The Human Factor* podcast Ep 31: Creating The Greatest Show on Earth | *The Human Factor Podcast* by SAP, https://podcast.opensap.info/the-human-factor/2023/05/22/the-human-factor-podcast-ep-31-creating-the-greatest-show-on-earth/ (archived at https://perma.cc/SUE7-25ZD)

TECHNOLOGY **IS** IN ALL ASPECTS of our lives

The role of technology in execution

14

Introduction

And so, we have arrived at a chapter on technology. Technology impacts on our lives in many ways, both at home and at work. Sometimes it can help us and be a pleasant experience. However, technology can also be frustrating and sometimes stressful, even for the most technically proficient amongst us. What causes these emotions, and can they be avoided?

During this chapter, we will explore technology from several different aspects:

- The evolution of technology in our lives.
- What is the difference between standardization and personalization?
- Why data plays such an important role in technology.
- Why connecting technology together is needed, and what makes this easier or harder.
- Why do the basics matter?
- The importance of being agile in today's ever-changing world.
- How will the emergence of AI enhance and/or disrupt our home and work experiences?
- Our perspective on approaches and considerations to make technology projects run more smoothly.
- And, of course, our tips and tricks for success.

The evolution of technology in our lives

Technology has been around for a long time. When the first cave dweller picked up a piece of wood and used it as a club, that 'technology' allowed them to consider leaving the caves and hunt. Clubs became axes and spears both to improve weapons, but also to till the land for crops. We are very creative as a species. We are always looking for ways to improve our lives. From the spinning wheel, through to steam power, electricity, the jet engine, the personal computer, the internet and more recently AI, suffice to say, technology has played a part every step of the way.

Today, we have technology in all aspects of our lives; cars, washing machines, lights and heating, television and mobile phones. The list is endless, and the same is true when we go to work also, though in some instances employees might feel that the technology at work is lagging behind the technology they use in their personal lives. As we entered the age of computers, it can sometimes feel like we are struggling to keep up with all the changes.

Moore's Law from 1965 famously tried to capture the pace of technology change. Intel co-founder Gordon Moore observed that the number of transistors on an integrated circuit will double every two years with only minimal rise in cost for the next ten years. People then colloquially use the law to describe the pace of change generally in technology. While we have left transformers behind, and Silicon Valley has hit limitations on just how small chips can go these days, technology itself continues to develop at pace, and today we live in a world of quantum computers and artificial intelligence (more on these later). As every generation in the past has probably felt, today feels both exciting and full of trepidation as to where technology will take us next.

Standardization vs personalization

After a very much abridged history lesson in the preceding section, another observation is how certain technologies rise above others in a competing market. Standardization was an approach that allowed for technology to be commoditized. It allowed for mass manufacturing and ultimately cost reduction to the consumer. But it came with a compromise; everything had to be the same. One size fits all.

But as we have seen throughout this book, humans don't readily fit this model. We are individuals, with personal preferences in both how we consume technology and our reactions to it. What we see with technology is that we tend to move through stages – first standardization, then personalization.

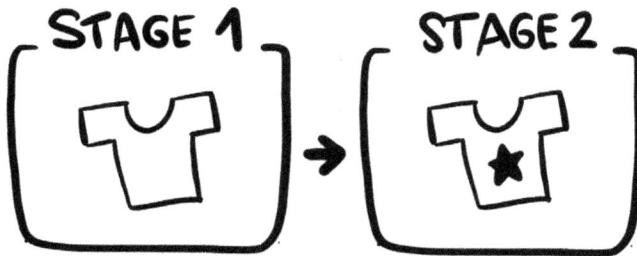

If we look at cars, for example, most these days have common features – electric windows, power steering, seat belts, ABS, air bags, satellite navigation and so on. As these supporting technologies became cheaper, most manufacturers realized that they had to add them without significantly increasing costs. However, the future direction of car technology is likely to be towards personalization: car owners deciding which services to add to their car to make them individual to their needs. Examples include concierge services, auto driving capabilities, streaming services for audio and video, and even being able to change the colour of the car internally and externally.

In 2023, BMW announced the world's first colour-changing car called 'The Dee'.[1] The Dee is an acronym standing for Digital Emotional Experience, and BMW described the car's capability to cycle through 32 different colours when they unveiled it at the 2023 Consumer Electronics Show in Las Vegas.

Personalization allows our differences to matter, but also allows us to differentiate as individuals. It allows us to consume technology in ways that are comfortable to us, but also to express ourselves through our technology. It is these human factors that will continue to shape technology advances in the future.

The importance of data quality

We have never had as much data gathering in the world as we do today. When we talk about volumes of data being collected, we no longer talk in terms of megabytes or gigabytes. The new sizes are terabytes and petabytes. How big is a petabyte?[2] It's roughly 11,000 movies filmed in 4k definition. If we wanted to sit and watch all those movies, one after the other, it would take us around 2.5 years (and an awful lot of popcorn).

What doesn't change, though, whether the data is petabytes or just bytes, is that the data must be high quality for it to be of value in our ability to execute. And this is the challenge within organizations – how to ensure that the data being used is:

- accurate
- relevant
- current
- accessible
- of some value

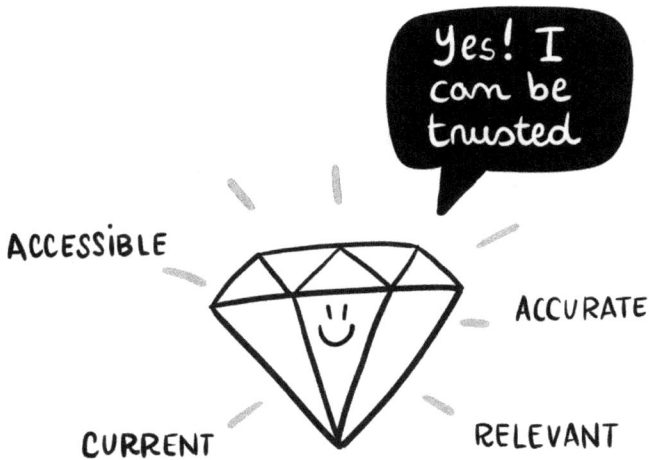

If the data we are holding doesn't fulfil these criteria, then why we are holding it needs to be questioned. What purpose does the data provide? Can it be trusted? Does it give insight? If we can get ourselves into a position where the data is high quality, then it can become a differentiator and potentially a competitive advantage.

If we are seeking to use the latest technologies such as AI (more on this later in the chapter), then we must ensure that the underlying data is high quality, otherwise we will see incorrect answers and biases reflected in the behaviour of that AI capability. The technology is only as good as the data that feeds it.

When we undertake technology projects, it is vital to ensure that we consider all aspects of our data, usually consolidated into a data strategy document. This document will typically outline:

- What data do we need to make our technology succeed?
- Where is our data recorded today (if at all)?
- How much data history should be migrated to provide value?
- What is the strategy for supplementing data if it isn't currently captured?
- What tools will we use to migrate from the legacy solution to the new solution?
- How will we test that the data has been migrated successfully?
- What will we do with any data that is not transferred into the new solution?
- Who will need to be involved from the organization (and outside the organization) to work on the data?

With the emergence of Software as a Service, and the development of improved memory storage space, the imperative to archive data has diminished, allowing organizations to store more and more data inside their applications. However, storing more and more data still requires project discipline and governance to ensure that it remains useful and relevant.

An example of how data can help and hinder our ability to execute comes in the management of data such as jobs and positions in the organization structure. We can capture many elements of a position within the structure, including pay information, position description, the positional hierarchy, the security and access permissions that the position grants, and the skills needed to successfully fulfil the position. This information gives enormous power to the structures we hold and how we manage our organization. However, we need to keep that data current and clean to provide maximum value. When people leave the organization, some companies do not have a rigorous process to govern how these positions are managed. The temptation is to leave the position empty, and to create a new one if a replacement hire is made. However, over time, our structures then become cluttered with erroneous information, and before long it becomes difficult to manage.

To ensure our ability to execute is at its best, we need to ensure that our data is at its best. This data hygiene ensures that we have the basics in place for success. We can then progress to where data can be used to create competitive advantage.

We discussed TSG 1899 Hoffenheim in Episode 33 of *The Human Factor*.[3] TSG 1899 Hoffenheim are a professional soccer club that plays in the top league in Germany, called the Bundesliga. They are not a rich club, but have managed to secure stable membership of the Bundesliga League since 2008, including qualifying for and playing in the Champions League. They describe themselves as a small village club, although that is being somewhat humble, given they have an average game attendance of around 24,000 and sales in 2023 of around €164 million. However, compared to Bayern Munich, for example, who average around 75,000 and sales in the region of €850m it's not so hard to see why they describe themselves that way. They focus very much on data and how they can use it for deep insight into player development.

We spoke with Dr Sascha Härtel, the Head of Performance, Coordination Science at the club. We wanted to get to the heart of how TSG 1899 Hoffenheim used data to maximum effect, to help them compete against those bigger clubs. Sascha explained the data they are seeking to gather from the players, and set it in the context of how listening to that data is a mutually beneficial process to both the player and the club. This was very important, as it required player trust in the process to establish why information was being gathered and what it was going to be used for:

The numbers of players who ask 'What are you doing with our data?' We like them to ask. We want to have players who are interested in these things because if the player understands why we do it, then it's much easier to work with them.

We delved into what data was being gathered, which included sleeping patterns, eating habits, health updates and general wellbeing information. What was crucial was that the combination of this off the field information, gathered directly from the players, coupled with on the field data gathered by technology meant that the club got a far deeper insight into how player performance was trending and why. A reduction in on the field performance could be medical or linked to emotional or psychological wellbeing issues, or even just attributable to a disruption in sleep patterns at home. Sascha summarized this approach as looking at the whole picture. The holistic view of the player and the team.

It's this observation that underpins many aspects around data – it's accurate because the club has explained why they are capturing it to the player, who then understands how it will be used. It's timely as they capture this on a regular basis. It's relevant, as it gives direct insight into aspects of the player's condition and wellbeing. Therefore, it can also be trusted and used by the club in player development.

If we return from the sporting arena back to the world of work, we are not suggesting that we start capturing our employees' sleep patterns. That would be a step too far for nearly everyone to even consider. But we should ensure we have a well-rounded, holistic and accurate view of our employees, including data around their work preferences, career aspirations, skills and performance.

Connecting technology

connected experiences

Now we have our data foundations in hand, we need to ensure that our information can be shared around our organization's ecosystem easily and efficiently. Connecting technology together can be a very frustrating endeavour. It should influence our buying decisions, whether at work or at home.

In a simple home example, would it be sensible to buy an Alexa device for the kitchen, a Siri device for the dining room and a Google assistant for the bedroom? Not if we want to have a harmonious house, as these competing devices are not compatible with each other and thus, would provide a very disconnected experience. If we have an IOS mobile phone, would we consider an Android tablet? Probably not as sharing our files, apps and games would be compromised across the two platforms.

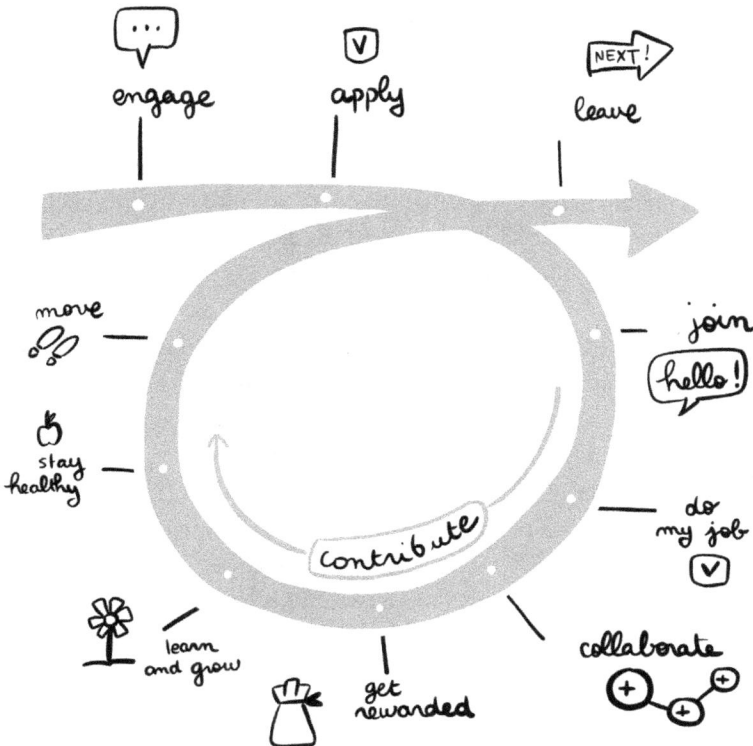

At work, we have more flexibility when considering our enterprise applications. Connecting our HR, finance, procurement, manufacturing and supply chain, expenses and other systems together is possible. However, what are the benefits and costs of doing this across multiple platforms, when compared with sourcing all those capabilities from an already integrated supplier?

Let's look at a general HR lifecycle that will exist in most organizations.

Even within HR, organizations face the choice of buying best of breed capability or a function-wide solution that provides capability across the whole process lifecycle.

However, when we look at the HR data and the related processes, they should be tightly connected so that HR can operate efficiently and with deep insight. For example, when joining the organization, our new employee already has data transferred from onboarding (for example, no need for additional paper forms to be filled in to provide bank account details), their company equipment can be ready on day one (laptop, phone, safety equipment, uniforms), payroll is already set up, competencies are transferred from the recruitment evaluation process and ready now to be enhanced by our performance and learning processes, a company induction can be initiated, and so on.

This connectivity of HR processes is now the expectation of the workforce, and this is the value of connecting all of the related capabilities. No more 'islands in a stream' of disconnected processes such as learning, performance or recruitment operating with third-party solutions that collect but don't share data easily and result in 'gaps in the floorboards' for data. No more nightmares for IT when one of the applications is upgraded and integrations cease to work.

We then see that the data doesn't stop at HR, but continues to flow around the organization in downstream processes such as travel expense management, finance management, procurement and project systems. By tightly connecting our HR processes and data to the wider enterprise, we can ensure that the value of HR data doesn't stop within HR. We can drive a consistent user experience to the entire workforce in an easy to use, easy to access manner through mobile or desktop, with the emphasis on being able to deploy self-service where you need to. With that tightly integrated capability, our workforce begins to move away from HR processes or finance processes and towards 'processes I need to do for my role', breaking down those functional silos.

COMMON ALIGNED ENTERPRISE MODEL

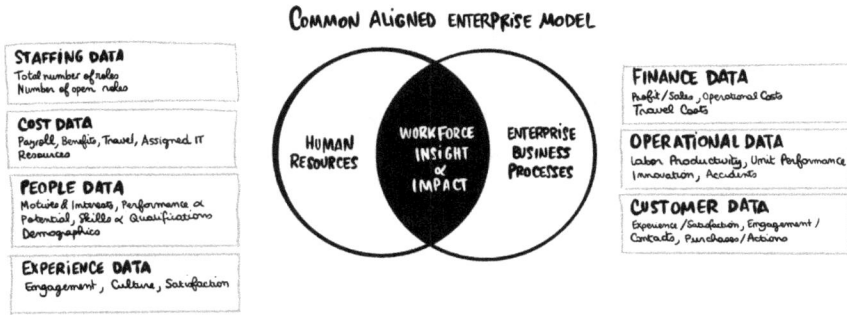

STAFFING DATA
Total number of roles
Number of open roles

COST DATA
Payroll, Benefits, Travel, Assigned IT
Resources

PEOPLE DATA
Motives & Interests, Performance or
Potential, Skills or Qualifications
Demographics

EXPERIENCE DATA
Engagement, Culture, Satisfaction

HUMAN
RESOURCES

WORKFORCE
INSIGHT
or
IMPACT

ENTERPRISE
BUSINESS
PROCESSES

FINANCE DATA
Profit/Sales, Operational Costs
Travel Costs

OPERATIONAL DATA
Labor Productivity, Unit Performance
Innovation, Accidents

CUSTOMER DATA
Experience/Satisfaction, Engagement/
Contacts, Purchases/Actions

At a data level, we can start to see benefits from aligned and integrated cross-functional data, including:

- a stronger connection between HR data, workforce capabilities, financial performance, operational efficiency and business results
- deeper insights from connecting together information that in the past was siloed
- a single source of truth for data across the organization
- real-time reporting and analysis
- more effective cross-functional collaboration
- reduced integration costs (both set-up and running costs)
- faster technology adoption
- decreased time to complete month-end processing
- a consistent user experience and integrated processes across systems (e.g. HR, finance, customer management, procurement, etc.)
- guidance for workforce management decisions by combining workforce data with business operations data found in financial, sales, supply chain and customer management systems
- the ability for organizations to calculate the business impact of workforce decisions by connecting HR data to business operations and financial data

During the summer of 2023, we spoke at length with Marc Starfield about the value and benefits of a connected enterprise. Marc is a Global HR Transformation and Programme Leader, and at the time was the Global Head of HR Programmes and Systems at Vodafone.

In our conversation, he got to the heart of what a connected enterprise represented.

It's important that the concept of these connected experiences should be seen as a collective of integrated experiences, multiple processes and data coming together, but also how you feel about the organization.

So, the connected enterprise is more than just integrating together the technology components. It's also about ensuring that the organization is connected to the employees within it. It's about how it feels holistically to those within it – the processes, the data, the experience.

And here is one of the key observations that we can make about technology:

Technology is an enabler for change to occur. On its own, it doesn't solve all challenges, nor address all aspects of a needed change.

Basics matter

So far, we have covered standardization vs personalization, our data foundations and our technology connectivity. These are some of the basics that all organizations should consider when looking at technology solutions. Basics matter.

What do we mean by that? This is a topic that has come up in many of the conversations we have had in our podcast series and with customers that we speak with. We have spoken with many customers considering organizational change and choosing technology to help enable that change. Unfortunately, some of those conversations have been distracted by 'whistles and bells' capabilities instead of ensuring that the organization has the fundamental basic capabilities in place. The basics are not the sexy capabilities of technology, but without being able to provide this basic capability to the organization, a solution will be building on sand, i.e. the foundations will be insufficient:

- At a data visibility level, can the organization report on how many employees it has, who they are, where they work, what they do and what do they need to perform well? Can employees be paid accurately, on time and efficiently? Can the data be trusted?

- At a technology level, do I have a single source of the truth? Is my technology integrated together efficiently without the need for manual intervention? Does my workforce have access to the capabilities they need to perform their role, and is this access secure and private?

- At a functional level, are the organizational processes connected together? Do our functions such as HR and Finance have the same definitions for key information such as Full Time Equivalent (FTE), and are they using the information consistently?

- Has the organization got the necessary resources in place to ensure a satisfactory level of service to the business? Are those people skilled, motivated and empowered to provide the best service they can? Is our operating model aligned to the delivery strategy outlined in our business strategy?

If the basics are built on robust foundations and trustworthy data, then technology can then enable change to lead to increased business value.

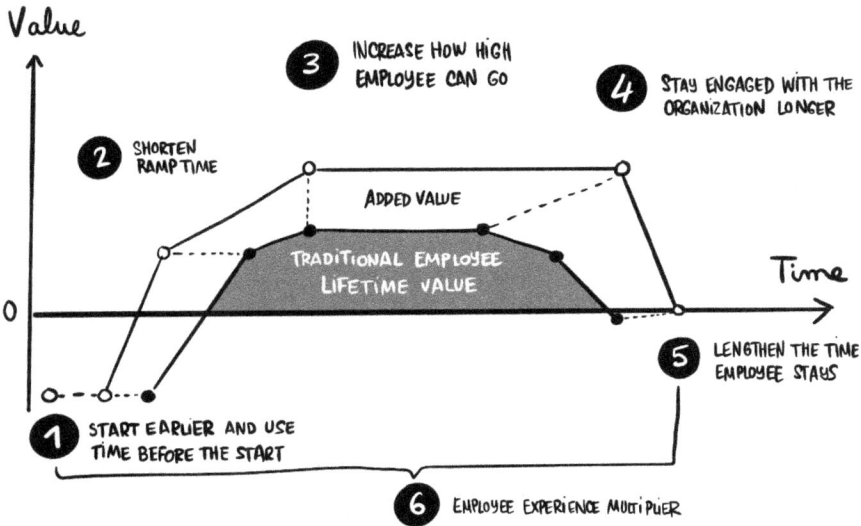

In the above figure, there are several key opportunities to add value:

- Source, engage and hire the world's best talent with a comprehensive, yet simple solution that provides guidance to everyone at every step.

- Offer a strategic, comprehensive approach to onboarding new hires and internal transfers.

- Provide a modern, personal and measurable approach to development and career planning that improves engagement and reduces complexity and cost.

- Deliver multiple reward models and compensation programmes and motivate your workforce with a strategic reward solution.

- Extend and scale your workforce succession and development efforts, assuming a more agile and strategic approach in line with business needs.
- Ensure every candidate and employee has what they need, when they need it, by actively listening to their feedback.

Agility at scale

As we have observed throughout the book, the only constant is change. Market conditions, user expectations, and technologies are constantly evolving. At home, if we want to try a new piece of technology, we have the luxury of being able to have a go with it and see if we like it. Maybe it's a new mobile phone, a wearable device, a digital assistant or a new app. At work, things are a little different. We have governance processes in place, legacy technologies to consider and we typically go through projects to evaluate, build, integrate and then assess new technologies. And this takes time, money and resource.

For example, at SAP, where we provide enterprise-wide capability, we need to be able to innovate at the pace of a start-up organization. Software as a Service capability provides constant innovation and the ability to be agile because the heavy lifting is done by us, the supplier rather than the organization itself. New capabilities and features can be added in every new release cycle.

However, no single supplier has a monopoly on innovation. At SAP we foster an eco-system of partners that help organizations stay at the forefront of technical capability. These partners work with us to certify that their technology integrates fully with our solution and is often plug and play in terms of speed of deployment. This then transforms the pace at which organizations can change, even at scale. Now, organizations can operate similarly to how we operate at home – try new capabilities quickly and easily and stay fresh and agile in the competitive world of work. Now technology has become flexible enough to allow us to execute our business strategy efficiently, but also agile enough to react to changing circumstances, requirements or conditions.

Emerging technologies

Technology does not stand still. As outlined earlier in this chapter, it changes at pace and new technologies can introduce opportunity and disruption. How can we harness the opportunity that emerging technologies offer while minimizing the potential for disruption?

The most obvious place to lead a discussion on emerging technologies is of course with artificial intelligence. It would be amazing if you haven't heard about AI from around 2023 onwards, as this has been all over mainstream media at various levels of hysteria. However, that is also a bit misleading. The term was first used by Alan Turing back in the 1950s, so it's a little difficult to still consider it an emerging technology.

Turing was a mathematician who is widely regarded as the father of theoretical computer science and artificial intelligence. He was immortalized in a stunning performance by Benedict Cumberbatch in *The Imitation Game*, a film focused on his work to help decrypt the German cipher system Enigma. He developed what became known as the Turing Test, which determines whether a machine could exhibit intelligent behaviour to such a point that it could convince the tester that they were conversing with a human being.

Of course, since the 1950s, the field has developed somewhat and despite a number of attempts to enter our mainstream lives in the past decade, only now does it feel like it is real and here to make a difference. But before we go further, what actually is artificial intelligence? In November 2022, ChatGPT was released by OpenAI. The GPT stands for 'Generative Pretrained Transformer'. (Probably a wise decision to go with the snappier acronym in this case.) This was the tool that really caught the world's attention and led to many playing with some of its early capabilities.

I asked ChatGPT to provide me with an explanation of what AI is. I asked it: 'Give me a 50-word summary as to what AI is, for the non-technical person to read.' It produced the following in the blink of an eye:

AI, or Artificial Intelligence, refers to computer systems designed to perform tasks that usually require human intelligence. These tasks include recognizing speech, making decisions, learning from data, and understanding natural language. AI is used in various applications like virtual assistants, recommendation systems, and autonomous vehicles to make our lives easier and more efficient.

However, ChatGPT is just one example of one dimension of artificial intelligence. Essentially the topic breaks down into three key areas – conversational AI, generative AI, and machine learning.

In simple terms, conversational AI is chatbots. It is the ability to converse with technology simulated to appear human, in order to find information. We have been using chatbots for a while, of course, with many retail organizations adopting them to help with e-commerce and customer interactions. This is technology that has been trained on libraries of questions and expected responses, and has then learnt from interactions to improve the responses provided over time (hence the intelligence).

Generative AI allows content to be created, such as text, images and audio. This has been the area of growth that maybe causes some of the discomfort around the technology, but also the area that opens it up significantly to create new boundaries.

Machine learning is the capability of technology to learn from the data it has been provided, to extrapolate data and draw new conclusions, and to perform tasks without explicit instruction. It's usually here that Skynet from the *Terminator* franchise is dropped into the conversation, and apocalyptic fears grow that machines will take over the world. Fortunately, we are not there yet (or at least, I think not).

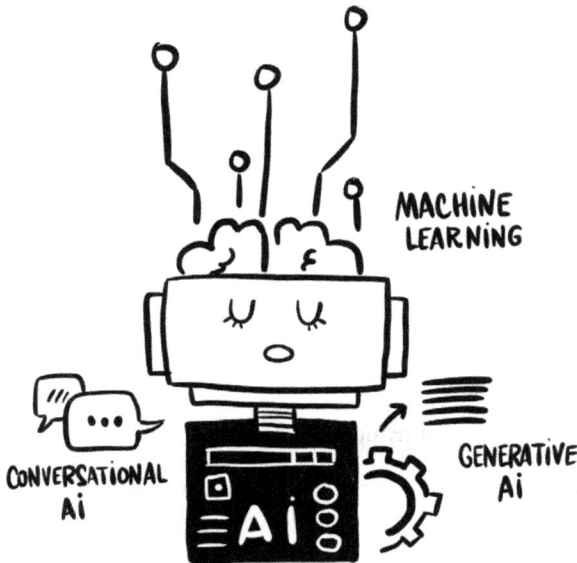

MACHINE LEARNING

CONVERSATIONAL Ai

AI

GENERATIVE Ai

There is usually a mixture of emotions when thinking about this technology, ranging from excitement and curiosity to fear and trepidation.

On the positive side:

- How can this technology help me do new and exciting things?
- How can this technology help me be more creative?
- How can I save time to spend on other things?

On the negative side:

- Will this technology take jobs away? And even closer to home, will it take my job away?
- Will it be misused by unsavoury characters or organizations?
- Can I trust what I am looking at any more?

How is AI disrupting (and you'd hope, improving) our personal lives and at work? As I said earlier, while this is an emerging technology, it's also been one we have been using for some time, but maybe not fully realized it. When we buy things online and the site provides recommendations – that is AI technology. When we watch streaming media and we provide rating feedback and receive recommendations as to what to watch next – that is AI technology. When we go online to order something and up pops the chatbot window, that is AI technology. The technology has already stealthily crept into our personal lives (some parts more annoyingly than others).

At work, we will see more and more areas that will adopt this technology going forwards. HR use cases today already include:

- creating job descriptions
- helping interviewers by creating questions to ask applicants
- helping employees with complex process or policy queries
- helping with complex processes such as retirement planning or organization redesign
- helping identify payroll fraud

If we look beyond HR and into industry sectors, the emerging power of AI is transforming how we interact with technology. For example:

- In medicine, AI has many applications including medical triage and diagnosis, complex symptom analysis, AI-powered drug discovery, and wearable devices and sensors.[4]
- In manufacturing, AI can help with predicting equipment failure before it occurs.[5]
- In retail, demand forecasting, inventory management, and customer sentiment analysis are just some of the ways that AI is transforming capability.[6]
- In education, AI already helps with educational games, intelligent tutoring systems, adaptive learning platforms and chatbots.[7]

We discussed AI with Andi Britt of IBM on *The Human Factor*. Andi is a Senior Partner with IBM. He leads their UKI Talent Transformation practice, providing talent management, digital HR, generative AI and organizational change management advisory services for clients. He is a regular speaker and presenter of IBM's research on the future of work, remote working, AI, HR re-invention, culture change, change management and employee engagement.

We asked him about the considerations that organizations are currently going through when considering AI:

> Most organizations realize that they now need to apply the accelerator on use of generative AI in their organization. But the problem is, they haven't yet built the brakes for their system and so they're slightly worried about pressing the accelerator without a brake or governance mechanism in place to ensure the responsible use of AI.

During the conversation we touched on many aspects of the technology, and there were many takeaways that are very useful. We talked about guardrails that should be in place. At IBM, their number one guardrail is that when they design, build or implement any AI tool, the purpose of the AI must be to augment, not replace, human intelligence.

In terms of the opportunity that AI presents to organizations today, Andi observed that it is an invasive technology. It will ultimately impact all industries in some shape or form. His view was that people who work with the tool will, over time, replace those who can't work with it.

Andi summarized his view of how the tool can be considered and used most effectively:

> If you can combine the things that humans are good at – empathy and creativity – and design with things that machines are good at, you actually come up with what is a brilliant human/machine partnership.

Considerations to help prepare projects for success

There are many examples of technology projects hitting the mainstream news negatively for:

- exceeding budget
- exceeding time

- scope creep
- misaligned requirements
- implementation challenges
- breakdown between organization and implementation partner
- non-achievement of business benefits

With the advent of Software as a Service, technology projects can run at high pace. With high pace comes the need for the organization to be as ready as they can when starting projects of this nature. The following considerations should be considered as early as possible in the project, ideally before the solution begins the design process:

- Is the target operating model for the future solution well understood? Is it clear who will perform what parts of the process, and how will the technology and the business be supported in its future to-be state?
- Is the decision-making process that will be used in the project clear, including if decisions need to be escalated due to disagreement?
- What is the approach to business process design that will be used by the project? Will it seek to adopt out-of-the-box capability as much as it can, or will it seek to adapt the technology to the organization processes?
- How and when will the change be managed and communicated to the business?

- What data will be needed for the project to succeed? Is the current data good enough quality? Can it be extracted? Does it have ownership? Who will approve changes if approval is needed? Is approval needed? How much data should be taken across into the new solution?

- What are the target business benefits? Have we baselined the current as-is state to allow for a comparison to the to-be state? What is the required timeframe to show a return on investment? Will benefits be cashable or non-cashable? Is there a robust case for change (see Chapter 2) to underpin the business benefits?

- Are the future business key performance indicators (KPIs) clear and known, so that the solution can be designed to provide them easily?

- Is the implementation partner a good fit for the culture of the organization? Do they have the right skills and services? Have they got good experience of doing this previously?

This is not an exhaustive list of readiness considerations. Nor will answering all these questions guarantee project success. However, they will serve as a robust foundation that will allow the project the opportunity to succeed.

In conclusion

The role of technology in execution is a huge topic. However, for sustainable success, it is important that technology is not positioned as the panacea for all issues. Whilst it can provide opportunities and is sometimes the driver for a change, only changing the technology is unlikely to achieve major benefits. We also need to consider adapting our behaviours and ways of working. We must see technology as *enabling* change to occur.

Tips and tricks

1 Data must be accurate, relevant, current, accessible and of some value.

2 Technologies should be tightly connected and, where possible, ownership of keeping them tightly connected passed back to the supplier.

3 Enterprise technology must be truly aligned with business goals and desired business outcomes, delivering value to the business and key stakeholders (not just the HR function).

4 Technology needs to be agile and flexible to ensure it stays relevant.

5 AI should augment human decision making, not replace it.

6 'By failing to prepare, you are preparing to fail' (anon.).

Notes

1 BMW Group (n.d.) CES 2023: World premiere of BMW i Vision Dee, www.bmwgroup.com/en/news/general/2023/i-vision-dee.html (archived at https://perma.cc/3XEZ-RJK4)

2 R Spurlock (2019) Petabyte – How Much Information Could it Actually Hold? Cobalt Iron, https://info.cobaltiron.com/blog/petabyte-how-much-information-could-it-actually-hold (archived at https://perma.cc/5SV4-3H5J)

3 *The Human Factor* podcast Ep 33: Turning Instinct into Insight | *The Human Factor Podcast* by SAP, https://podcast.opensap.info/the-human-factor/2023/07/31/the-human-factor-podcast-ep-33-turning-instinct-into-insight/ (archived at https://perma.cc/Y58D-NLD4)

4 K Basu, R Sinha, A Ong and T Basu (2020) Artificial Intelligence: How is it changing medical sciences and its future? *Indian Journal of Dermatology*, **65** (5), pp. 365–70, https://doi.org/10.4103/ijd.IJD_421_20 (archived at https://perma.cc/GJV2-SMDW)

5 C Dilmegani (2020) Top 12 AI applications in manufacturing in 2021, AIMultiple, https://research.aimultiple.com/manufacturing-ai/ (archived at https://perma.cc/P9C6-JV4L)

6 B Morgan (2019) The 20 Best Examples Of Using Artificial Intelligence For Retail Experiences, Forbes, www.forbes.com/sites/blakemorgan/2019/03/04/the-20-best-examples-of-using-artificial-intelligence-for-retail-experiences/ (archived at https://perma.cc/LT3U-SW7Q)

7 University of San Diego (2021) 43 Examples of Artificial Intelligence in Education, https://onlinedegrees.sandiego.edu/artificial-intelligence-education/ (archived at https://perma.cc/6U8M-9SLG)

8 *The Human Factor* podcast Ep 45: AI for HR | *The Human Factor Podcast* by SAP, https://podcast.opensap.info/the-human-factor/2024/06/18/the-human-factor-podcast-ep-45-ai-for-hr/ (archived at https://perma.cc/LR4G-DBFT)

SUSTAINABLE

Success

DOESN'T HAPPEN

by

ACCIDENT

The dynamics of teams 15

Introduction

So far in our journey into the human factors at play in our home and work lives, we have focused on the organizational view and the individual view. But there is typically another layer of complexity to add into the mix – that of being part of a team. We have all been part of a team at some point in our lives, either at home and/or at work. That could be a sports team, a pub quiz team, or even when you think about it part of a family team. At work, we might formally work in a team structure, or be part of a virtual or more dynamic team structure that changes depending on the project or deliverable being worked on.

But what does being part of a team mean in terms of the human factors at play in these structures? How is the team formed? Is it a healthy and successful balance of skills and personalities? Or are there some challenges that hold the team back? What happens when our own success conflicts with the team success? How do we reward success at a team level, and how does a team react to adversity? And let's not forget, we have a whole chapter looking at what success means, and how it can be relative, so how this works at a team level is that extra dynamic we want to talk about here.

There are many ways for teams to operate. There is no one-size-fits-all approach. There is more than one way to construct a team, and more than one way to operate within a team. However, there are common aspects that have led to success regardless of what the team is. This chapter will look to discuss these different aspects. Some topics may seem familiar – for example, the role of a leader is an area we have dedicated an entire chapter to – but we also need to put that leadership lens on how it works and the factors at play in team structures, which is what we will do here.

We will use some of the conversations from our podcast series (who would have guessed, eh?) and we will lean heavily on our favourite passion, the world of sport, but there are so many parallels to our home and work lives that we feel these anecdotes and observations can provide us insight into how team dynamics influences us in so many ways

As usual, we will finish with our thoughts on tips and tricks to consider back in our lives. For now, what is it we mean when we say the word 'team'?

What is a team?

We always like to start by setting a common baseline for the topic. We all know what a team is, right? It's a group of people that come together with a common goal or objective. We are all very familiar with teams in sport, and many of us will have our favourites which may have been chosen due to geography, style of play, stars within the team or even 'hereditary' teams passed on within our family and influenced by their favourites.

We will all likely be involved in, or at least connected to, a team or multiple teams at work. The HR team, the IT team or Finance, or Procurement. We might be a store team, or a route team. We might be in a team of like-minded roles like a driver team or a project manager team. Even those who work as an individual contributor could still be part of a team including themselves and their line manager or supervisor.

There are some groups that might initially also look like teams, but don't fit the definition sufficiently. Committees and councils for example look like teams, but don't necessarily share that common purpose. They might even be a group that are operating against each other and either consciously or subconsciously trying to sabotage each other.

In terms of size, there is no upper limit of the size of a team, and a lower limit of two members is the generally accepted minimum level. We will also see teams within teams. This book has been created by a team of people and organizations all working in harmony to create it. Inside that team are smaller teams – your illustrious co-authors are a team of two, supported by a team of peer reviewers, supported by our creative teams, and then even spanning multiple organizations such as SAP and Kogan Page, our publishers.

There are many, many books on bookshelves around the world that dissect team dynamics and what makes for a successful team. We will explore the surface of those discussions here. The goals, membership and dynamics of all these different types of teams is different, of course, but what is common are the underlying human factors that bind the teams together (or destroys them). It's those factors that we are going to look at in more detail in this chapter.

The power of a team

Let's first look at what being in a team can bring in terms of inspiration and purpose. In our definition, we outlined that it was a group of people who shared a common objective. Being part of a team can provide much more than a common objective, though. It can provide purpose, direction, clarity, support, complimentary skill sets, and even connect with us at an emotional level to provide inspiration, pride, wellbeing and many others.

Now, let's not just have rose-tinted spectacles on. A team can also do none of those things, or even worse, the opposite of those things. Some teams can be incredibly toxic and damaging, but for now, let's stay with the positives.

In Chapter 8 on the relativity of success, we went to the world of Hollywood and explored the story behind the Jamaican bob sleigh team. Let's explore another recent film and explore how the team evolved to reach success (putting to one side the emotional heartstrings that the films are designed to tug on).

The American Samoa football team was generally regarded as one of the worst football teams on the international stage. During the qualification competition for the 2002 World Cup, they were beaten by Australia, setting a record for the worst margin of victory with the 31-0 result. In 2011, they were the joint lowest ranked team in the FIFA world rankings, which ranks all member association teams as a means of comparison. Currently that list of rankings contains 211 teams. The documentary film *Next Goal Wins*, released in 2014, follows their journey to improve the team against the backdrop of the qualifying campaign for the 2014 World Cup. The story revolves around the key decision to hire a new coach for the team, Thomas Rongen. Rongen was an experienced player and coach when he accepted the coaching position with American Samoa.

The film explores how Rongen approached the task of improving the team, including recalling some players from overseas that had more experience and skill, clarifying and communicating the purpose of the team, and improving the inter-team dynamics in areas such as supporting each other and aligning values.

The outcome was ultimately that the team failed to qualify, but in relative terms (see Chapter 8 for a further exploration on the relativity of success), the team succeeded in improving. They recorded back-to-back wins against Tonga and Cook Islands in 2015 and set their highest world ranking position of 164th.

The story is inspirational and emotional (thank you, Hollywood, for playing with our heart strings), but also is informative on the human factors at play in the team dynamic. The team itself had only a limited pool of members to choose from. Unlike domestic football, which can use players from any country, the international teams have strict limitations on who can and can't represent their country. With this limitation, therefore, Rongen had to use other techniques to drive that improvement such as:

- widening the skills pool as wide as possible (i.e. recalling players from overseas and appealing to their national pride) – in our HR language, maximizing his ability to recruit the best he could
- clarifying and reinforcing the common purpose of the team, including focusing on short-term improvement goals rather than long-term ambitions
- creating a support mechanism within the team to improve relationships and dynamics at a personal level

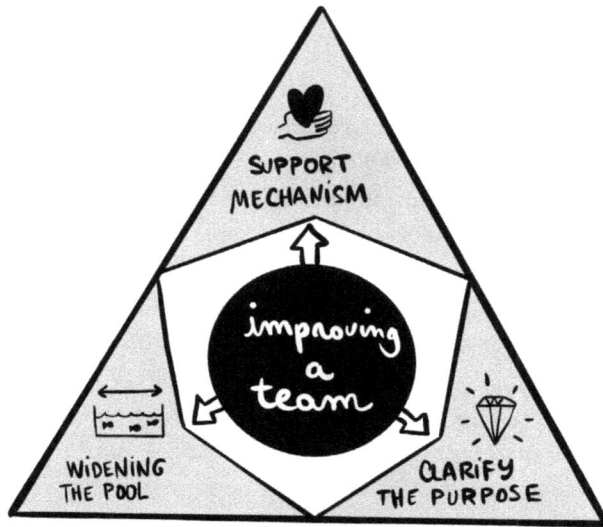

The team improved because of all these approaches and became more powerful as a team than as a collection of individuals when they first hired their new coach. The documentary received universal praise from audiences and critics for the story it told, and in 2024 still has a 100 per cent approval rating on the review aggregator site Rotten Tomatoes. As such, it was also made into a Hollywood film in 2023 starring Michael Fassbender as Thomas Rongen.

Now we have finished our popcorn, we can move on from the world of film and explore some of these factors in more detail, starting with team composition.

Team composition

As we said earlier, we aren't going to go into a thesis of a perfect team, but there is no doubt that composition does affect the team dynamic. For that additional reading, the study 'Enhancing the Effectiveness of Team Science' published by the National Library of Medicine, is an excellent body of work studying teams from several dimensions, including a chapter on team composition and assembly.[1]

At work or at home, typically our teams are comprised of people with complimentary skill sets. There may be overlaps in some skill areas, but it's unlikely that there will be many cases of exact skill matches. Sports teams have different players suited to the style of the team – defenders, attackers, goalkeepers, scrum halves, bowlers, batters and so on. In work, our teams will have technical and softer skills in the team members depending on the reason for the team formation and team objective.

A perfectly composed team for one objective may not be so perfect for another objective. Sometimes diversity of skills is an advantage, and sometimes it dilutes the skill depth too much to be effective. However, teams go beyond just skills. The team members also have traits such as introvert/extrovert, risk averse/seeking, individualistic/team orientated, and so on. Another significant dynamic is the role of each team member within the team – leader, challenger, doer, thinker, supporter, etc (and noting that there are several other schools of thought on team roles, for example as defined by Belbin).[2]

It is the combination of all these factors that contribute to the overall success or failure of a team (or, of course, any of the levels between these two outcomes). So what can we say about team composition if we are not going to go into detail on all these factors? It's that team composition is very important and needs sufficient attention whenever forming a team or analysing the performance of an existing team. We must remain cognizant of how these factors can affect team outcomes as well as any individual contributions to the team outcome.

But there are so many other factors that we must also consider with respect to teams, beyond just its members who form it. Let's drill down into one of the factors of team composition, that of cultural impact.

The importance of culture for a team

In our conversation with Professor Damian Hughes on *The Human Factor*, we talked about cultural architects and assassins.[3] Professor Damian Hughes is an international speaker and bestselling author who combines his practical and academic background within sport, organizational development and change psychology to help organizations and teams to create a high performing culture. He was appointed as a Professor of Organizational Psychology and Change for Manchester Metropolitan University in September 2010. He is also the co-host of *The High Performance Podcast*, exploring the psychology behind sustained high performance.

CULTURAL
ARCHITECT

CULTURAL
ASSASSIN

Damian shared with us how culture can be influenced by many different types of character. We discussed two in particular – cultural architects and cultural assassins. In the most basic definition, a cultural architect is someone who supports and respects the team and works to influence positive outcomes. A cultural assassin is typically the opposite of that, operating in a negative manner and likely projecting negativity to other team members.

In our conversation we talked about how these different types can manifest themselves in the culture of the team. We delved into how high performers typically bring an intensity to the team. Sometimes this intensity can be uplifting and focused, raising the performance of others in the team. However, sometimes it can be overwhelming, intimidating and destructive to the team. It can create that climate or culture of fear within the team dynamic.

> Intensity can either light the candles of everybody else in the organization, or they can overwhelm us.

Sometimes, a cultural assassin may not know they are one. We discussed how, if given the right feedback and that feedback being received and acted upon, they can become architects by understanding the power they wield within the team dynamic and utilizing it in a different way.

However, sometimes, the assassins must leave the team for the team to prosper. We talked about Michael Jordan and the Chicago Bulls. During the 1990s, the Chicago Bulls were the most successful basketball team in America. They won six championships in a period of eight years and were widely regarded as one of the greatest teams in NBA history. Michael Jordan was the most famous of these players and dominated the media. Damian observed though that initially Jordan's team behaviour was more of a cultural assassin.

Phil Jackson, the manager of the team, recognized this and adapted the team dynamics so that the whole team could step up in those critical match moments rather than it only being Jordan. The team evolved from being a one-man dominated team to an all-round powerful team, using Jordan to empower others to perform and raise all their standards. Thus, Jordan went from being an assassin to an architect.

This same dynamic can occur in the workplace, and requires a similar intervention to ensure that the culture of the team is positive and healthy, rather than toxic.

But what happens when the team goals differ from those of the individuals within the team, or the organizational goals?

Team goals vs individual or organizational goals

Most of the time, the goals for a team will align to the goals of the individual and/or the goals of the organization. Let's take our sporting analogy again. A sports team will have goals to win matches, tournaments and trophies. As individuals within that team, we will also have those common goals, and as an organization, if the team is performing well, the organization should be succeeding. Right? Maybe not. How many times have we used the phrase 'take one for the team' – that is, sacrifice your own progression for the wider benefit of the team? It comes up quite often when we think about it.

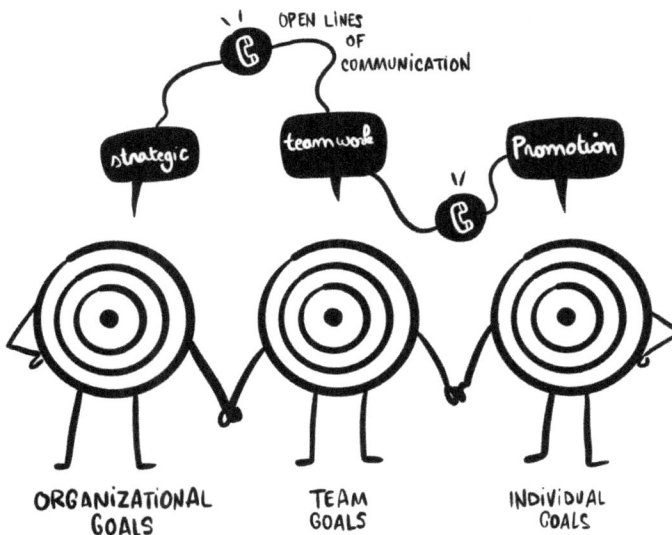

This conflict can cause tension between different goal structures. As an individual, I may have goals around promotion and advancement, but the team I am in may value teamwork as a priority goal. Recognizing those points of tension can help reduce the conflict, but potentially not eliminate it. Not all situations will have a win-win outcome unfortunately.

The same can be said for organizational goals vs team goals. The requirement to ensure alignment between different teams to drive towards the organizational goals is sometimes missed, and then the resulting cross-team tensions can ultimately cause harm to the organization.

One of the key ways to alleviate the potential for conflict is to have open lines of communication both within the team structure as members, but also outside the team in terms of articulating what the team purpose and goals are. Communication is key for many other aspects of the team dynamic, and we will now look at that topic in a little more detail.

Communication within a team structure

We had a very insightful conversation in 2022 with Paul Gustard.[4] Following a very successful rugby union playing career with Leicester Tigers, London Irish, Saracens and Barbarians, Paul has gone on to further success as a coach for Saracens, England, Harlequins, Benetton and, in 2024, at Stade Français.

We wanted to dig deeper into how teams operated, and what could affect the dynamics and success of a team. It was a wonderful insight into elite sport and how teams are managed, with so many parallels to the world of work and business. We discussed many different aspects of this topic, including:

- the key principles behind the formation and shaping of a team
- the major ingredients of a successful team
- how a team grows and matures
- how to introduce autonomy into a team with respect to decision making
- the importance of feedback to the success of a team

Throughout the episode, one of the common threads was on the importance of communication. There were many quotes I could lift from the discussion, but a few really stood out in terms of summarizing well the critical nature of communicating and communicating well to ensure success.

COMMUNICATING WELL
TO ENSURE SUCCESS

> The most important thing for the group is to have absolute clarity about what you're trying to achieve.

We have covered this in several chapters of this book – i.e. clarity of the intended outcome. Without this clarity, the team lacks direction and the mechanism of evaluating success. How can a team know if it has ultimately succeeded if the outcome isn't well defined and communicated? We have observed in sports, in business, in life that having clarity of outcome can drive success, or at least the relativity of success (see Chapter 8 for more on this topic). But Paul also warned: 'We can't leave it to the outcome to decide the feedback.'

Success is not always possible, but that shouldn't inhibit trying new ideas and taking risks, provided those risks are calculated ones.

In Rugby Union, the team on the field comprises 15 players. But looking at a club or international organization, the team are supported by many others behind the scenes, and thus are comprised of multiple teams all (hopefully, see the previous section on goals) aligned to a common set of goals. But Paul broke his communication style into two distinct areas:

1 the number of messages being communicated

2 the number of people to communicate to

He followed a 'power of three' and 'power of four' style. No more than three key messages, and trying to limit his communications to no more than four people at a time. Clearly this isn't for all communications, but he found it especially effective for these mini communications to really ensure high quality outcomes. Paul does also offer tips to communicating to bigger audiences too, and especially to try and create a bond between the orator and the listener.

Finally, he shared that the team needs also to be able to discuss and ideate:

> It's important that the group or the team feels that you're able to talk and share ideas freely.

The important part of this quote from my perspective wasn't that the leader felt that the team could talk and share freely (how many times does a leader say 'my door is always open'?), but that the group itself felt that way. Reaching that level of culture and team dynamic will truly open that team for a more likely successful outcome.

But what happens if the team is already successful? Easy right? Just keep doing what they are doing. But that doesn't account for those human factors, and just assuming that a successful team will continue to be successful is a recipe for failure. How do we build sustainable success into the team dynamic?

Success and sustainability for a team

It's one thing to create a successful team (not to diminish the difficulties of doing that, of course), but it's another to sustain that success on an ongoing basis. It's not uncommon to see a dip in performance after a team high, whether that be a drop in standards, appetite or a change in team composition. What we were especially interested in, during our conversations, were the ingredients to sustaining that success and how to retain it time after time. What was very clear was that sustainable success didn't happen by accident. It required a deliberate strategy and focus to ensure that all the elements needed for success were given the necessary levels of attention and that bad habits didn't start creeping in.

In this chapter we are using a lot of sporting stories and analogies, but as observed in the last section, they are relevant for any team, whether for play or for work. The conversations we have had have validated that many times, and probably why we see so many successful sports stars hit the corporate speaking circuit after their playing careers are over.

But before we get to sustainable success, our team must achieve success. As noted previously, we discuss success in Chapter 8 in some depth, but success is often linked with the phrase 'high performance'. What does that phrase mean, though?

I'm reminded of a story told to us by Danny Donachie (who is introduced more fully in Chapter 5 on the predisposition of a human being). Danny was the medical director at Everton Football Club, and he observed that as he entered the gym at the club ground, there was a sign that read 'High-performance behaviours only'. When he reflected on it, he didn't understand what that meant and struggled to find anyone there who did understand it.

How often do we see these motivational signs on walls of offices and meeting rooms that, upon reflection, lack substance or specificity? Now, I'm not now going to go into depth on what high performance is (that is done very well in other books on the market), but simply want to raise the point that success and high performance do not come about due to platitudes on walls. And neither does sustained success.

When we do have the luxury of observing a consistently successful team, there are common traits that we are likely to observe:

- a clearly defined purpose for the team with a clearly articulated and defined outcome to be achieved
- an adherence to maintaining standards – i.e. going beyond a 'that'll do' level
- a team structure that is made up of individuals that reinforce each other and have complimentary skill sets
- a leader, or leaders, within the team that can maintain the team appetite for more success
- a team that celebrates success but doesn't over-indulge in it and is ready to reset when needed with clarity and focus
- team members that take accountability for their own performance and contribute to other team members' success

In our conversations with Maggie Alphonsi we talked about some of these ingredients, and her first observation was to not expect harmony in a team environment. One of those human factors that can emerge is ego, and that can cause tension within a team. But rather than fear conflict and tension, it can be harnessed for good and lead to team members improving each other as a result. Knowing how far you can push each team member in a positive way to give more, without tipping over into that point where it becomes counter-productive.

Her other observation was that sustainability itself implies 'over a period of time', and in that period of time it may not be possible for the team membership to stay the same. Some people leave for other things, and new people join. The people that join need to be brought into that team harmony in a non-disruptive way, so that success itself is not disrupted. So, what can we learn from others about how to do that?

Joining an existing team

Joining a successful team can be very intimidating, especially to the more junior joiners. We chatted with Paul McVeigh in one of our episodes. Paul was a Premier League footballer, who came over from Northern Ireland to join Tottenham Hotspur as his first club in 1996. He talked to us about the first time he walked into the senior dressing room and saw Jürgen Klinsmann and Teddy Sheringham, and was somewhat overwhelmed by the experience. Those feelings of 'Am I good enough to be here?' surfaced for him, and he took time to build his confidence to a point of believing in his right to be a part of that team.

But there are ways for teams to help new people join them. The All Blacks, one of the most famous and successful rugby union international teams, had to actively consider how new players would join the squad.

What they did was create a small black book that would be given to all new team members. The book, beautifully crafted in fine leather is a visual whakapapa. 'Whakapapa' is a fundamental principle in Māori culture, and reciting your whakapapa proclaims your Māori identity and links yourself to land and tribal groupings.[5] The intent of the black book is to remind those joining of the heritage, principles, values, standards, code of honour, ethos, heroes and character of the team. It intentionally leaves blank pages, waiting for the recipient to fill in their own journey.

What this is doing therefore is showing the new team member what being a player for the All Blacks means, what is expected from them, and inspires them to bring their best self, but also to impart their own personal footprint on that legacy. What better way to be welcomed to an already successful team? But also for us as authors, a great way to share some insights in how to integrate new people into an existing team.

Going back to Paul Gustard, we also asked him about recruitment, and his approach. His mantra was person before player, and during the recruitment cycle he would very much focus on getting to know the person rather than focusing on the skills they brought to the team:

> Understanding the person that you're about to recruit, their family, their drivers, what makes them tick, what does a good day look like for them when they're at their best? What does a bad day look like for them when they're in the shadow? What do they feel inspired by? What do they enjoy doing? You suddenly see people respond differently in the conversation.

It's not always possible to explore all these elements when introducing a new person to the team, especially in a work context, but the introduction of the player doesn't stop when they have been recruited. They also need to be inducted and observed in the early part of their role within the team. Introducing them to the ways of working, the culture, the expectations of them, and all those other factors that will turn them from a new team member to a successful part of a successful team.

We can't always be face to face with our team, though, especially in a work context. So how do we continue to maintain things like culture if our team is more virtual, remote, or dynamic?

Virtual or dynamic teams

The Covid-19 lockdowns meant that we all had to operate in a different way. The enforced separation meant that we had to think and act differently in how we worked, and this was also true of how we operated as teams. Suddenly we were all operating with a lot more independence and teamwork required significantly more effort. Most of us were forced on to Zoom or Microsoft Teams for endless meetings. If anything, teamwork became a chore to some. Endlessly staring at a monitor image of our team rather than working physically alongside each other.

To some, though, the pandemic brought teams more together. My own team was already remote, operating in different parts of the world, and we would rarely meet face to face. Personally, I worked more closely with my team during lockdown than before, and I felt it actually made our team stronger, but I suspect this is more likely the exception. This was because we made more conscious effort to meet, including socially, and to be aware of each other in terms of working style, personal home life considerations, and awareness of actively trying to be more co-operative with each other.

Before that point, it would have been easy for an outside observer to deduce we were more a collection of individuals than a team. Post-lockdown, we now not only perform better, but we also have a more underlying culture within the team of co-operation and support.

Teams that are virtual, remote or dynamically created and then disbanded must have even more emphasis on the areas we have been talking so far – purpose, clarity of outcome, good communication and retention of culture. This is because we lose out on some of the information that we would typically impart in face-to-face interactions. The tell-tale body language signs, the cultural considerations, and the extra strain on communication styles.

However, does our leadership style change when we go from line management to team management? How many leaders should a team even have? We need to shine that spotlight now onto team leadership to round out our discussion on team dynamics.

Team leadership

'Too many cooks spoil the broth.' We are all aware of the saying. And the traditional belief was that teams needed a single identifiable leader to function at its best. In terms of a hierarchical structure, I think that's very valid. Knowing who is accountable for making decisions needs to be clear to all, and that leader (or leadership structure) needs the respect of the hierarchy to be effective.

However, does that mean that there can be only one leader? No, it doesn't. Having a team of leaders can be extremely effective, especially if the nominated leader is struggling or absent. It means that others can step in and take that accountability and maintain the function of the team. Maggie Alphonsi talked with us about this being one of the big differences she observed between the England team that came runner up in the 2010 Women's Rugby Union World Cup, and the England team that went on to win it in 2014. The England team first had to develop its basics better (see our chapter on the basics), and they observed other teams, looking for good practices to adopt. As a result, they improved their fitness, strength, conditioning and ball handling skills. But that was still not enough to land the cup in 2010.

In the period of reflection and change between 2010 and 2014, they focused a lot on the more human factors of team dynamics. That increased awareness of self. They did a lot of work on personality types within the team and creating stronger emotional connections to each other.

The other major change was from a team with a single leader to becoming a team of leaders. This allowed them to be more dynamic on the field, in the heat of the moment, by utilizing that combined leadership rather than all the pressure being on one person to lead. There became that accountability within the team for all its members to help each other, to raise their collective standards rather than be a collective of individuals. During the conversation, Maggie observed: 'You have a CEO, or sometimes I've seen co-CEOs, but it's important that others understand that they are also leaders and contribute to the overall strategy.'

I think the other area of importance, particularly from the leadership perspective, is to recognize the whole contribution to success. We recounted the NASA story about the janitor and that the janitor recognized his part in the team. Whether the story is true or not, it is a lovely way to think that is how teams work, but that's not always the case. Danny Donachie told us a story about Roy Keane from Manchester United. At the club, the players would have to sign footballs regularly, and one week there were a couple of players that hadn't signed the footballs. Roy gathered all the players together in a meeting and told them it wasn't good enough. 'The lady who gets these balls signed is just as important as any of you is in this organization and you need to treat her with the respect that she deserves.'

It's a wonderful example of a leader in the team ensuring that the whole team gets recognition and inclusion, rather than just those who perceived themselves as important. We heard similar anecdotes from a team member inside Manchester City about how Pep Guardiola recognizes the whole team, including backroom staff, in the club's success, and by doing that cultivates inspiration and loyalty. That it's not all about the star players, but that everyone plays their part in the success achieved.

We've covered a lot of ground in this chapter already, but we need to also go back to those human factors again for one important last point. That teams are made of humans, and we need to be mindful of that and 'see the person'.

See the person

Our final section here is to remind ourselves that at work, or in our sports team, or pub quiz team, we are all people. We are all different. If we treat everyone the same, we are missing the point that we are all different, and we react to things differently. Sometimes, when standards might have slipped a bit, a leader might raise their voice when giving feedback. One person might respond positively. But another might take that approach poorly and have a negative reaction.

We must ensure that people are seen and treated in ways to get the best out of them. Paul Gustard summarized it well when he observed:

See the person, not the player.

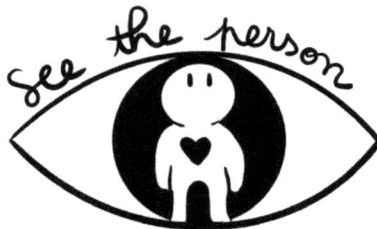

In conclusion

We set out at the beginning of this chapter looking to understand the additional human factors involved when we add a team structure into the mix. We have explored many different aspects of these team dynamics and yet we barely scratched the surface. I have used a number of sports stories and reflections to emphasize points being made, but in reality these could be stories from any walk of life, whether they be at home or at work. The same principles, observations, and pitfalls still apply regardless of which context we are looking at how teams operate.

Let's reflect and conclude with another Hollywood film example. This film followed the story of the Homeless World Cup, which was initiated in 2003 and runs each year. In 2024, Netflix released *The Beautiful Game*, which follows the England squad as they enter the tournament. Not a documentary this time, so a pinch of salt is needed when drawing conclusions from the film, but here was a story that explored what being in a team really meant and how it gave its members more individual power as a result.

As the competition name implies, it follows the world of football (soccer if you are reading this on the other side of the Atlantic Ocean). Its teams are comprised of players that have been homeless between the previous and current tournament years.

The film explores what binds the team together, nominally the shared goal of winning the competition, but throughout the film the real purpose is to grow as individuals and support each other through their difficulties outside the competition. It focuses on the underlying purpose of creating relationships, supporting each other and working towards a restoration of self-esteem through team success. Again well received by critics and audiences, it taps into our emotions because it focuses on the human factors that underpin team dynamics, and highlights some of the factors that we explore in this chapter.

Tips and tricks

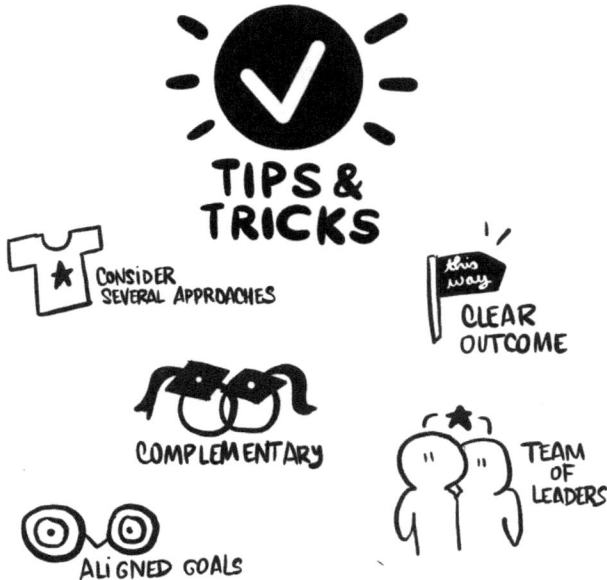

1 Teams are made up of individuals. One approach not does not necessarily suit all, and we should always consider how to get the best out of everyone.

2 Look to build complementary skills and personalities into the team structure rather than too many similar types.

3 Establish a clear, definable outcome for success for the team to work towards.

4 A team of leaders can adapt more readily in the moment to adversity or unforeseen changes.

5 Ensure goals are aligned at an individual, team and organizational level.

Notes

1 *Enhancing the Effectiveness of Team Science* (2015) Eds. N J Cooke and M L Hilton, Committee on the Science of Team Science; Board on Behavioral, Cognitive, and Sensory Sciences; Division of Behavioral and Social Sciences and Education; National Research Council, Washington (DC): National Academies Press (US)

2 Belbin (1981) The Nine Belbin Team Roles, www.belbin.com/about/belbin-team-roles (archived at https://perma.cc/V8DH-E9KA)

3 *The Human Factor* podcast Ep 8: Building a High-Performance Culture and Sustaining It | *The Human Factor Podcast* by SAP, https://podcast.opensap.info/the-human-factor/2021/10/18/the-human-factor-ep-8-building-a-high-performance-culture-and-sustaining-it/ (archived at https://perma.cc/WNN9-E733)

4 *The Human Factor* podcast Ep 20: The Dynamics of Teams with Paul Gustard | *The Human Factor Podcast* by SAP, https://podcast.opensap.info/the-human-factor/2022/08/18/the-human-factor-ep-20-the-dynamics-of-teams-with-paul-gustard (archived at https://perma.cc/8SBH-G4A7)

5 New Zealand Ministry for Culture and Heritage Te Manatu Taonga (2019) What is whakapapa? Te Ara, https://teara.govt.nz/en/whakapapa-genealogy/page-1 (archived at https://perma.cc/BH64-JMKS)

Our reflections 16

Taking the time to write a book of this nature, coupled with the amazing conversations on the podcast, is an extremely rewarding experience. It speaks to our natural curiosity and desire to learn. It has opened our eyes to things we haven't seen, heard or experienced and this is one of the biggest takeaways. We don't believe that mastery can be attained in any of the topics covered, because the context in which we live and work doesn't stand still.

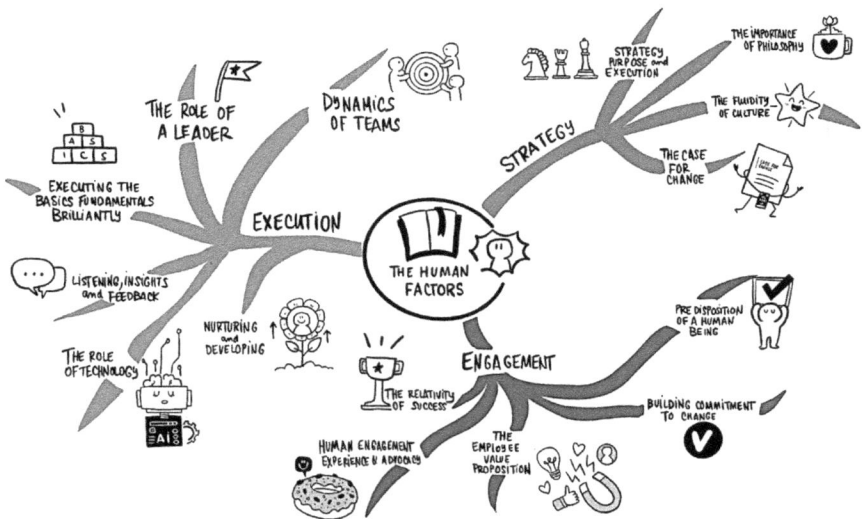

The human factors are a connected web of interdependencies. So many moving parts that influence the success of organizations and the growth and prosperity of individuals. As we were writing the chapters, it became so evident the overlap and dependencies that existed.

Following the spirit of the book and the podcast, we wanted to share what our current top five takeaways are; the things that really resonate with us and the things that we keep coming back to.

1 *The basics matter.*

o They really do. They feed into our motivation as human beings. They are core to our growth, development and progression; a key factor in whether we are committed or compliant and whether we go home most days and say, 'I had a good day.'

2 *Culture is intangible but permeates everything we do.*

- o It really does. We can't see it or touch it, but we feel it every day. Culture can either be a force for progression and prosperity or an environment that feels less supportive and at times toxic. In our view it can make or break the overarching experience for all employees.

3 *The role of the leader has never been more important.*

- o The champion of change, the facilitator of growth and development, and the executor of the basics every day. The leader today arguably influences the overall experience of an employee more than anyone.

4 *Success is relative.*

- o Everything in life is relative to the person and the situation they are in, and success is the same. Success means different things to different people and should never be assumed but we strongly believe irrespective of the activity that being able to track if the needle is being moved in the right direction is always imperative.

5 *The human experience lies at the heart of everything we do and don't do.*

- o Experience is an emotion. It influences how we feel every day. It is truly an amalgamation of many moving parts and dependencies. It requires great thought, amazing design and consistent execution.

Writing this book has been a wonderful experience for us both. Stripping away our assumptions or any pre-conceived notions has been a true learning experience. At the very outset we challenged ourselves to provide practical advice and takeaways from each of our chapters and to ground the topics in a pragmatic and relatable way. We wanted to ensure you as the reader could take away some tangible tips, tricks and advice that you can use back in your workplace or even for your own personal development.

We are blissfully aware that we have not covered all the 'human factors' as there are many more to cover, but these are the ones we believe very much form the foundation for individuals and organizations to flourish on a day-to-day basis.

We often described our quest on the podcast as 'peeling back the layer of an onion' and that quest will continue. There is so much more to uncover, discuss and debate in this forever changing world in which we live and work. As we say, the only constant in life is change.

INDEX

Page numbers in *italic* denote information contained within a figure or table; those in roman numerals denote information within the foreword.

acceptance (change) 108, *109*, 110
accountability 51, 54, 187–88, 199, 201, 218, 297, 301
achievement 93, 94, 191, 192, 193
'act' principle 116
Adams, Helen 36
Adler Mannheim 229
adversaries 41, 42
advocacy 41–42, 63, 128, 137–38, 167, 177–79, 180, 227
  see also champions
affiliation (relationship building) 93, 94, 131, 134, 137, 176, 191–92, 199, 289
  see also connections
affiliative leadership *195*
Affleck, Ben 151
age, and perception of success 158–60
agility 81, 129–30, 274
AI (artificial intelligence) xvii, 12, 172–73, 266, 275–79
alcohol 95
Alexa 173, 269
All Blacks 298–99
Alphonsi, Maggie 81, 152–54, 187, 217, 218, 297, 301
Amaechi, John 119, 200, 235–36
ambiguity 27
America Samoa 289–90
anchoring 49, 54–58, 251
anger *109*, 110
Any Given Sunday 118
Apple xvii, 76
appreciation 131, 233
APS Intelligence 200, 235
Argo 151
argument and justification 33–34
art sector 114
articulation 41, 79, 82, 112–13, 114, 126
artificial intelligence (AI) xvii, 12, 172–73, 266, 275–79
assumptions 115, 116, 117, 181
authentic self 96
authenticity 32, 79, 80, 84, 96
authoritative leadership *194*
automation 11, 59, 214

Averbook, Jason 214–15
aware self (self-awareness) 95–98, 102, 152, 154–56, 203, 301

balanced scorecard 136
Barcelona Football Club 75
bargaining *109*, 110
baselines 29, 43, 54, 150, 160, 201, 281, 287
'basics' 208–11, 306–07
  technology 272–74
  as a way of life 211–19
  see also clarity; connections; employee satisfaction; feedback; goal-setting; process management
Bayern Munich Football Club 75, 267
Beautiful Game, The 303
behaviour (leadership) 193–96
'being best' (competition) 32, 76
Belbin team types 291
belief 202
beliefs 73, 133
belonging 82–83, 133, 202
Bentley Motors 167, 169–70
Bergin, Elaine 29, 113–14
'Big Picture, The' 55
black book (All Blacks) 298–99
BMW 264
board of directors (C-suite) 20, 40, 51, 110–11, 112, 253
  see also CEOs
Bolt, Usain 147
Boots 36
Boston Consulting Group 130–31
Bracey, Glenn 96–97, 154–56
Brailsford, Sir David 218
brand loyalty 16, 63, 76, 79, 80, 128, 167, 177, 302
Brin, Sergey 76–77
British Cycling 218
Britt, Andy 278–79
BT Group 137, 178–79, 227
Bundesliga 267
business partnering 12

C-suite (board of directors) 20, 40, 51,
    110–11, 112, 253
    see also CEOs
Camerer, Colin 59–60
Carrington Training Ground 218
Catrin *see* Jones, Catrin
Centre of Excellence teams 12
CEOs 51, 52, 55, 80, 115, 254, 301
champions 52, 120, 137–38, 227, 307
    see also advocacy
change 20, 30–31, 106–08, 202
    case for 26–43, 112–13, 281
    consequence of 32–33
    and organizational dynamics 113–14
    resistance to 39–42, 108–12, 118–19
change curve model 108–12
change drivers 28–30
change evangelists 42
change fatigue 118–19
change management 20, 26–44,
    114–17, 280
    programme failures 107
change names 31
change plans 117, 120
chatbots 276, 278
ChatGPT 275–76
Chicago Bulls 292–93
Cirque du Soleil 82, 172, 254
clarity 99, *197*, 201, 202, 289, 295
clarity sessions 99
climate (organizational) 63–65, 196–98
cloud-based technology 169, 172, 235
    see also SAP SuccessFactors
coaching 97, *195*, 203
coercive leadership *194*, 195
collaboration 174, 188, 250, 271
collaboration tools 172
commitment 61, 128, 139, *197*, 246, 247
    see also employee engagement
committees 287
communication 14, 22, 40–41, 54–60,
    67, 75
    change 111, 280
    EVPs 139
    internal 137
    within teams 294–96
    see also articulation; empathy; listening
compassion 199, 200, 202
competence 209
competition ('being best') 32, 76
complacency 66, 115, 215
compliance 14, *111*, 112, 116, 136, 174,
    191, *194*
compliance function 52, 57, 107
conflict (tension) 48, 294, 297

connections 215, 301
    see also affiliation (relationship building)
connective technology 269–72
conscious preferences 90
consistency 40–41, 60, 100, 177–78, 199,
    202, 270, 271, 273
consulting sector 145–46
Consumer Electronics Show 264
consumer perception 62, 126, 129
consumerization 226–27
conversational AI (chatbots) 276, 278
Cool Runnings 147–48
councils 287
Covid-19 pandemic 16, 253, 299–300
Cruyff, Johan 75
Crwst 100–01, 127–28, 177–78
cultural architects 292, 293
cultural assassins 292–93
culture 48–54, 65–67, 99, 217–18, 307
    communication 54–61
    high performance 150–51, 291–93,
        296–97
    negative 157, 174
    perception of 61–63
    positive 156–57
    and success 156–58
    and team building 291–93
    toxic 64, 156, 157, 174, 288, 293
    versus climate 63–65
Cumberbatch, Benedict 275
curiosity 157, 200
cynicism 59

Damon, Matt 151
data quality 265–68, 281
data storage 266
data strategy documents 266
data visibility 272
decision making processes 27, 280, 294
'Dee, The' 264
definitions consistency 273
DEI&B 51
    see also belonging
deliverables with a business and customer
    return 175, 176
democratic leadership *194*
denial *109*, 110
'desired' culture 51
development 100, 199, 233,
    244–58, 273
    see also learning
digital capabilities 175, 214–15
discontent 26–27, 82, 107
discovery 29–30
discretionary effort 61

disengagement 57, 135, 174, 180, 189,
213, 245
see also employee engagement
doables without efficiency 175
Donachie, Danny 96, 97, 297, 301–02
dress codes 80
drills (practice) 210, 215, 216
dynamic teams 299–300

education sector 278
Edwards, Michael (Eddie 'The Eagle') 148
emerging talent reviews 250
emerging technology 274–79
emotional intelligence 187
empathy 33, 76, 94, 253, 279
employee development 100, 199, 233,
244–58, 273
see also talent development; training
employee engagement 99, 110, 137, 166–67,
174–81
see also commitment; disengagement
employee satisfaction 212–13
employee surveys 82–83, 179–80
employee value propositions xv, 11, 12, 54,
79, 123–39
employees 52
expectations of 65, 131, 132, 188
mobility 131, 256
retention 128, 233–34
turnover 18, 57, 136
see also advocacy; champions; employee
development; employee engagement;
employee satisfaction; employee
surveys; employee value propositions;
loyalty; succession planning
employer branding 129
empowerment 10, 99–100, 101, 196,
202, 273
England Rugby 81, 153
'Enhancing the Effectiveness of Team
Science' (National Library of
Medicine) 290
Enigma 275
Equatorial Guinea 148–49
Eric the Eel 148–49
Erich Gutenberg Award 130
Esau, Jayne 136
Esau, Robert 201
ethics 52
Everton Football Club 297
excellence 94, 100–01
existing teams (joining) 298–99
experiential flow 230, 231, 238
experimentation 156–57
exposure management 251–53, 255–56

expression 156–57

failure *144*, 145, 146, 157, 161, 176
Fassbender, Michael 290
feedback xv, 18, 56–57, 65, 117, 181, 213,
225, 234–39, 302
feedback framework 236–38
feedback loops 20, 230, 255
feelings 116
see also employee engagement;
organizational climate
Ferguson, Sir Alex 246, 252
finance teams 35
First Half, The (Logan) 159
Fishbowl 130
Five Guys 126–27, 132
five stages of death (grief) 108–12
flexibility 132, *197*
flexible working 132
see also hybrid working; remote working
football industry 64–65, 73–75, 96–97, 118,
218, 246–47, 252–53, 289, 297–98,
301–02
Ford, Henry 245
Fosway Group 228–29
four-circle model 189–90
Fresh Perspective Resourcing 124–25

Gagnon, Marie-Noëlle 82, 254
gains 107
generative AI 12, 276, 278
generative pretrained transformers
(GPTs) 275
Glassdoor 64, 130
goal-setting 56, 100, 117, 136, 145–46, 161,
293–94
see also SMART objectives
Goleman, Daniel 187, 189
golf basics 27, 28, 210, 211
Good Will Hunting 151
Google 16, 76–77, 79
Google Assistant 173, 269
governance 10, 13–14, 254, 266–67, 274
Goyder, Caroline 236–37
Great Place to Work List (*Times*) 55
Green, Harriet 8, 17–18, 79, 115, 116,
247, 256
Grylls, Bear 96
Guardiola, Pep 75, 79, 302
Gustard, Paul 217, 294–96, 299, 302

habit formation 59–60, 108, 110–11
happiness 99–100, 137, 174, 212–13
happiness index 212–13
'hard yards' 114, 118

Harrington, Jane 31–32
Harrods 100, 177
Härtel, Dr Sascha 229, 267–68
Hasso Plattner Founders' Award 157
Hawkins, Ann 36
HBR culture building model 52, 54, 56, 57, 65
Hieatt, David 15, 53, 77–78, 99
high performance culture 150–51, 291–93, 296–97
Hiut Denim 15, 53, 77–78, 79, 99
Homeless World Cup 303
hope 199, 202
HR (human resources functions) 12, 51, 56
HR AI applications 278
HR initiatives for HR's sake 175–76
Hughes, Professor Damian 291–93
human experience (user experience) 76, 164–74, 180, 181, 226–28, 270, 307
human predisposition 87–103
humility 203
hybrid working 132, 202

IBM 278–79
iceberg model 90–92
ideation 296
Imitation Game, The 275
imposter syndrome 97, 98, 155–56
in-the-moment feedback 181
incremental performance gains 218
individual goals 293–94
individual ownership 67, 99, 199, 238, 257
INEOS 218
influence 94–95
infrastructure 11–13
    see also process management; technology
insights 224–25, 228–34, 239, 248–49
Intel 263
intelligence gathering 231–34, 239, 247–49, 255
intensity 292
intent 95, 126, 198, 200, 203
internal communications 137

Jackson, Phil 293
Jobs, Steve 76
Johnson, Michael 149
Johnson, Nicola 31
Jones, Catrin 100–01, 127–28, 178
Jones, Celyn 114
Jones, Osian 100–01, 127–28, 178
Jordan, Michael 292–93
justification 33–34

Keane, Roy 218, 301–02

'keep-me-ups' 94
Kennedy, President Jack 16
key performance indicators (KPIs) 14, 136–37, 138, 247, 249, 281
key talent reviews 250
Kübler-Ross change curve model 108–12

labelling 237
Lankston, William 99–100, 137, 212–13
Lanning, Michael 126
leadership xv–vi, 19–20, 52, 81, 119, 136, 153, 184–203, 301–02, 307
    see also board of directors (C-suite)
leadership role 191–93
leadership styles 193–96, 200
Leapgen 214
learning xv, 57, 117, 136, 200
    see also development
legacy systems 10, 216, 266, 274
legislation 13, 107
Leyland, Emily 124–25
Leyland, Laura 124–25
likeability (leadership) 199
line managers 52, 99, 231, 255, 287
listening 65, 67, 117, 137, 224–34
    see also feedback
Logan, Gabby 159–160
long-term leadership 194–95, 196
low mood 109, 110
loyalty 16, 63, 76, 79, 80, 128, 167, 177, 302

machine learning xvii, 276
macro view 116
Mad as Birds 114
managers 52, 65, 99
    see also line managers; senior management team
Manchester City Football Club 75, 79, 302
Manchester United Academy 250
Manchester United Football Club 218, 246, 252, 301–02
manufacturing sector 36, 264, 278
Martin, Russell 74, 79, 82, 217, 253
McClelland, David 90, 91–95, 187, 189, 190, 191
McGuiness, Paul 246–47, 252
McVeigh, Paul 217, 298–99
meaningful work xv, 16–18, 133–34
measurement (metrics) 14, 117, 120, 148, 150–51, 219
    EVPs 135–38
    see also employee engagement; key performance indicators (KPIs)

medical sector 278
mediodorsal thalamus 27
'meet me where I am at' principle 172
mentors 82, 203, 249, 251, 254–56, 258
Michaels, Edward 126
micro view 116
Microsoft xvii
Microsoft Teams 172, 300
mid-life 158–60
mid-life crises 158
Mid Point with Gabby Logan, The 159
middle management 52
mindfulness 97
mini celebrations 58
mission statements 14–18, 22, 42, 78, 119
mobile workforce 131, 256
Moore, Gordon (Moore's Law) 263
motivation 87–103, 187
Moussambani, Eric 148–49
Murray, Henry 90, 92
muscle memory 216

NASA Space Team 16–17
nature versus nurture 89, 92
negative culture 157, 174
    see also toxic culture
net promoter scores 64, 138
neuroscience 27
Neville, Gary 218
Next Goal Wins 289, 290
Nike 16
non-conscious motives 91, 92–95
norms 93–95

onboarding 56, 132, 135, 270, 273
OpenAI 275
operant methods 90, 92
operating model 9, 10–14, 280
operational effectiveness 7
organizational change 20, 26–44,
        114–17, 280
    case for 26–43, 112–13, 281
    consequence of 32–33
    and organizational dynamics 113–14
    resistance to 39–42, 108–12, 118–19
organizational climate 63–65, 196–98
organizational culture 48–54, 65–67, 99,
        217–18, 307
    communication 54–61
    high performance 150–51, 291–93,
        296–97
    negative 157, 174
    perception of 61–63
    positive 156–57
    and success 156–58

and team building 291–93
    toxic 64, 156, 157, 174, 218, 288,
        293, 307
    versus climate 63–65
organizational dynamics 113–14
organizational health 135, 136
organizational resilience 66, 82
organizational values 16, 17, 66, 153, 157
Osian *see* Jones, Osian
ownership 67, 99, 199, 238, 257

pace-setting leadership *194*
Page, Larry 76–77
pain avoidance 107
'Painting Britain Red' (Warburtons) 56
partner ecosystems 12, 274, 281
Pavlov's motivation theory 92
perception 62, 126, 129
perennial challenges 9–10
performance management xv, 56, 96
    incremental gains 218
performance reviews xv, 136, 213–14
Perring, David 228–29, 230
personal standards 152, 154, *197*, 201, 202,
        218, 297
personality 217
personalization 132, 168, 171–72, 264
personalized power 94
petabytes 265
philosophy (principles) 11, 71–84
    leadership 188, 198–201
popularity 201
Porter, Michael 7, 126
positive culture 156–57
power 93, 94–95, 192–93
'power of three (four)' rule 295
practice drills 210, 215, 216
Premier Farnell 59, 247, 250, 256
Primitive Culture (Tylor) 49
problem statements 29–30
process management 11, 112, 169, 170,
        214, 273, 280
production teams 53
productivity 174, 180
project opportunities 251
psychological contract 54, 129
psychological self 97, 154–55, 156
purpose, approach, mindset framework 37–
        39, 157

quality philosophy 76, 77–78, 79,
        127–28, 178
    see also data quality
questioning 82, 229, 239
'quiet quitting' 64, 157, 174

RACI model 187–88, 248, 249
RBL Group 62
readiness 136, 246, 250, 254, 256
recognition 57, 60–61, 202, 302
recruitment 32, 56, 132, 136, 173, 217, 299
reflection 102, 152, 160, 301
refresher sessions 117
reinforcement theory 58, 60–61
relationship building (affiliation) 93, 94,
    131, 134, 137, 176, 191–92, 199, 289
    see also connections
relative success 147–49, 150–51, 161, 218,
    289, 307
remote working 216, 278, 299–300
repetition 58–60, 216
resilience 66, 82
resistance to change 39–42, 108–12, 118–19
resourcing (sourcing) 11, 33, 273
respect 63, 201
respondent methods 90
responsibility *197*
results focus 199
retail sector 36, 99, 127, 201, 276, 278
retention (employee) 128, 233–34
    see also turnover
reviews 217, 250
reward systems 57, *197*, 273
    see also salaries
Rhein-Neckar-Löwen 229
Rijkaard, Frank 75
risk management 52
Rongen, Thomas 289–90
rugby sector 81, 152–53, 294–96, 298, 301
rule of seven 59
rule of 6-9 58–60

salaries 79, 131
SAP 82–83, 157, 173, 235, 245, 274, 288
SAP SuccessFactors 59, 170, 172
scepticism 34
scorecards 136
secondments 251
self *96*, 190–91, 193
    psychological 97, 154–55, 156
self-awareness (aware self) 95–98, 102, 152,
    154–56, 203, 301
self-care 200
self-control 93, 94, *95*
self-directed teams 187
self-esteem 27–28, 157, 303
self-preservation 110
Selfridges 177
Sendra, Dr Caitlynn 167, 170
senior management team 51–52
see also board of directors (C-suite)

shadow culture 53
Shah, Dr Vikas 39
shock 110
short-term leadership *194, 195, 196*
Silicon Valley 263
simplification (simplicity) 40–41, 115,
    127, 219
Siri 173, 269
skills pools 131, 289, 291, 297
Sky Sports 159
Skynet 276
SMART objectives 18–20
smart watches 171
smartphones 133, 226–27
social media 179
social norms 93–95
socialized power 94
software as a service 266, 274, 280
Sony xvii
sourcing 11, 33, 273
sponsors 114, 116, 120
stakeholder management 34–36,
    113–14, 120
standardization 171, 264
standards 152, 154, *197*, 201, 202, 218, 297
Starbucks 16
Starfield, Marc 271–72
Strack, Rainer 130–31
strategic alignment 14–20, 22, 56, 75, 129
strategy 6–10, 20–22, 126
    see also goal-setting; mission statements;
        strategic alignment; vision
streaming media 277–78
subconscious (unconscious) mind 90, 97
success 80–83, 142–62
    celebrating 67, 297
    metrics 14
    sustaining 296–98
    see also mini celebrations
succession planning 57, 136, 249–51, 274
super designers 11, 13
surveys 82–83, 179–80

talent 'ceilings' 252–53
talent development 100, 250
    see also employee development;
        succession planning; war for talent
talent reviews 250
teams *197*, 287–88, 289, 297
    Centre of Excellence 12
    composition 290–91
    dynamics of 216–18, 286–304
    goals 293–94
    leadership of 301–02
    self-directed 187

Teams (Microsoft) 172, 300
technology 13, 19, 36, 59, 131, 168–71,
    215–16, 260–82
  cloud 172, 235
  digital 175, 214–15
  see also Alexa; automation; collaboration
    tools; legacy systems; smartphones
tendency 89
tension 48, 294, 297
Terminator 276
Theaker, Mike 37
'think' principle 116
time constraints 81
Timpson, James 212–13
Timpson Group 99–100, 137, 212–13
Tinch, Eric 20, 40–42, 110–11, 119
Tottenham Hotspur Football Club 298–99
toxic cultures 64, 156, 157, 174, 218, 288,
    293, 307
training 51, 96, 210, 218, 230, 245
transactional excellence 175
trust 99, 255
TSG 1899 Hoffenheim 229–30, 231,
    267–68
Turing, Alan (Turing test) 275
turnover 18, 57, 136
  see also retention
2002 Rugby World Cup 289
2010 Rugby World Cup 81, 153, 301
Tylor, Edward B 49

Ulrich, Dave 62–63
uncertainty 27, 30

unconscious preferences 90, 97
understanding *see* self-awareness (aware self)
unique selling proposition (USP) 8
upside-down management models 99
user (human) experience 76, 164–74, 180,
    181, 226–28, 270, 307

value 127
value propositions 125–28
  see also employee value propositions
values 16, 17, 66, 74, 91–92, 98,
    153, 157
values re-assessments 102
Verhoeven, Michiel 235
virtual teams 299–300
vision 50, 82
voice driven AI 173

Walgreens Boots Alliance 36
WalkMe 173
war for talent 17–18, 124, 130
Warburtons 49, 55–56, 61, 66
'whakapapa' 298–99
Willetts, Helen 137, 178–79, 227
Winston, Sally 132
work, purpose of xiv–v, 16–18, 19, 61,
    133–34
work experience 168
World Pastry Awards 177

Yell, Sue 49, 55–56, 61, 65–66

Zoom 48, 300

Looking for another book?

Explore our award-winning
books from global business
experts in Human Resources,
Learning and Development

Scan the code to browse

www.koganpage.com/hr-learning-
development

More from Kogan Page

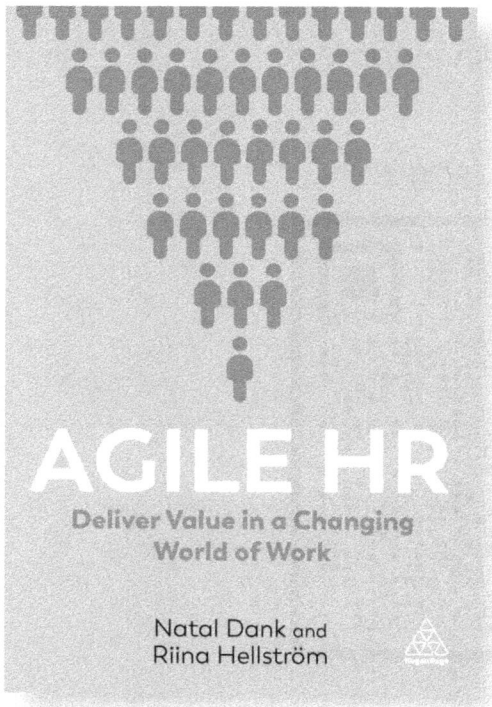

AGILE HR

Deliver Value in a Changing World of Work

Natal Dank and Riina Hellström

ISBN: 9781789665857

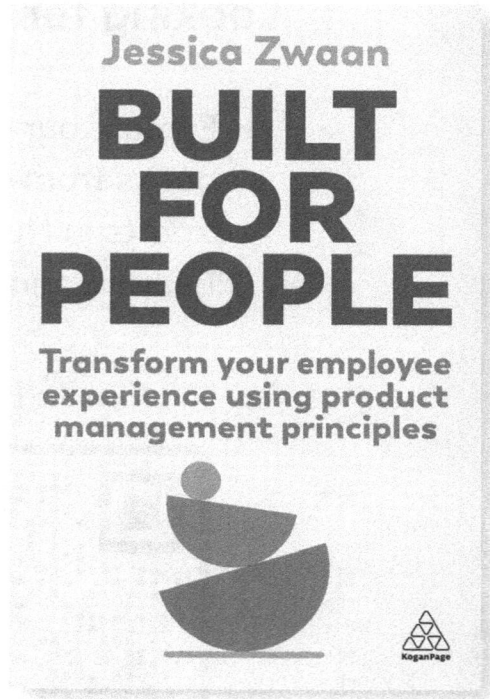

Jessica Zwaan

BUILT FOR PEOPLE

Transform your employee experience using product management principles

ISBN: 9781398608023

www.koganpage.com

From 4 December 2025 the EU Responsible Person (GPSR) is:
eucomply oÜ, Pärnu mnt. 139b – 14, 11317 Tallinn, Estonia
www.eucompliancepartner.com

www.ingramcontent.com/pod-product-compliance
Lightning Source LLC
Chambersburg PA
CBHW071540210326
41597CB00019B/3070